George Burley...

George Etell Sargent

GEORGE BURLEY:

HIS HISTORY, EXPERIENCES, AND OBSERVATIONS.

GEORGE BURLEY:

HIS HISTORY, EXPERIENCES, AND OBSERVATIONS.

BY G. E. SARGENT,

AUTHOR OF THE "STORY OF A POCKET BIBLE," "CHRONICLES OF AN OLD MANOR
HOUSE," "ADVENTURES OF A CITY ARAB," ETC.

LONDON:

THE RELIGIOUS TRACT SOCIETY;

56, PATERNOSTER ROW; 65, ST. PAUL'S CHURCHYARD;
AND 164, PICCADILLY.

CONTENTS.

———————

Contents.

INTRODUCTION.

IN the following story the writer has endeavoured to show that there is no real happiness in sin; but that it is injurious, in every way, though in various degrees, to its votaries, and to all who are brought within their influence. It is as plainly seen in common life as it is faithfully declared in the Bible, that "the way of transgressors is hard"; that "the triumphing of the wicked is short"; that "one sinner destroyeth much good"; that "no man liveth unto himself"; that whatsoever a man soweth that shall he also reap; and that "he who soweth to his flesh, shall of the flesh reap corruption." These truths the writer has sought to illustrate.

On the other hand, it has been his aim to show how, in the words of the psalmist, the way of a young man may be cleansed by his taking heed thereto, according to God's Word. To make this manifest, it was not necessary to select as the hero of a story, a youth of large acquirements or splendid talents. It was better that he should be one of commonplace abilities (rather stupid than otherwise if the reader please to consider him so); not removed by any wide distance from the ordinary pathway of every-day life, and not exposed to any violent vicissitudes. There is, in fact, enough in the common walks of existence to try every man's work, of what sort it is, and to prove to him the need of seeking a strength infinitely greater than his own, to enable him to persevere in that patient continuance in well-doing, which leads to true glory and honour in this life, and to immortality in the life to come.

This Divine strength cannot, however, be obtained except in God's own appointed way. Nor can peace and happiness be ensured but by a believing approach to the source whence they flow. "If any man thirst," said Christ, "let him come unto ME and drink." "He that cometh to ME shall never hunger; and he that believeth in ME shall never thirst."

Let the reader receive this great truth, act upon it, and fall in with the arrangements which God has made for human welfare, through the Lord Jesus Christ, and his safety is secured; for "HE is faithful who hath promised." It does not necessarily follow that a young man who makes religion the principal thing in his estimation and pursuit, will get riches, or even be successful, as the world in general counts success. But he will have what is infinitely better—a conscience void of offence towards God and towards man, and an assurance of endless prosperity and soul-satisfying wealth in His presence where there is fulness of joy— at His right hand, where are pleasures for evermore. Nevertheless, as a rule, it will be found that all the virtues inculcated by the Gospel are favourable even to worldly success, so that in its narrowest signification, the Scripture statement holds good, that "Godliness is profitable unto all things, having promise of the life that now is, and of that which is to come." While, similarly, almost every day's observation brings home to us the result of the psalmist's life-long experience—"I have seen the wicked in great power, and spreading himself like a green bay tree. Yet he passed away, and lo, he was not: yea, I sought him, but he could not be found."

GEORGE BURLEY:

HIS HISTORY, EXPERIENCES, AND OBSERVATIONS.

CHAPTER I.

HURLY BURLY.

"'LL tell you what, Mr. Bix, I can do nothing with him. He is the most mischievous urchin I ever did come across. Yes, you are; you know you are," added Betsy, in a tone of reproachful sorrow, giving my arm a sudden wrench, which extorted from me a piteous cry of "Oh don't then; oh!"

"You know you are full of mischief, and you only five year old," said Betsy, who still held my arm with a forcible grip, from which I vainly struggled to escape.

"Gently, Betsy, gently," said my grandfather, taking out his snuff-box and solacing himself with a huge pinch of what in after-years I knew to be that damp, clogging, luscious delicacy called Prince's Mixture. "Don't dislocate the boy's arm, Betsy. Oh dear, oh dear! What a thing it is to have other people's children thrown upon one's hands!"

"'Tis the third pane of glass he has broken since he came to live here," resumed Betsy; "and—would you believe it, Mr. Bix?—the little rebel only laughed when he had done it, as if it were good fun and nothing else, to hear the shivered glass rattling down on the stones."

"It was the ball did it," I said, sobbing; in fact, Betsy's eloquence was accompanied on my part by cries and tears, for a good reason why.

"And who throwed the ball when he was told not to?" Another twitch of the arm. "And there's your poor grandfather, which takes such care of you and loves you so, will have to pay for the damage done. Three panes of window-glass in a month, and five shillings a pane if a penny! But there," said Betsy Miller, "what's the use of telling *you* how much it will cost?"

"I don't care," said I, in desperation.

"There, Mr. Bix, you hear what he says; and now you'll believe, I hope. 'Don't care,' says he. Pretty well for a five-year old, I think."

"Oh dear, oh dear!" again groaned my grandfather, helplessly. "He must have a switching, Georgey must. Give him a switching, and see if that won't make him mind you, Betsy."

"I have smacked him, Mr. Bix; I just have," said Betsy, triumphantly. And so she just had. "I smacked him till my fingers are all of a tingle," said she. I didn't know about the fingers, but I knew that *I* was all of a tingle.

"Well, then, what is to be done?" My grandfather took another pinch of Prince's Mixture. "I tell you what we must do, Betsy. We'll—ah, yes—we'll send him to school."

"I don't want to go to school; I want to go home; I want my mother," I wailed piteously.

And hereupon rose a sorrowful responsive cry from Betsy Miller, whose mood suddenly changed, and who, catching me up in her arms, kissed me again and again as she mingled her tears with mine. "Poor little orphan!" said she, as our noses rubbed together. "Poor little innocent! And he doesn't know, he doesn't, what has happened. And to think I should have been smacking him, too! Oh dear me!" And then she kissed me again.

MR. ANTHONY BIX, MY RESPECTED GRANDFATHER.

"There, there, there, that will do, Betsy. Take the boy away and let me have a little peace. I am busy, and can't be disturbed every hour of the day. Give Georgey a cake; ah, yes, give him a cake. Here's a penny; go out and buy him a cake, Betsy." And thereupon my grandfather extracted the coin from his waist-coat pocket, pushed it into Betsy's hand, and shuffled away to his office (as he called a little room on the ground-floor), leaving me in the custody of his servant and housekeeper, who forthwith re-commenced hugging me, calling me a "pretty dear," and wish-ing her fingers had been blistered before she had laid them on me. Remembering the "smacking" I had so recently received, I wished so too, if blistering (whatever that meant) would have softened the strokes. I got my cake, however, which was some recompense for the indignity I had suffered; and for some time I heard no more of school. In the course of the day the broken window was mended, and I heard no more about that.

This being the first event of my life on which my memory now rests with any degree of certainty, I take it as the starting-point of my story.

I was an orphan. This fact was so often repeated in my hear-ing that I was not likely to forget it. For instance, a day or two after the day of sorrow just mentioned, I accompanied Betsy to a little shop in one of the smaller streets of our neighbourhood, and heard something like the following dialogue :—

"A nevvy of yours, Miss Betsy?" asked the wife of the shop-keeper, fixing her eyes on me.

"No ma'am; no kin of mine. My master's orphan grandchild, ma'am, Mr. Bix's; which his mother died a little better than a month ago, and got no father; and his mother, my master's only daughter, ma'am, as you can't remember, not being living here at that time when she was married, seven years ago, and never had no chick nor child but this one as come along two years after; and his father died, ma'am, of the ague as had been hanging off and on a twelvemonth or more ; and then the widow carried on the farm, for the husband was a farmer in a small way, ma'am ; and then she took with a fever and died, and left nothing but debts behind, and this little orphan ; and so Mr. Bix has taken him, and brought him home, and paid the debts ; and there's the money, ma'am."

This last part of the speech referred, be it understood, to the shillings and pence just expended, and not to my mother's debts.

"Thank you, Miss Betsy," returned the shopkeeper.   "And so he is an orphan, is he ? pretty little man !   And his name ; what may be his name, now ?"

"Hurly Burly, ma'am," replied Betsy, with an unmoved countenance, and quite in a matter-of-fact way.

"What a funny name !   It never can be his right name."

No, not quite my right name, which was George Burley ; but it was near enough for common purposes.   The fact is, Betsy had given me the nickname a month before, and Hurly Burly stuck to me many a year afterwards.

"And what is the old gentleman going to do with such a mite of a thing ?" asked the woman, when my name had been duly canvassed.

This was more than Betsy could tell.   She guessed, however, that there would be time enough to find that out by-and-by. Meanwhile the old gentleman would not have much trouble in keeping me in victuals, and drink, and clothes ; and as to lodging, and such like, said she, there was plenty of room in the old house for twenty such as I.

And so there was ; and this is as good a place as any to describe my grandfather's house, or rather the house in which he lived. But I must take another chapter for that.

CHAPTER II.

SOME ACCOUNT OF THE OLD HOUSE IN SILVER SQUARE, ITS OWNER, AND ITS OCCUPANT.

T was a substantial, brick-built house, in one of the smallest and dullest of London squares. I give the more ambitious title, otherwise it would be better described as a court. Originally, I believe, the square or court was a garden, inclosed by high walls on three sides, and shut in on the fourth by a mansion and stables, and other domestic offices, belonging to a certain Sir Miles Silver, a great City merchant, and an alderman of London, who, perceiving the population around him increasing year by year, sat himself down to count the cost, and then demolished his flower-beds, uprooted his fruit-trees, pulled down his stables, also his garden wall, and built a parallelogram of some twenty or five-and-twenty dwelling houses on the site of his former garden, leaving his own mansion standing in the centre of one of the sides of the square, conspicuous by its superior grandeur. Eventually the middle of the square exhibited a shrubbery inclosed within iron railings, the houses received their tenants, and Sir Miles' pleasant garden was thenceforward known as Silver Square.

All this happened a hundred and fifty years ago, and Sir Miles dying and leaving no issue, his title became extinct, and his name unremembered as that of a living man, while his estate passed to another line. Meanwhile the square, which was just outside the city boundaries, became hemmed in by busy streets and busier factories; its houses were gradually blackened by smoke, and the shrubbery degenerated into a piece of waste ground, covered only with shabby turf, excepting that one of the original shrubs—a mountain ash, I believe—had survived the general desolation, and had shot up into a tall, scraggy, unhealthy, straggling tree, putting forth a few yellowish-green leaves in early spring, to shed them again before the summer was past and gone.

But it was a thriving estate, this Silver Square. Being stoutly built, the houses had stood the wear and tear of time, and had borne the brunt of cold and heat, sunshine and storm, with very few signs of decay ; and, always commanding a succession of well-to-do respectable tenants, their value had increased with the increasing prosperity of the immediate neighbourhood.

It was in the great house of the square—the original mansion of Sir Miles Silver—that my grandfather passed an almost solitary life, as the factotum and general agent of its owner, who, living abroad on the rents of the property, was fortunate in having a faithful retainer to see after his interests. Concerning this invisible owner, whose name was Falconer, I have little to say here, save that he was reported to be a man of eccentric habits, who, having been educated for the bar, suddenly took a disgust, not only towards his profession, but also towards his country, and, abandoning both, retired to a secluded valley in Switzerland, whence he corresponded, very occasionally, with his agent, Mr. Anthony Bix.

For a quarter of a century the old house had been my grandfather's home. I have spoken of his life as having been almost solitary during that period ; but it was not entirely so, for he had a wife and two children when he first entered on residence. Mrs. Bix, however, did not live long to enjoy the comforts of a well-furnished house and a decent competency, added to the dignity of her husband's stewardship. She lived but a year or two after this was entered upon, and my grandfather never thought of a second wife.

Of the two children my mother was the elder, and was her father's favourite companion until she left home on a visit to a distant relative in one of the midland counties. There she met with the young farmer who eventually became her husband and my father. There is no occasion to expand my story in this direction, Betsy Miller's explanation being mainly correct: it is enough to say that, when my grandfather visited my mother in her illness, he promised he would take care of little George; and, accordingly, after her death and funeral (of which, strangely enough, I have no recollection), I accompanied him to London.

Respecting the younger child of my grandfather a solemn silence was always maintained. His name was William, and he was not dead. This was all I knew respecting him until three or four more years of my life had passed away: and it will be time enough to introduce him into my story when he actually makes his appearance.

My grandfather was a little wiry man, about sixty years old when I first made his acquaintance. He was always very formally, and yet neatly habited, in a style of dress which, even in the days of which I am now writing, was old-fashioned, though not altogether singular. For there were a few gentlemen in those days, as my older readers will remember, who delighted in tasselled Hessian boots, tight elastic pantaloons, of a dark gray colour generally, white neckerchiefs of voluminous fold and innocent of starch, no shirt-collars, but full shirt-frills and ruffles; and powdered hair, which imparted, by its prodigal sprinklings, a sort of millery appearance to the collar and shoulders of the broad-skirted black coats of the wearers. Conjure up to your mind's eye one of these spectres of the past; add to it a countenance expressive of mingled shrewdness, simplicity, good-nature, and irritability, and you have before you Mr. Anthony Bix, my respected grandfather.

He was always very full of business, or fancied himself to be so, which with some persons (as I have observed in after-life) amounts to exactly the same thing. He had rents to collect for his patron; repairs to overlook for the tenants; accounts to keep, in which every penny received or expended on behalf of the Silver estate was scrupulously set down; and occasional correspondence to keep up with Mr. Falconer. I may as well add here that, since the time of that gentleman's voluntary expatriation, he had only twice revisited England. I shall have occasion to state the cause of these visits in a future chapter.

And now, looking back on what I have already written, I find that I have not yet described the house which was, through my childhood at least, to be my home. To begin at the beginning:— the front door was massive, and almost wide enough to admit a stage-coach, and was attained by a flight of five or six stone steps, flanked by heavy iron balustrades, which, in their turn, were ornamented by a pair of link-extinguishers, the uses of which were a mystery to me for many a long day. Entering the aforesaid door, you reached a large hall, flagged with diamond-shaped stones, alternately black and white, which gave to the floor the general aspect of an immense chess-board; an illusion which might have been kept up by certain marble busts and statues, very brown with age, which were ranged round the hall on brackets, and represented with sufficient accuracy the kings, queens, and knights of the aforesaid game; and by a goodly number of leathern fire-buckets, hung round the walls on brass hooks, which might aptly enough have stood for the pawns. A few very heavy chairs standing against the walls, and a marble table in the middle of the hall, completed its equipment, and left almost room enough for the aforesaid coach to turn in, supposing it had once obtained entrance.

On either side of the hall, doors opened into various apartments, large and lofty, as befitted so magnificent a portal and ante-room. At one time, no doubt, these rooms had been richly furnished; and even yet they retained traces of former grandeur in chairs, tables, sideboards, and uncomfortable couches, black with exposure, and rickety with age; also in large antique paintings in tarnished frames, which almost covered the wainscoted walls. Yet over all was cast so sombre an air; and so chilly an atmosphere pervaded these rooms, even on the hottest summer day, that you would not willingly have chosen to inhabit them. And they were not inhabited. Once a week they were in turn entered by Betsy Miller, who carefully dusted the old furniture, swept the floors, and then retired shivering; but this was all, and the grim portraits on the wall, which, on these hebdomadal visits, appeared to follow with their piercing gaze every movement of brush and duster, till Betsy was ready, as she said, to scream out, were left again to their repose.

A broad and grand staircase rising from the hall, and enriched by balustrades of carved and polished oak, conducted to a suite of apartments on the first floor, also very sombre and very dismal, in spite of rich carpets, and gorgeous curtains, and bright colours on the walls. These rooms, also, were deemed too sacred for frequent intrusion, but were kept in due order and passable condition by the industrious hands of Betsy Miller.

A lighter staircase led to many chambers on the second floor. Two or three of these were state bedrooms, solemn enough to strike terror into a young heart like mine, by the hearse-like plumes which surmounted the heavy old bedsteads and the dark silken coverlets. Our bed-chambers were at the back of the mansion, and were reached by another flight of less pretentious stairs; but the most cheerful part of the house was that which contained the small parlour in which my grandfather, his housekeeper, and myself took our daily meals; the large and airy stone kitchen in which these meals were prepared, and where the housekeeper usually sat when her morning's work was done; and the little office—once a butler's pantry—which was fitted up with a desk and high stool, also with a set of shelves containing day-books, ledgers, and rental-books, also with a number of brass hooks ranged along the wall, just under the ceiling, from which depended files of dusty papers. These rooms all overlooked a paved yard, shut in on the other side by a high stone wall, which, in its turn, overlooked a churchyard, and was a favourite promenade for all the cats of the neighbourhood. This, then, was my home.

CHAPTER III.

MY GRANDFATHER'S HOUSEKEEPER.

MY chief companion for many a month and year after my entrance upon this new home of my childhood was Betsy Miller. Not that my grandfather neglected me, or was indifferent regarding me; but I should have interfered with his methodical habits if he had admitted me too much to his society; and, for my part, I preferred that of his housekeeper. For Betsy, after that one punishment, inflicted on me with no light hand, never treated me with severity. I could not then have accounted for the change in her manner towards me, but I am sure now that it arose from the tender compassion and sympathy awakened in her breast by my wailing cry for my mother. I do not think that, in general, my grandfather's housekeeper was very soft-hearted. She hardened herself, like a flint, against the importunities of street beggars. She shut the door in the faces of the more genteel mendicants with whom London abounds, and who, attracted by my grandfather's reputation for wealth—for he was supposed to have well feathered his nest—found their way to the old house with begging-petitions, subscription-lists, or cases of distress. She scolded, with no want of zest, the tradespeople with whom she dealt if their wares were found to be deficient in weight or measure, or defective in quality. She boxed the ears of a great lubberly boy, till they were red as fire, whom she had caught in the act of defacing her white door-steps with charcoal scrawls. But, after that one experience of her vengeful power which I have formerly mentioned, I was exempt not only from blows, but from hard words. I was her " darling," her " precious little treasure," and I know not what besides. No wonder, therefore, that I clung to her as to a guardian-angel, and conceived an affection for her which time did not diminish.

When I first knew her, Betsy Miller must have been forty years old. She had lived with my grandfather about fifteen years, and, not being given to change, she contemplated living with him fifteen years longer, at the end of which time she intended leaving active service and " settling down." She was a tall, bony, high-cheeked woman, with sharp gray eyes, and reddish-coloured hair; and she was as precise in her dress, in her way, as my grandfather was in his. She lived on terms of easy, yet respectful familiarity with my grandfather, who would no more have thought of interfering with her in her household duties than she would have thought of dictating to him in respect of his business affairs: thus they got on exceedingly well together.

My manner of life for some time after the first introduction to my grandfather's house requires but little description. Through the day I followed Betsy Miller's footsteps pretty closely. If she was at work in the upper part of the house, I was by her side. When she descended to the kitchen, I was seated at the table watching her preparations for cooking. Had she occasion to go into the neighbouring streets on shopping excursions, I accompanied her. And when her daily household occupations were over, the good creature devoted herself to my recreation. Sometimes, on fine summer evenings, she took me by the hand, and strolled with me, away from the busy streets, to suburban green fields, where, seated on the sward, she would tell me of her own country home, far away, where she had lived till the fit took her to get a situation in London, twenty years ago; how the fit took her in consequence of her being badly used and deceived by her John (who wasn't her John now; not he, indeed), and she couldn't bear to live in the place where he lived any longer; how she had had two or three hard services, where she was worn down to skin and bone, before she went to live at Silver Square; how she had, three times in twenty years, gone to see her friends at her native place, till she found everything and everybody were strange to her, and she to them; and how she had made up her mind at last that it was of no use minding, and the best thing for her was to settle down for good, as she intended to do some day.

She told me stories of her young life which would be of no particular interest to repeat, though I thought then that there never had been, and never would again be, another such a heroine as Betsy Miller. And then, having emptied her budget for that time, and the grass on which we were sitting getting damp, my nurse would hurry me away to treat me with curds-and-whey, or new milk, purchaseable at some wayside dairy, before returning to our nest at Silver Square.

Otherwise, on wet or wintry evenings, I should have been found perched on a high chair by the kitchen table, opposite to Betsy Miller, watching her busy hands as they plied the needle. If I remember rightly, stocking-darning was her fondest achievement; but, failing this, my nurse had almost enough to do in making new clothes for me, or mending old ones. On one occasion, when

I had been sitting wrapped in speechless admiration of Betsy's industry for a full hour, and she had been unusually taciturn, she suddenly broke out :

" Did anybody ever try to teach you to read, Hurly ? "

" No, Betsy ; I don't know that anybody ever did," I answered, ponderingly.

" Nor yet to spell, Hurly ? " more anxiously still.

" Nor yet to spell," said I.

" And you don't know a great B from a bull's foot, I'll be bound."

I confessed my ignorance.

" And I have been sitting here all this time, like a booby, and never thought of it ! Why, what will ever become of you if you grow up such a dunce ? Let us begin this precious very minute."

So I began that precious very minute to learn the alphabet out of an old primer which was stowed away among Betsy Miller's treasures, and which had laid the foundation of her erudition some thirty-five years before. It was dog's-eared, and grimed, and torn, but it served the purpose ; and if the pupil was not bright, the teacher was persevering and patient.

From that time we had occupation enough for winter evenings ; for, when the difficulties of the primer were surmounted, Betsy had other rudimental books which she brought out, one by one ; and, whatever I may owe to subsequent teachers, my first debt of gratitude on this score is due to my grandfather's house-keeper.

These, such as I have described them, were our week-day occupations and habits. On Sundays I was taken regularly twice a-day to the old city church, the burying-ground of which ad-joined our paved yard. Sometimes my grandfather led me there ; but it was oftener Betsy Miller, who very rarely missed either service. On the other hand, my grandfather was only an occa-

sional attendant upon them.   Even in those days, when London
did not go "out of town" on Sundays, as it does now, the city
churches were not generally thronged with worshippers; and our
church was no exception to the rule.   A few of the old-fashioned
high-walled square pews had pretty regular occupants; and the
seats in the aisles had always a scanty scattering of the poorer
people of the neighbourhood, principally elderly women and
children, with a few servant maids.   But there were always many
more places vacant than filled, both in pews and aisles,—a fact
which my nurse very pathetically deplored.

" Where can people expect to go to when they die, if they don't
go to church when they are alive, Hurly?" she sometimes said;
and I presumed that she was only too right in her inferences,
though I confess to the feeling, which I dared not then express,
that I would have preferred a ramble in the distant fields on a
fine sunny Sunday afternoon to being shut up in my grandfather's
square pew.   To tell the truth, those Sunday services, as I now
remember them, were uninteresting to me, as a child; for no
attempt was ever made to stamp upon them vitality and reality.
It was my duty to go to public worship, I was told; but there
the teaching I received at home ended.   Nor was there much
that was enlivening in the manner in which the services were
conducted.   The liturgy was read in a monotonous, unimpressive
tone; the singing was little more than a solo, performed by the
clerk, who had a harsh, unpleasant voice; and the sermons, however excellent, were (I think) far above the comprehension of a
child.   In process of time, indeed, I learned to pay some attention
to the prayers and lessons, which I could follow from my book;
but the sermons were profound mysteries to me, which I did not
attempt to fathom.   Perhaps they were mysteries for this very
reason; but I am not sure, for Betsy Miller, who was my oracle,
on one occasion confidentially declared her inability to understand

them. This was enough for me; for how could I attempt that in which she failed?

I knew nothing of the clergyman who officiated, and whom I never met with or saw save in the church. He was elderly, and had the reputation of being a great scholar; but he led a life of extreme seclusion, and rarely appeared among his parishioners except when compelled to do so by his public duties. This may partly account, perhaps, for the little apparent effect produced by his ministrations. But I cannot be sure even of this.

My Sunday evenings in Silver Square were more pleasant to me than the previous parts of the day in church. For then, seated with Betsy Miller in her apartment, with a large Bible open before us both, she read to me (or I to her when I had sufficient scholarship) the wonderful histories of the Old Testament, or the Gospels of the New, until, in process of time, I had the leading events of both well impressed on my memory. Sometimes, for a change, Betsy would reach down an old copy of "The Pilgrim's Progress," or an equally ancient copy of "The Holy War,"—both being embellished with extraordinary engravings; and then we passed away the hours with Christian on his perilous journey, or with the Mansoulians in their wonderful town. These two books, with the big Bible, formed our Sunday library, which we never dreamt of enlarging. These readings might have been more profitable to me than they were, had I had "some one to guide me." But Betsy never attempted to explain or enforce. It was a duty to read the Bible and good books on Sunday, she said, just as it was a duty to go to church. But this was all. It did not occur to her mind, I fear, to ask even herself, "Understandest thou what thou readest?" and certainly she never put the question to me. For a long time, therefore, I had confused notions that the allegories referred to were true histories. Better this, however, than for me to have taken the true histories to be allegories, as some have done, but which I certainly never did.

I am aware that these annals of childhood are trite and sufficiently uninteresting ; I shall pass over, therefore, any further notice of them, and, in my next chapter, take a stride of some four years in my private history.

CHAPTER IV.

THE VERY SHABBY MAN WHOM I MET IN MR. FILBY'S SHOP.

WAS between nine and ten years old ; but long before this time I had become pretty familiar with the neighbourhood for some distance around Silver Square ; and I had lately made myself rather useful to my grandfather in a variety of ways, among others, as an occasional messenger to more distant parts of London.

I was one day sent to a law stationer's in Fetter Lane for some small order, which was written down in a note ; and, while waiting to hand this to the proprietor of the shop, I was struck by the sound of my grandfather's name once or twice repeated by him to an exceedingly shabby-looking man with whom he was in conversation, and who was speaking very earnestly, though in a low tone, as it seemed to me, of entreaty.

"I tell you no, Bix ; I couldn't think of it ; couldn't indeed," I heard the stationer say.

The shabby man muttered some more earnest words, the purport of which did not reach me ; but I noted him more closely. He was tall, slight, and haggard. His dark hair hung in long flakey tangles over his cheeks. He was unshaven ; or, rather he carried an ugly scrubbing-brush of beard of at least a week's growth upon his chin and upper lip. His countenance was sallow, almost to yellowness; originally it might have been a handsome face, but there was something stamped on it which made it appear repulsive to me, though I did not know why. I do know why now: that something was vice and profligacy.

I have said that the man, who was perhaps about thirty-two or thirty-three years of age, was shabbily dressed. His coat (a tight military frock, once blue, now faded to a dull kind of green) was white at the seams, out at the elbows, and ragged about the cuffs. It was buttoned so close up to the wearer's chin that no scrap of waistcoat or shirt was visible; and a high black military stock, without shirt collar, was buckled tightly round his neck. He wore drab kerseymere trousers, very dirty and threadbare, strapped over a pair of fashionably-made boots, which I observed were old and split out at the sides. The man was evidently steeped in poverty; at the same time there was a pretentious air of breeding about him which told of better days.

The conversation continued: it was plain to me that the poor fellow was pressingly entreating some favour, which the other was determined not to grant.

"I wonder you should have the face to come to me with such a story," said the stationer bluntly.

"Necessity, sheer necessity, Mr. Filby," returned the suppliant. "You have known me a good many years, sir," he added.

"Yes, I have, Bix," said Mr. Filby.

(Bix again! what did it mean?)

"The more the pity, perhaps you are disposed to say, Mr. Filby," rejoined the shabby fellow.

"Just the very words I was thinking of," retorted the stationer; "at any rate, I should be better off now if I had never known anything of you. You cannot deny that."

I could see that a dark flush for a moment suffused the stranger's cheek; but it passed away, and he smiled. "I don't deny that you have some little cause of complaint against me, Mr. Filby," he said, softly; "but nobody knows where the shoe pinches so well as he who wears it."

I looked down at the shabby man's feet, and wondered, in my boyish curiosity, whether his shoes pinching him had caused them to open at the seams; meanwhile the stationer, who understood the figure, which I did not, replied:—

"You never said a truer word, Bix" (Bix again! thought I); "the shoe has pinched me so sharply that I don't mean to put it on again."

"On my word and honour——" the man began, but was cut short by Mr. Filby with "Your what, Bix? Your *what?*" spoken, as it seemed to me, in a tone of disgust. "Don't talk to me about word and honour," he added.

"You are very hard, Mr. Filby," said the shabby man, with a groan which touched my tender feelings; "but you shall have it your own way, sir. 'Tis the way of the world; when a poor wretch is down, keep him down—keep him down. Tread on him, trample on him; kick him—he can't help himself." And as he began to cry, or so I thought, I pitied him yet more exceedingly, and set Mr. Filby down in my mind as a very cruel man, especially when he said, angrily:—

"And who wants to tread, and trample, and kick? You come here into my shop without being sent for, and ask me to do this, and that, and the other to bolster you up, and when I tell you civilly that I can't and won't be mixed up with you and your schemes, because I have suffered enough from you already, you talk of being trod on, and trampled on, and kicked! That isn't civil language, sir."

"Don't be angry, Mr. Filby: pray, don't," pleaded the man,

in a piteous tone. "I should not have applied such words to you, sir—you who have stood my friend when nobody else would. But others have trampled on me and kicked me; you know they have, sir, you know it, Mr. Filby." The last words were spoken rather indistinctly, by reason of a handkerchief, which the speaker snatched hurriedly out of a hat lying on the counter, being applied to his face.

"Pho! pho!" exclaimed Mr. Filby, impatiently; "don't tell me about being deserted by your friends. I know all the rights and wrongs of that. There's never a man that I ever knew who had better friends than you have had, Bix, if you would have kept them. Talk of treading and trampling and kicking! Why, that's what you have been doing to every one of your friends these ten years past, and long before. I don't want to reproach you," added the stationer, cooling down a little in his warmth, "but when it comes to running down friends, you know, I have a right to speak out."

"I never meant running you down, Mr. Filby," said the shabby man, submissively. "But really now——" and he whispered again in so low a tone, as he leaned over the counter, that the words did not reach my ear. I could judge, however, that he was pressing some point very eagerly; and he wound up by saying, more loudly and energetically, "I should be able to repay you all—repay you all, sir."

Mr. Filby was obdurate, however, or appeared to be. "One word is as good as a thousand," said he, firmly. "I'll not do it, Bix. I've done a deal more than I had any right to do, out of respect to your connexions; but there must be an end somewhere; and the end is come. As to repaying—pho, pho! But when I say I won't do anything more," he added, relentingly, "I don't mean but what——there," and he slipped something into the suppliant's hand—" if that trifle will be any use."

"Thank ye kindly and heartily: it will give me a few more means, Mr. Filby, before——." He applied the handkerchief (a brown cotton one) to his face again, and smothered the rest of his sentence in it. Then, carefully putting on his hat (it was brown, crushed and *seedy*), he withdrew lingeringly from the shop, leaving Mr. Filby at liberty to read my note.

"Dear, dear, dear!" said he, looking down upon me with a curious expression. "How remarkable, though; really! So you come from Mr. Bix, eh, my boy? He is your grandfather, isn't he?"

"Yes, sir."

"And do you know that gen——that person who was talking to me just now?" he asked presently, as he was tying up my parcel.

"No, sir."

"And needn't want to," said he.

I returned home by way of Holborn. At the part of that street called Holborn Bridge there was in those days, and I believe there is now also, a large retail spirit house. I was passing by the door, when it opened, and nearly stumbling over me, out came the shabby man, wiping his mouth with the self-same brown cotton handkerchief which a quarter of an hour before had concealed and dried his tears of repentance.

"Hillo, young fellow!" he exclaimed, with a rich, liquory tone; "*he* didn't send you after me, did he?"

"Who, sir?"

"Old Filby—the stingy rascal. You were in his shop, you know, when I came out."

"Yes, sir: no, sir, he didn't send me after you," I said; and I passed on, with a catching of my breath, induced by the strong fumes which issued from the unclean mouth, which had stooped down to question me, greatly wondering what it could all mean; but with all sentiments of sympathy dissipated.

CHAPTER V.

MY GRANDFATHER'S PATRON MAKES HIS APPEARANCE.

ON my reaching Silver Square I proceeded at once to my grandfather's room, to deliver up the parcel; and, to my astonishment, found him closeted with a stranger.

"Lay it down, George, and——" he looked at the door, and nodded.

"Do not send the boy away, Mr. Bix," interposed the stranger, speaking with a foreign accent. "Your grandson, of whom you were speaking, I presume?" he added.

"My grandson, Mr. Falconer," replied my grandfather, gravely.

"Come and shake hands with me, my fine fellow," said the gentleman, with a smile. "You and I must be friends—and shall be, I think," he continued, as he drew me towards him, and looked me keenly in the face.

He was a singular-looking person. In the present day there would have been nothing extraordinary in his appearance; for he had a fine, flowing, silky, though very gray beard, which descended to his breast; but, as I am writing now of days in which close shaving was the fashion, the singularity was marked and striking. There was such a kind expression of countenance, however, and so much quiet humour in the sparkling of his large dark eyes, that I could not but return his gaze with confidence. "Yes, we shall do capitally well together," he said presently, as he smoothed down my hair with his broad, but delicately white hand, while he yet detained me between his knees.

He was strangely clad, wearing as an over-garment a kind of

c

loose gabardine, of light colour, and of some delicately fine and soft material. This was fastened round his waist by a broad band of red leather, and, being thrown open in front—it being a hot day in summer—a silken waistcoat was displayed, only partly covering a shirt of dazzling whiteness, fastened at the collar by a narrow riband, while the collar itself lay folded down over the wearer's shoulder. Other portions of the gentleman's attire were equally uncommon, including a hat of Leghorn straw, conically shaped and broad-brimmed, which lay on the floor at his feet. If I add to the above that the visitor might have been at least sixty years of age, though he seemed scarcely so much, my description may suffice.

"This gentleman is Mr. Falconer, of whom you have sometimes heard me speak, George," said my grandfather, by way of explanation. And then, without waiting a reply, he went on with the business, or conversation, which my entrance had momentarily interrupted.

"But why, my dear sir," said my grandfather, "should you be lodging at an inn, while you have a house of your own here, where you have a right to command every attention?"

"It is kind of you to say so, Mr. Bix," returned the *émigré;* "but there is my servant and my luggage."

"I think you will manage to find room enough in this house, sir," returned my grandfather, with a smile.

"Doubtless; but you have only one female servant in your establishment—my old friend Betsy, I see; and she might disapprove of visitors."

"Only one servant, combining housekeeper, cook, housemaid, and parlourmaid in one person," continued my grandfather; "but Betsy Miller is a woman of much strength of mind and many resources; and I will answer that she shall be equal to the occasion. At any rate, we will secure extra help if that be all; and, seriously, it must never be said, Mr. Falconer, that you were not admitted into your own house after so many years' absence."

"It shall be as you please, my friend," said Mr. Falconer, who seemed to have been wearied with previous discussions of the subject; "and in that case I will take the liberty of sending my luggage to-morrow."

"Meanwhile, your rooms shall be prepared, sir," added my grandfather. "And if it will please you now just to examine these vouchers, and go through the accounts"—my grandfather laid his hand on an immense pile of papers as he spoke.

"My dear friend, we will take some other time for that, if it must be done at all," said Mr. Falconer, in a sort of serio-comic dismay: "though why it should be done I cannot tell. I am perfectly satisfied with the balances you have been so good as to forward to me from time to time. And at any rate we won't plunge into business the first hour of our meeting."

My grandfather looked disappointed. He had kept his books in such apple-pie order, and had so long looked forward to a personal settling up of the accounts, that he was perhaps surprised that his eagerness was not shared by his patron. There was no help for it, however; and the conversation turned to other matters, in the course of which, being set at liberty by Mr. Falconer, and obedient to a silent motion from my grandfather, I left the room. Presently I heard the opening and closing of the hall door; and then I knew that the visitor was gone.

I had intended to tell my grandfather of the strange, shabby fellow I had seen in Mr. Filby's shop, and of his being repeatedly called by my grandfather's own name. But the newer surprise had put the older one out of my thoughts, and through the rest of that day there was such a running to and fro on the part of Betsy Miller, and such anxious preparations for Mr. Falconer and his servant, who were expected on the morrow to take up their abode in the house, that I had no time to speak either to my grandfather or my friend Betsy.

In the course of the following day arrived Mr. Falconer's luggage, in charge of his servant, a brisk foreigner, who, being unable to speak English, was obliged to carry on all communications with my grandfather and his housekeeper in dumb motions. Meanwhile, Betsy had slipped out on the previous evening and hired a woman to assist her in her house-work. So, by the time Mr. Falconer appeared, later in the day, we were all in a high and polished state of readiness to receive him.

Our visitor, or rather our master and patron, remained more than two months at his old house in Silver Square. Whether my grandfather ever inveigled him into his office, and compelled him to look into the state of his affairs, I am uncertain ; but I rather think he did, for on one occasion I observed a peculiar smile of satisfaction on my grandfather's countenance, which indicated that a burden had been removed from his mind. I am not uncertain on one point, however : namely, that never in my life had so much pleasure-taking fallen to my lot as was comprised within the few weeks of Mr. Falconer's residence in London. Scarcely a day passed, indeed, without some sight-seeing of a pleasurable nature, and in which the white-bearded gentleman did not choose me for his companion. Of course it would be easy to set this down as caprice on his part; but it is as easy, and more truthful, to say that Mr. Falconer avowed his partiality for the society of children in general, and that I happened to please and amuse him while he ministered to my pleasure and amusement. How many sights I then saw, and to what extent I was treated with almost all kinds of delicacies all the time this dissipation lasted, I am not able to say now with any degree of certainty ; but I very well recollect a fit of temporary illness which came upon me, entirely owing to stuffing—so the doctor who was called in to prescribe for me said—to *stuffing;* and I remember an embargo, in the form of an earnest and pathetic entreaty, was laid by Betsy Miller upon Mr. Falconer's taking me into any more confectioners' shops during the remainder of his stay in London.

CHAPTER VI.

A MYSTERY CLEARED UP, AND ANOTHER ENTERED UPON.

NE day—it was the day after my sickness, just referred to —I was alone in the house with Betsy Miller, my grandfather having stepped out on a business call upon one of the tenants in the Square, and Mr. Falconer having walked out in another direction, attended by his foreign servant.

The door-bell rang.

"It is only your grandfather come back, Hurly," said Betsy. "Go and open the door for him, please; my hands are all puddingy."

And so they were, for Betsy was preparing dinner. I went into the hall, therefore, and opened the door.

Not to my grandfather, however, but to the self-same shabby, gin-drinking mendicant whom I had some time before met in Mr. Filby's shop. I knew him at once by his greeny-blue frock-coat buttoned up to the chin, by his greasy military stock, his dirty drab trousers, and split boots; most of all, however, by his sallow and sinister countenance.

" Hallo ! " said I, in the extremity of my surprise.

I said, "hallo!" a second time, when the man, pushing me aside, and taking no further notice of me (for, though I recognised him, he did not remember me), walked into the hall, threw his seedy hat down on the marble table, and asked, in a loud, insolent voice,—

" Where's the old man?"

" Who, sir?" I wanted to know, as I cautiously retreated from the intruder and edged my way towards the habitable part of the house.

" Old Bix," returned the man, sharply. " Where's old Bix? And how long has he set up a house-boy?"

" I am not a house-boy," said I, indignantly. " Mr. Bix is my grandfather. What do you want?" I added, rather more boldly, for I heard Betsy's footsteps approaching from the kitchen.

" Your what? Your grandfather?" exclaimed the shabby man, stretching out his hand towards me; but I was beyond his reach, and the marble table was between us. " Do you mean to tell me that you are Polly Burley's boy?"

I was spared the trouble of replying to this question by Betsy Miller, who now appeared upon the scene, and who, rapidly passing me, advanced to the side of the intruder, and, regardless of her " puddingy" hands, seized his outstretched arm and looked him steadily in the face.

" You here, William Bix?—you here again?" she said, sternly.

" Yes, I am here, and here again," he replied, with an attempt at bravado; though it was easy to see that he quailed beneath the eye of the indignant woman.

" What do you mean by it?" she asked.

" Mean? What do I mean by it? I mean that I have a right to come to—to wherever my father is; and I'll have my right too. Mean? I mean that I want food, and I'll have it: that I want money, and I'll have it. I am not going to be frightened away by your looks, I can tell you, Betsy Miller. Come, now, hands off, woman, and let your master know that I am here. Or shall I find him for myself? That will be the best way, I suppose;" and so saying my uncle William (for I knew now who the shabby man was) suddenly disengaged himself from Betsy's hold, swung himself round, and was stalking to the door of my grandfather's office, when, once more, the determined woman confronted him.

"Not another step, William Bix. Take another step that way, and——"

"Tcha!" exclaimed the man, fiercely. "Do you think you have got a boy to deal with? The time's past and gone when you could do what you liked with me. Let me pass, I say;" and he attempted to evade the faithful guardian, but to no purpose.

"Take another step that way, William, and as sure as you stand there a living man, and I stand here a living woman, you shall be lodged in Newgate before night. You know me of old, and that, if ever I said I'd do a thing, the thing was done."

Uncle William made a feint of laughing; but it was a failure, and his cheek became blanched. Also, instead of making any further advances towards the office, he seated himself on the marble table, swinging his feet, as he replied,—

"I know you to be as obstinate as a mule, and as vixenish as a cat; but talk of Newgate to me—to me, ha, ha!"

Betsy made no immediate reply, but, drawing a chair towards her, she sat down at about three feet from the intruder.

"I sit here till you leave the house you have brought such sorrow on, William Bix," said she; "and I wonder you are not ashamed to look me in the face."

"Why should I be ashamed to look you in the face?" he asked, sullenly.

"Because I know your wickedness. And that's the reason you are not ashamed, I suppose. The more wicked people are, the less shame they have. But, if you have any shame left in you," she added, "I should think it would come uppermost at seeing yourself exposed before a child like that." Betsy pointed to me as she spoke.

The unhappy man muttered something which I did not hear, and then more loudly asked, "And what's the boy to me?"

"Nothing to you, William; nothing, nothing. May he ever be kept from being anything to you, or having anything to do with you. Poor little fellow!"

I may just repeat here, what I have before written, that beyond the fact of my having an uncle somewhere in the world, all knowledge of his antecedents had been kept from me, both by my grandfather and by Betsy Miller. The reader may suppose, therefore, how much I was taken by surprise, not only by the unexpected invasion, but by Betsy's strong and stern language, which, put together with what I had heard in Mr. Filby's shop, and seen that same day, gave me a fearful idea of my uncle's wickedness, which was not abated when he burst out into a discordant laugh, and said, mockingly—

"Poor little fellow! Oh, that's the song, is it? The poor little fellow had better keep out of my way, then. What business has he here?"

"More business than you have, William Bix," rejoined Betsy, promptly; "and once more I ask you why you are come back to London, and to this house above all others?"

"I've told you before that I am come for what I can get—money, money; and money I'll have, or I'll know the reason why. Where's my father?" he again demanded, in a bullying tone.

"Your father is out," responded Betsy.

"And you in the house all alone?" asked my uncle, with eager, flashing eyes. "But of course you are; and I have a good mind to——." He glanced around him, and seemed preparing to spring from his seat on the table; but a look from Betsy seemed to cause him to shrink from his half-formed purpose.

"You have a good mind to take what you can get, I suppose you mean to say," she said, calmly; "but you won't do it, William. And I can tell you something else: you will get nothing by waiting here. And you would be anywhere else rather than here at this minute, if you knew——." Here she suddenly paused.

"If I knew what?"

"What I am not going to tell you. I have altered my mind; and you shall wait as long as you please. You said just now that you came for food. Is it true that you are hungry, William?"

The very question seemed to rouse his craving appetite. "Do I look as if I had been feasting lately?" he asked.

He did not look like it. I had been watching the invader all the time the singular and, to me, inexplicable conference had been going on. It is little to say that I had then never seen a more famished-looking man, with cheeks so hollow, and eyes so wildly staring; it is more to the purpose that I have never since seen hunger so strongly marked on any countenance. My uncle looked badly enough when I first saw him in Mr. Filby's shop: he looked worse now. I have no doubt that Betsy Miller noticed the poor fellow's hungry looks, for her compassion was evidently roused, in spite of her indignation.

"You shall have food," she said; "but you must eat it here." And then she directed me to go into the kitchen and bring a loaf and cheese, and a knife.

I obeyed, and Betsy, taking the knife in her own hands—the pudding being dried on them by this time—cut a large slice and handed it to my uncle.

He took it and ate it—rather, let me say, devoured it, as a dog might.

"I must have drink too, he said," chokingly, when the bread and cheese had nearly disappeared. Betsy whispered to me, and I again went into the kitchen, returning with a jug of water.

"This! Is this all you are going to give me?" said he, seizing the jug and looking into it with disgust. "Water! only water!"

"Only water. It would have been better for you if you had drunk only water all through your life, William Bix," said Betsy.

"And now," she continued, when the recently fed man was wiping his mouth after his repast, "you had better go."

"I have not got all I came for yet," he answered.

"Do you want to kill your father outright?" she asked, reproachfully. "Haven't you done enough already to shorten his life? But what's the use of asking you such questions, William? It will be better for you to go before worse comes of it."

"I don't mean to go till I have got what I came for." He spoke with greater confidence, now that he had eaten, and drunken, and was refreshed. "I can wait; time isn't of much object to me," he said, insolently.

"And I can wait too," rejoined Betsy.

At that moment came another ring at the hall door, and my uncle's countenance was lighted up with a sort of malignant triumph. "Ah! I thought he wouldn't be long," he said; adding, "and I warn you, mistress, to leave me alone with the old man. A pretty thing, indeed, for a woman like you to be thrusting yourself in between a man and his own father."

"Open the door, Hurly," Betsy whispered to me; and I did so. It was not my grandfather who entered this time, but Mr. Falconer, followed by Alphonse, his Swiss servant. Mr. Falconer spoke to me in his cheery way, directly I opened the door, and then he passed on—

To come to a full stop the moment his eyes rested on my uncle

REAPPEARANCE OF A NE'ER-DO-WELL.

William, who, pale, trembling, and dismayed, seemed at once to shrink within himself at that steady, silent gaze, as at some dreadful apparition. Then he stealthily removed himself from the table, picked up his hat, retreated step by step backwards, until he was within a few paces of the yet open door; when suddenly turning, he would have darted through the doorway, but was arrested by a firm commanding word from Mr. Falconer.

"Stop!"

In another moment the two men stood confronting each other.

"Is this the way in which your promise is kept, William?" demanded my grandfather's patron sternly.

"What was I to do, sir? what am I to do?" whined the wretched man, in tremulous tones. "Look at me, Mr. Falconer: see to what I am reduced."

"By your own abominable vices and crimes. But I will waste no words upon you. You came for money, I suppose. How much?"

My uncle's eye kindled covetously, in spite of his evident terror, as he saw a purse drawn from Mr. Falconer's pocket. "It isn't for beggars to be choosers, sir," he said.

In another moment I heard the chink of money, and my poor uncle's murmured thanks.

"Silence! You offend more by your fawning than by your past ingratitude," said Mr. Falconer. "And now, listen to me. Let me but know that you ever enter this house again, uninvited, and the consequences of your former crime shall fall on you. Now begone!"

There was no need for a second command. In another moment the culprit was out of sight, and the door closed upon him.

"Do not tell your grandfather of this visit, Hurly," said Mr. Falconer to me presently, after he had held a short explanatory whispered consultation with Betsy Miller; "it would cause him a great deal of pain; and you don't want to do that, I am sure."

I said truly that I did not, and promised faithfully to keep my part of the secret. But it dwelt long on my mind. What could the mystery be?

CHAPTER VII.

MY UNCLE WILLIAM.

"WHAT are you thinking of, Hurly?" demanded Betsy Miller, suddenly looking up from her work. This was on the evening after the occurrence mentioned in my last chapter.

I was thinking of my uncle William; and I told Betsy so.

"You hadn't ought to be thinking about him. He is not worthy of it. He is a bad man, Hurly," said she.

"I cannot help thinking about him, Betsy," I rejoined; adding an impertinent question—"Were you not thinking about him too?"

"That's different," replied Betsy, quickly. "I have got a deal to think about that shouldn't come into a little head like yours. Wait till you are older."

"I can't help thinking—how can I, now?" I wanted to know.

"You should think of good things and good people; but I suppose that's too dull work for you. Any way, William Bix is a wicked man, and the less you think about him the better for you."

This might be very true; but then, if I could not help thinking about him, I could not. I stated this view of the case to Betsy very strongly, and it puzzled her.

BETSY TAKES ME INTO HER CONFIDENCE ABOUT WILLIAM BIX.

"I have seen uncle William before to-day," I remarked presently.

"What do you say, George Burley?" asked Betsy, in a tone of alarm, mingled with such stern reproof that I hastened to apologise and explain.

"I couldn't help it, could I, now?" I pleaded, when I had told of my former meeting with my uncle in Mr. Filby's shop, and what had passed there.

"And why did not you tell me of this before?" she demanded.

"Because I left off thinking about him till I saw him again to-day," said I. "That was right, wasn't it?" I asked, laughing at having turned the tables on my reprover. Betsy Miller, however, did not see the point of my retort.

"No; it wasn't right," she rejoined. "You ought to have told me, and then I should have guessed what I had to expect; and, if you ever come across that man again, and he dares to speak to you, mind you tell me every word he says, Hurly."

"So I will, then," I promised; "but what makes uncle William such a bad man?"

"What curious questions you ask, boy! What makes him bad? Why, what makes other people bad? What does the Bible say about it? But I see what it is," added my teacher; "you want to know the meaning of what you saw and heard this morning. Very natural, Hurly, but not proper."

"Why not proper, Betsy?"—so I went on.

"Because there's a deal that goes on in the world that little boys oughtn't to know."

This was bravely said by Betsy Miller. Nevertheless, I could judge by certain signs, which were intelligible enough to me, who had unconsciously studied my chief companion of the last four years, that Betsy was uncertain whether or not to take me into her confidence, but that the inclination to do so preponderated. According to my custom in such cases, therefore, I dropped the subject, and began to talk about something else.

The innocent *ruse* succeeded. Betsy got more and more fidgety, till presently she returned abruptly, of her own accord, to William Bix.

"What a dreadful wicked man that uncle of yours is, to be sure, Hurly," said she.

No response.

"You would like me to tell you all about him, now, shouldn't you?"

"You said it wouldn't be proper, Betsy."

"No more it would be for you to know *all*. Dear me! As if all *could* be known that bad people in this world do!" (this by way of interjection). "But it will be a warning to you, Hurly, to know a little of what your uncle has done." And, with this introduction, Betsy plunged at once into the following narrative.

CHAPTER VIII.

THE HISTORY OF A REPROBATE.

"IT was more than nineteen years ago that I came to live here at Silver Square along with your grandfather, bless him! It was the best move I ever made in my life, Hurly; for, as I have told you often and often, I had been knocked about like a shuttlecock between two battledores, till there wasn't much life left in me. But master was pleased with my looks, and I was pleased with his, and I was pleased with the place, and pleased with having no missus set over me; and—

there, you know all about it. I began a new sort of life, and here
I am now.

"When I first came, your grandfather had been a lone gentleman six or seven years, and had been terribly put upon and
robbed by a wicked maid-servant, who left at a day's notice, and
might have been took up and tried for what she had done, only
master was merciful, and didn't treat her as she deserved; and
why I tell you of this is because it comes partly into your uncle's
story. My dear, I am not going to tell you all that was found
out about that creature, so don't think it; but her name was
Sarah Warner. Warner, indeed! I'd have warned her.

"To go on with what I was saying. There was your poor
grandfather, all lonely, and badly cut up in his mind, one way
and another; and there was your dear precious mother, who was
about fifteen years old at that time; and she was the very best
young person I ever knew: so gentle and good, Hurly, as you
would have known well of your own knowledge if she had been
let to live. But that wasn't to be. And I little thought, when
she went away into the country for a holiday, that it was to go on
to a marriage, and end in a death; but that *was* to be, you see."

"You have told me about that very often, Betsy," said I,
interrupting my good friend: and so indeed she had; and as the
upshot of her reflections always went to prove how much happier
my mother would have been, and how much longer she would
have lived, if she had not married my father, I had felt myself
getting inwardly rather restive under the infliction. It was very
well in Betsy to cry up my dead mother: I had no objection to
that; but she need not have cried down my dead father; so I
thought, in my childish way. I think that Betsy guessed what
was passing in my mind, for she said hastily—

"You are right, Hurly; it is your uncle's story I began upon,
and not your mother's. He was about thirteen years old—William

Bix was—when I first came here, and a very pretty boy he was, too, to look at: bright sparkling eyes, curly black hair, and such a pleasant, merry manner with him. You would not think it now, would you?"

No, I should not have thought it. I could not have imagined that the haggard, wretched, brutalized-looking man whom I had that day seen, had ever been a pleasant, merry, blooming boy.

"But he was, though," said Betsy Miller, when I expressed my surprise. "He had lost his innocence when I first knew him, but not his innocent looks. It takes some time to get rid of *them*," continued she; "but be sure of this, Hurly, as certain as ever men or boys, women or girls, make up their minds to be downright bad, and give themselves up to it, the face begins to alter, and keeps on altering till there is not a bit of the old look left. And another thing, Hurly: the more like angels they might have been in beauty, the more like devils they come to be in ugliness."

How solemnly Betsy said this I am not able to write down; I can only remember it the more vividly, because, strange as the remark seemed then, I have so often in later years observed the same thing, that I am convinced of its general truth.

"Yes, Hurly," continued Betsy, "your uncle was a fine-looking boy, and uncommonly proud of him his father was, though, as I have told you before, your mother was his great favourite. But he loved William so well that he would not believe anything wrong in him. Wrong enough there was, however. I never reckoned myself sharp-sighted after people's faults; but what are you to do, you know, when they blaze out before your face? And that's what William Bix's faults did. It didn't take long to let me into the knowledge that Sarah Warner, who had been living with your grandfather over five years, had been at work, turning all that might have been good in the boy into evil. Oh dear! it frightens me now to think of the awful deeps of wickedness there were in that poor boy's heart; he let it out sooner than he would have done, I dare say, because he thought I must be such another as his old teacher and tempter. And when he found out that it wasn't so, he had said and done too much to blind me."

" It was Sarah Warner, then, who made uncle William so wicked," said I.

" It was, and it wasn't, Hurly. She hadn't made Miss Mary—that's your mother—wicked. 'Tis my belief"—here Betsy's voice dropped almost to a whisper, and her low tone became very solemn—" 'tis my belief that Sarah Warner was set on by the devil, or one of his agents, to corrupt both them young people; but one of them prayed to be delivered from evil, and also resisted the devil, and the other did nothing of the sort. So you see, Hurly, there was blame and sin all ways, and sorrow enough, you may be sure.

" As to what William Bix did to show his badness," continued Betsy, " for one thing, he was the most outdacious story-teller I ever knew. There was no believing a single word he said; he would stand, and look you in the face, so open-like and innocent, and say that black was white, or white black ! If you had even seen him do a thing, and he knew you had seen him, not a bit of difference did it make to him; if it suited him to deny it, deny it he would, and almost persuade you that he hadn't done it. Then, he used the most awful words; dear, dear ! I have put my hands to my ears many a time, to shut out the sound of his wickedness, and my flesh has been all of a creep while he was standing by, as bold as brass, with his mouth full of cursing, as the Bible says. And as for thieving, there was nothing that came in his way that he wouldn't lay hands on if he took a fancy to it. I soon found that I must lock up everything, especially money; if I didn't it was sure to be gone. And locking up did not do either; for he found out how to pick locks, or got false keys, and that was the first thing that opened your poor grandfather's eyes to your uncle's wickedness."

"Didn't you ever tell of him, Betsy?" I asked, not unnaturally.

"Tell of him! Yes, I did, Hurly. I told of him so often that I very nearly lost my place by it. Your grandfather wouldn't believe any harm of William. It was all my jealousy, he said. And then the boy would put on such a smooth face to his father, and make believe to be so innocent, and stand out so boldly for his being in the right, that all I got for my pains was to be told that I had prejudiced myself against the poor motherless boy, and wasn't to take any more stories about him to his father, otherwise I might find another place where there was not a boy to be in my way. After that, my mouth was shut, you see; and all I could do was to join with Miss Mary—your mother, Hurly—in trying to mend the young rebel; but he only laughed at us, my dear, and dared me to tell any more stories about him.

"At last, the time came when your grandfather's eyes were to be opened, Hurly, whether he would or not. It was when your uncle William was about seventeen years old that it happened. But I must tell you first that he had had a good education, and was very clever too. Learning was no trouble to him; and as he took care to mind his behaviour at the great city school where he went every day, and wasn't very sharply looked after, perhaps, by the masters, he left with a decent character, I believe, only, as I have heard, he was so well known for his want of truthfulness that he got the name of 'Lying Bix' among his schoolfellows, which wasn't a pretty name to be called, was it? Otherwise, he passed in the crowd, I dare say, as many a clever, wicked person does for a time; but only for a time, Hurly, mind that. There comes a finding-out time, sooner or later.

" When your uncle left school," continued my informant, " he could write a beautiful hand, like copperplate print, almost ; they told me, too, that he was a famous Latin scholar, and maybe he was. I have heard some people say," observed Betsy, after a pause, " that all you have got to do to keep folks from going wrong is to give them school-learning. It isn't any such thing, Hurly. Learning is good when there's good use made of it, of course it is ; and I'd have you get as much as you can, my dear ; but it is only good when there is a good use made of it, mind that. It won't keep people from being wicked if they mean wicked ; it only helps them on in it, and makes them more mischievous than they would have been, just as it has your uncle William.

" Well, he came from school, and was bound apprentice to a doctor. And then he began to show more openly what was in his heart. He found out a set of other young men, as wild as himself ; and they led one another into all sorts of wickedness almost. There was one wickedness, however, that he did not give in to, and that was drunkenness. He did not take to that till years afterwards, when he grew desperate and left off caring what people thought of him ; then he began to drink, and took a liking to it, as you have seen, Hurly.

" But if he wasn't a drunkard he was a dicer ; and that was as bad, or worse," Betsy went on.

" What is a dicer, Betsy ? " I asked, interrupting her.

" A gambler, Hurly : a man that plays at dice and cards, and such games as you know nothing about, and need not want to, for money ; sometimes losing and sometimes winning, sometimes cheating and sometimes being cheated."

I was as wise now as I had been before, and very little wiser. I made no further remark, however, and Betsy went on with her story.

" Many is the time I have sat up till twelve and one, and two

and three o'clock in the morning, to let in my gentleman after he
had been spending the night in play of this sort, and all the while
he was pretending that he had been kept up all night mixing
medicines or seeing patients.   You may be sure that he could not
go on so without spending a deal of money, and, if he couldn't get
it by fair means, he would get it by foul.   And so it was he got
found out at last: he robbed his master, and he robbed your
grandfather by means of the false keys I told you of.   There was
a pretty to-do, you may be sure.   His master was for having him
sent to prison as a thief, but your grandfather could not bear the
thought of such a disgrace, and so he made up to the doctor what
he had been robbed of.   As to master William, he pretended to be
so sorry for what he had done, and made such promises not to do so
any more, that he got forgiven.   There was no going back to his
master, though ; and as nothing else could be done with him then,
he led an idle life at home, for three years and more, doing nothing
useful, but lots of things on the sly that he ought to have been
ashamed of, you may be sure.

"I cannot tell you how often his father had to pay his debts,
and to pay money that wasn't debt, to get William out of trouble ;
nor how many people he deceived and robbed in one way or another
(Mr. Filby was one of them).   At last, however, when his poor
father was driven almost out of his mind to know what to do,
he wrote the whole story of his wicked son, and sent it to Mr.
Falconer, to ask his advice.   And what do you think Mr.
Falconer did, Hurly ?"

"I don't know.   What did he do, Betsy ?"

"Why, he came all the way from—from wherever his home is—
hundreds of miles beyond the sea, and, after he had done and said
all he could to comfort your grandfather, he took your uncle
William in hand.   What passed between them nobody ever knew ;
but the end of it was that, when Mr. Falconer went back again to

his home, after stopping in London a month, he took William away to live with him, hoping that, when he was separated from his old bad companions, he would mend.

"It was very good of him," said I.

"Of course it was, Hurly; and, if William Bix had had a bit of gratitude in him, he could have been turned from his wickedness then, one would have thought. And it was hoped that he would—at least, his father hoped so, for he made great promises. And, indeed, for two or three years it seemed as though these promises would be kept, for he sent beautiful letters home, and also Mr. Falconer wrote to say how steady William had become.

"But it was all of a piece with your uncle's former doings, Hurly. He was only laying by for more mischief, and mischief came at last.

"One day, eight or nine years ago, Mr. Falconer suddenly came across the sea to London, when he wasn't in the least expected; and the minute I opened the door at his knock, I knew by his looks that something had gone wrong with William Bix. And something had gone wrong. I told you just now, Hurly, what a nice hand he wrote. Oh, he was clever, he was! Well, would you believe it? he had learned to write so like Mr. Falconer that hardly anybody could tell the difference; and when he thought he was perfect in it, he wrote Mr. Falconer's name to some papers —some money papers, you understand—and got them changed away for money, lots of money, Hurly—hundreds and hundreds and hundreds of pounds—and then ran away with it."

"Where did he run to?" I asked.

"Nobody knew for certain; but Mr. Falconer was not far off from right when he guessed that he had found his way back to London; for in London he was, and in London he was found, after a good deal of searching, among his old set of wicked companions, living like a prince on the money he had brought with

him. He had not shown his face in Silver Square, you may be
sure of that; but here he was made to come to give account of
himself to Mr. Falconer and your poor dear grandfather, who was
more dead than alive.

"What they said to one another I never knew," continued
Betsy, "for they were shut up together, them three, in the great
drawing-room, for more than two hours. At last they all came out
into the hall; Mr. Falconer was leading your poor grandfather by
the arm, and half supporting him, while the tears were running fast
down his cheeks—your grandfather's I mean—and he was sobbing
as though his heart would break. After them walked out your uncle,
as bold as brass, with a wild scornful brightness in his eyes, though
his cheeks were pale enough. There wasn't a word said, Hurly;
but your uncle walked straight to the hall-door, let himself out, and
shut it after him. Then Mr. Falconer led your grandfather away
to his own room, and there they sat together all the rest of the day.

"Your uncle never came back again, at that time nor afterwards,
till yesterday, as you saw him. And after a little while your
grandfather began to get more like his old self again—but never
quite—no, never quite; and it is my belief that a sight of William
Bix, like as he was to-day when he came here, would be the death
of him. A mercy he wasn't in the house when your uncle came;
and a mercy Mr. Falconer had the dealing with him. He won't
come again directly, I'll warrant."

"But, Betsy," said I, when it seemed as though she had come
to the end of her story, "you told uncle William that you could
send him to Newgate if you liked."

"And so I could have done, and so I can do now if I have a
mind, Hurly; but this is what you wouldn't understand if I were
to tell you, perhaps," said Betsy, with an air of conscious superiority which she sometimes naturally assumed towards me. I
fancy, moreover, that she thought she had been communicative

enough for one time. At any rate, she drew the line at this part of the history, and began to extract from it the obvious moral, for which I was not unprepared ; namely, that sorrow is sure to spring, sooner or later, from sin ; that whatsoever a man sows, that shall he also reap, and that the way of transgressors is hard ; and that, when talents, and opportunities, and education are misused and abused, they become a curse to the possessor and to the world, instead of a blessing.

This was the summing up of Betsy's narrative, which had lasted so long that it was past my bedtime when she came to an end. I went to bed, therefore, but not to sleep ; my mind was too full, and my thoughts were too much exercised with the story I had heard, for that.

What a new world had been opened to me in that true history ! It was as though a curtain had been drawn up, and I had obtained a glance of things that had indeed previously existed, but which had hitherto been beyond my apprehension. And how I trembled in soul when I thought myself to be within reach of the dangers which had brought such ruin upon my unhappy relative.

My poor uncle William ! He was a happy, innocent boy once, and only to think what he had come to ! And why not I ?

There was one hope for me—I remember thinking this, in the midst of my mental perturbation—and this hope was that God could help me if I sought His help. It was something to me then that I had an unwavering and undisturbed faith in all that I had ever read in the Bible. My knowledge was, of course, very defective ; and my doctrinal views probably were very unsound, but I believed that God could help me if He would, and the petition I know not how often repeated welled out from my overburdened heart, " Lead me not into temptation : Lead me not into temptation : Lead me not into temptation : but deliver me from evil ! "

I do not mean to say that I had, at that time, any or much right conception of the nature of sin, as an act of rebellion against an infinitely holy God ; I dare say, if I had seen my uncle in very prosperous circumstances, and had been told that he was a wicked man, I should not have been very much troubled. But it was brought home to me now that sin is an evil thing and a bitter ; and something for even a boy to avoid. So far, then, the sight had been salutary to me ; while the cry still went up—" Lead me not into temptation ; but deliver me from evil ! "

And so, with this petition on my lips, I fell asleep that night. On the following day I endeavoured to learn more particulars about my uncle William ; but Betsy was not to be drawn out (so she said), she only hoped that I might profit by what she had already told me. And with this answer I was obliged to be satisfied until in process of time my curiosity almost subsided.

Many years afterwards, however, I came to understand what Betsy Miller's hint about Newgate meant ; and I may as well put it down here. It was, in effect, as follows :—

Mr. Falconer remained some days in London after the distressing meeting already described ; and before he recrossed to the Continent he had a private interview with Betsy Miller.

" You have some regard for your master, I think, Mrs. Betsy," said the eccentric man.

" A good deal, sir," said Betsy.

" Right. I am glad of it ; and I can tell you he has a high esteem for you. And, as that is the case, I presume you are not likely to leave his service for some time to come ? "

" No," said Betsy, " unless he turns me away."

" Good again. Now, about that unhappy lad. I shall leave you in charge to protect your master from him. You know what he has been doing."

Yes, Betsy knew this ; and she knew that, if the young profligate were not restrained by fear of consequences, there was nothing he would hesitate to do. She knew this, and quite expected that he would some day, sooner or later, be the ruin and death of his father. All this she fully believed, and acknowledged in the course of the conversation that followed. But what could she do to prevent it? If William would come to his father's house, and rob him and bully him out of his money and his life, like a highwayman, as he was only fit to be, how could she prevent it?

"It shall be in your power to put a stop to it at any time, my good friend," said Mr. Falconer, "if you have only courage enough to act up to my directions when he intrudes."

"I'll do anything you tell me, if it is for my master's good," said Betsy, boldly.

"Listen, then," returned Mr. Falconer. "The young man has robbed me, you know, to the amount of five hundred pounds. I care nothing, or little, about the loss, as far as I am concerned; and, though I might recover some of the plunder, I shall not attempt to do it. It will all be spent soon enough, no doubt; and there will be the end of it. But I have got a paper to which he forged my name, and he knows it; and he knows, too, that it is in my power to transport him for life, for that forgery. Now, I have passed my word to him that, for his father's sake, I will not prosecute him, on condition of his leaving the country, and never troubling my good friend Mr. Bix any more with his presence. Well he *has* left the country. He sailed for America yesterday. I saw to that. So, for the present, your master is safe from personal annoyance. But I have no faith in the young man's promises, and I am afraid that, when he has spent all the money he has with him, he will find his way back to England, and to Silver Square. What do you think, Betsy?"

"I should say most likely he will, sir," said the confidante; "especially if he thinks there's anything more to be got out of his poor father. And think that he will, so long as both of them live."

"Just my opinion," said Mr. Falconer; "and so I have taken measures to meet that difficulty. I have placed the forged paper in the hands of a sharp London lawyer, and given him instructions to set the police to work, and have William Bix arrested the moment he causes any fresh trouble. The lawyer's name is Fawley: he lives in Hatton Garden. Stay, here is his address. You will take care of it?"

"I'll take care of it, sir," said Betsy.

"And all you will have to do, in the event we have supposed, will be to give Fawley a hint that the young man is in London, or send for him if you are in any trouble of any sort through William. He will do all the rest."

"I'll mind your direction, sir; but would it not be better for Mr. Bix himself——"

"No, he is too tender-hearted. I look to you to protect him."

And Betsy promised again that she would take care of her old master; and on this understanding the conference ended.

As I have said, it was many years afterwards that this matter came to my knowledge, and I am unable to fill up the blank which it will be seen has been left in William Bix's history. It is easy to be conjectured, however, that, having lived the life of a rowdy in America till the remnant of his plunder was dissipated, and then having preyed upon society till it was no longer safe for him to remain in that country, and fancying, too, that his trouble in England was blown over, he worked his way home to levy fresh contributions from his father, when he met the unexpected check I have already described.

I have only to add here that he did not make his appearance again at Silver Square. The apparition of his injured benefactor, and Betsy's threat of Newgate, probably frightened him. Happily, too, for my poor grandfather's peace and comfort, the fact that my uncle William had returned to England was successfully kept from his knowledge.

I shall have more to tell of William Bix in some future chapter. At present, however, I dismiss him from the scene.

CHAPTER IX.

MR. FALCONER'S STORY, SHOWING WHAT A FRIEND HE HAD.

THE principal object of Mr. Falconer's present visit to England was to seek out a distant relative—some cousin of the fourth or fifth degree—with whom in earlier life he had bitterly quarrelled. As the cause of that quarrel was identically the same as that which drove him from home society, and fathered upon him the eccentricities of which I have already spoken, I may be permitted to refer to it, throwing upon the circumstances the light of information I obtained some years after the days of my boyhood.

Mr. Falconer, or Jack Falconer, as he was then called, and Frank Tozer, were schoolfellows and fast friends—as fast friends, at any rate, as two boys could be, one of whom was a half-spoiled favourite of fortune, and the other a poor dependant. I am afraid—indeed, the fact is beyond dispute—that the boy Tozer had been impressed with the necessity of paying court to, and treating with extreme deference, the heir-apparent to the great Silver estate; and there is no doubt that he played the *toady* exceedingly well. The natural result followed: Jack Falconer was very well pleased with the worship paid to him by his cousin, and was probably exorbitant in his demands for more; while, on the other hand, the character and the principles of the boy-worshipper became deteriorated. I dare say he had no real regard for the fortunate relative, and made up for his servility to him by overbearing conduct towards almost all others. At all events, after the two youths had left school, which they did at the same time, Jack Falconer was remembered as a good-natured fellow, who was always ready to do a kindness to a schoolfellow, while Frank Tozer was spoken of as a big bully, a sneak, and an undermining mole.

Frank Tozer's entire dependence was on the liberality of Jack's father, an easy-tempered, extravagant man, who had somewhat diminished the annual value of his estate by sundry mortgages raised upon it to meet some passing whim, but who so far took charge of Frank's fortunes as to pay for his articles to a London attorney, and to allow him a sufficient maintenance during the term. But, to mark the difference in position and prospects between the two youths, Jack, on leaving school, was sent to college, preparatory to his studying the law under a celebrated conveyancer. Eventually, he entered at one of the Inns, ate his dinners at the Hall, and came out into the world as a budding barrister.

While these several stages in young Falconer's history had been developing, his far-off cousin, Frank Tozer, had toiled through his articles, and, by the further help of his relative and patron, had taken offices (two small rooms on a second floor, containing an old desk, an older carpet, and three worm-eaten chairs) in a little court leading out of Bishopsgate Street. Whether the office ever attracted any clients was a question which principally concerned the young attorney—not entirely, however; because, clients or no clients, an attorney must eat, drink, and sleep; and, wanting clients, Frank's means for these necessaries of life came from the rents of Silver Square.

A FALSE FRIEND.

E

Frank Tozer was always a welcome guest at the house of the elder Falconer. It is presumable that he played his cards well (to use a sporting phrase); or, in other words, that the facile subserviency he had practised towards his schoolfellow Jack had, by some years' further experience, become almost a second nature to him, and was exercised with increased facility towards Jack's easy-going and self-indulgent father. A great show of submission, some cheap services in the way of his profession, occasionally rendered, with a sufficient admixture of flattery, made his society acceptable to the failing sexagenarian.

Perhaps even these easy efforts were not needed; for Jack Falconer, who was now living under his father's roof, retained his old liking for his former schoolmate, and courted his society. It was Jack's weakness—an amiable, if not a common one—that he could see no blemish in any of his friends; and he was as far as possible from suspecting that the affectionate yet deferential bearing of Frank Tozer towards himself was almost entirely prompted by self-interest.

"I wonder how it is Jack doesn't see through that sneaking fellow," was a remark sometimes hazarded by some common acquaintance.

"All the better for Tozer that he doesn't, and all the happier for Jack Falconer," was the probable reply of another common acquaintance. A mistake this; for it is never well to deceive, even unintentionally; and, in the long run, it adds to no man's happiness to be deceived.

For the time, however, young Falconer was happy enough in this deception, and gave so many proofs of his friendship to Frank as might have warmed his heart into something like true reciprocity, if it had been a whit more pervious than it was to such softening influences.

The death of the elder Falconer about this time drew the young barrister and attorney into still closer connections, and strengthened their friendly bonds by a kind of mutual interest. On the part of young Mr. Falconer (no longer to be called Jack, except by very privileged intimates), it may be stated that he found his affairs in considerable confusion, needing a clear head and an industrious right hand to disentangle them, and put them in due order. Frank Tozer readily undertook this drudgery, and, being a better lawyer than his friend, though his friend was a barrister, he really made himself of some service. On the other hand, the new owner of the Silver estate was not only sincere in his verbal acknowledgments of his friend's good offices, but he was also profuse in rewarding them; and as Frank Tozer, in addition to this, was a legatee for a few hundred pounds, under the will of old Mr. Falconer, his circumstances were considerably improved, though he was still comparatively needy. Nor did it appear that he made any great advances in his profession, or any large addition to the number of his clients.

While affairs were in this state, Mr. Falconer did what most men naturally do, at least once in their lives—he fell in love. The object of attraction was a young lady, his junior by several years, who had then recently been introduced into the circle of society in which Falconer occasionally moved. Julia Marmaduke was an orphan, and had inherited a fortune of about four thousand pounds, which her friends, who were anxious to see her "well married," magnified to twenty thousand—insinuatingly, of course. But Mr. Falconer knew better than this; and if he had been anxious to secure a money prize in the matrimonial lottery, he most assuredly would have passed this young lady by. Had Julia's fortune, however, been sunk in the sea, hundreds of fathoms deep, it would have made no difference to the enamoured lover, who was perfectly satisfied with his own share of the good things of this life, and admired the charmer for the loveliness of her person, the gaiety of her manners, and the mental qualifications which she was supposed by him to possess.

It may be imagined that Falconer, with so many advantages in his favour—such as youth, manly spirit, good property, engaging manners, and a well-cultivated mind, and with the awkwardness of inexperience rubbed off by contact with the world and by his legal training—would have found no difficulty in arriving at an amicable understanding with the lady of his affection. This would be a mistake, however : and, strange as it may sound, it is often seen in affairs of this nature, that those who are most favoured by circumstances are the most diffident of success. It was so with Falconer, who fluttered like a dazzled moth, for weeks and months, around the pretty Julia, before he could pluck up courage to offer his own heart in exchange for her hand. He made the venture at last, however, and succeeded, almost to his own astonishment, but not at all to that of the amused lookers-on, who had long before settled the matter in their minds, to his satisfaction and their own.

And now Falconer was in an elysium of earthly delight. But I have no occasion to enlarge on this part of his history, and shall only say that it was soon understood that the courtship, if sweet, was to be short, and that, in a few weeks, the bachelor home of the wealthy young barrister would be a bachelor home no longer.

Alas ! the enamoured lover little suspected how short-lived his exultant happiness was to be. I never read that touching lamentation of David, in the fifty-fifth psalm, without being involuntarily reminded of Mr. Falconer. "It was not an enemy that reproached me ; then I could have borne it ; neither was it he that hated me that did magnify himself against me ; then I would have hid myself from him. But it was thou, a man, mine equal, my guide, and mine acquaintance ! He hath put forth his hands against such as be at peace with him ; he hath broken his covenant. The words of his mouth were smoother than butter, but war was in his heart; his words were softer than oil, yet were they drawn swords."

In plain terms, Mr. Falconer was deceived both in the character of the lady whom he would have made his wife, and in the fidelity of his friend. It is an old, old story, often repeated with many variations; and it need not be retold in full here. It is enough to say that Falconer became the victim of a base plot on the part of his treacherous friend, who, dazzled with the young lady's fortune, and encouraged by her coquetry, secretly determined to have her himself for a wife. In carrying out this design, he first poisoned Miss Marmaduke's mind against her lover, by most wicked and unfounded charges affecting both his moral character, and his supposed wealth; and when these insinuations had taken effect, he made passionate protestations of admiration and love; and persuaded the foolish and fickle girl to entrust her future happiness to his keeping as her husband.

All this was done with so much secrecy that the first intimation Mr. Falconer received of the utter prostration of his hopes, was in the astounding intelligence that the false friend from whom he had parted on the usual terms of confidential familiarity, only a few days before was married to Julia Marmaduke, and, with his newly married wife, had left London on a wedding tour.

The effect produced on poor Jack Falconer by this sudden blow was intensely sorrowful. For a time he sank into a kind of mental lethargy, bordering (so the physicians said) on madness. Recovering from this he formed the determination of quitting for ever, as his home, the land in which he had suffered so terrible a disappointment. I have already shown that this determination was carried into effect; and though the deceived and disappointed man gradually recovered some degree of serenity of mind, he could never be prevailed upon to abandon the seclusion he had voluntarily chosen, and re-enter the society in which his dearest hopes had been laid low.

A few more words will complete this episodal history. On their return to London the bridegroom and bride found themselves —not, perhaps, to Frank Tozer's great surprise—peremptorily excluded from the society in which Julia had once moved. Whether or not then, or how long a time, or how shortly, afterwards, she woke to a sense of her folly and disgrace, and discovered that she had been the dupe of a designing and heartless man, it is not for me to say. All that is necessary to add here is that, finding himself shunned and execrated by all his former acquaintances, Frank abandoned his offices in the Bishopsgate Street court, together with his very few London clients, and (with Julia's money, or part of it) was reported to have bought a practice in the country, but in what part of the country no one took sufficient interest in him, or in his wife, to inquire. In the course of a few months, therefore, they had both faded not only out of knowledge, but almost out of remembrance.

CHAPTER X.

WANTED, AN HEIR.—MY FIRST JOURNEY.

IN the previous chapter I have found it necessary to narrate some events which transpired in the lives of other persons many years before I was born. It will be presently seen how intimate a connection there is between those events and what I have further to write. I may say, also, that, though I have headed these papers with my own name, no small portion of them will be occupied with the sayings and doings of the various people with whom, in the days of my childhood, boy-hood, and youth, I was brought into contact. With this expla-nation, if explanation be required, I resume my history.

I have said that Mr. Falconer's principal object in his return to London was to seek out the faithless pair who, thirty years before, had so deeply and treacherously injured him—not for the pur-pose, be sure, of taking a late and tardy revenge upon the false friend and fickle dame, nor even to satisfy a vain curiosity; but, judging from what really did afterwards take place, that he might condone the past offence by showering benefits on the offenders.

Anger—however righteous and justifiable—must be very deep and implacable to last thirty years; and, as Mr. Falconer was essentially a generous man, I am persuaded that his resentment had long since faded away. Still, in the earlier years of his voluntary banishment; his mind had been too acutely sensitive to the wrong he had suffered to permit him to make any inquiries respecting Frank Tozer and his wife, while a kind and considerate reticence had been maintained by such of his friends at home as might have informed him of their destiny. It is not wonderful, therefore, that in the long lapse of time, no tidings either of their continued existence, or of their place of abode, had ever reached him. Nor is it strange that, when he eventually roused himself to make those inquiries, he found none of the few who remained to him of the old circle of his acquaintance who were competent to answer his questions satisfactorily. The Tozers? They knew nothing of the Tozers. Ah! Miss Marmaduke that was? Yes; they just remembered the young lady, and the circumstances of her marriage; but she and her husband left London years and years ago, and where they went, or whether they were dead or alive, no one could tell.

"My dear Jack," said Mrs. Meredith, an elderly and very

infirm old lady, on whom Mr. Falconer called one day, I being his companion ; and, as she spoke, she pressed his broad, big hand with hers, which was thin, wrinkled, and tremulous—" My dear Jack, why are you so anxious to know anything about that very treacherous man and his poor, silly wife ? They are far beneath your notice ; and I hoped that, by this time, you had almost entirely forgotten them."

Mr. Falconer shook his head gravely. " My memory is too sadly retentive," he said ; " and, as old age creeps on, I find that former scenes and circumstances stand out in bolder relief than they did twenty years ago."

" Old age, indeed ! " returned the lady, with a smile. " You must not begin to talk of old age yet. Wait till you have passed beyond the threescore and ten years of the psalmist, as I have : and then, indeed, you may say that old age is creeping on. But you are right about former scenes being revived as we grow older ; I have long experienced that strange phenomenon. I don't believe there is such a thing as real and entire oblivion : memory does not get old. But you have not answered my question : to what end do you go about distressing yourself in seeking to know that which would be far better buried in ignorance ? "

" Simply, my dear lady, that I may bury my past resentment in an act of justice. And I can tell you, moreover, that my remembrances of the past do not distress me, as you imagine : they only soften me. I think of poor Frank as my boyish companion and friend, of the many acts of mutual kindness that passed between us."

" All sheer selfishness and guile on his part," interposed the old lady, sharply.

" I did not think so then, and though I have since fancied it might have been so, I do not wish to think it now," said Mr. Falconer. " But, if they were, I have, as I have just said, an act of justice to perform.   I have no other relatives in the world than Frank and his wife, and his children, if they have children."

"I see.   The great Silver estate is not to go begging, then?"

"No, nor to furnish picking for lawyers, either, if I can help it.   I intend, before I leave London, to make my last will and testament."

"And you want an heir.   But do you tell me, Mr. Falconer, that you have lived all these years without having made a will?"

"No; I have not been quite so unwise.   I made a will thirty years ago, when I was smarting with disappointment, and burning furiously with resentment.   You may guess what sort of a will that was.   I made another twenty years ago, which, ten years afterwards, I revised.   But I am not satisfied."

"Well, I have no right to pry into your secrets, my dear Jack, nor to criticise your actions," said the kind old lady.   "I would help you if I could; but I really have not the slightest recollection of having ever heard what became of those people.   By the way, have you thought of looking into the law lists, or making inquiries at the Stamp Office?   Attorneys have to take out a license to practise, I believe."

"Yes; in common with hawkers and other worthies.   And you may be sure that I have left no stone of this sort unturned; but without success.   Poor Frank seems to have slipped out of existence."

"Perhaps he may have done this in reality.   Why not advertise, and offer a reward to any one who can give information on the subject?"

"Ah, this is the advice my friend Bix gives me; and it will have to be my last resource, though I would have avoided the publicity if I could," returned Mr. Falconer.   "However, there seems to be no alternative, and it shall be done."

I very well remember this conversation, though at that time I did not perfectly understand it. Presently it turned to other subjects of less interest to my story, and then we took our departure.

About three weeks after this a letter for Mr. Falconer arrived by post, and was put into his hands as we—that is to say, he, my grandfather, and I—sat at breakfast. Breaking the seal, Mr. Falconer commenced reading the letter; then he hastily rose and left the room, apparently disturbed and agitated. He soon returned, however, and apologized to my grandfather for his rudeness, as he called it.

"No unexpectedly bad news, I hope, sir?" said that gentleman.

"Startling, but not very strange, perhaps. My advertisements have taken effect, at any rate," said Mr. Falconer, gravely.

My grandfather raised his eyebrows and nodded.

"Poor Frank is dead," continued my grandfather's patron, with a sigh—"has been dead ten years; and Julia—but read the letter for yourself, Bix, and tell me what you think of it," he added, passing the epistle over to his faithful steward, who carefully adjusted his spectacles, and obeyed the instructions.

"A rather singular letter," he remarked presently.

"Ah, you would say so, I knew that. But what is to be done next?"

"That is for you to decide, Mr. Falconer," said my grandfather.

"I don't know about that. Tell me what you think," returned the patron.

"The lady seems very desirous of renewing old friendships, sir," observed Mr. Anthony Bix. "Hurly, my boy," he added, turning to me, "there's a note on my office-table I want taken to Fleet Street; run with it, and wait for an answer."

Understanding this to mean that I was one too many in the conference, I withdrew and departed on the errand. On my return the subject of the letter seemed dropped for that day and the next. On the day after that, however, I was made aware that Mr. Falconer intended to take a journey into Kent in the following week, and that I was to accompany him.

Since my first introduction to Silver Square I had never been beyond the outskirts of London, and I was delighted enough with the thought of the trip, especially when I learned that we were to travel not by the ordinary conveyance of a stage-coach (the time of which I am writing being long before railroads were thought of), but in a grand carriage hired for the occasion, drawn by post-horses.

I pass over the intermediate days to the eventful morning when, equipped in my Sunday suit, and with a small bag containing a change of clothes (for our journey was planned for several days), I sprang into the carriage by the side of Mr. Falconer, the silent Alphonse having packed himself into the rumble behind us. Our adieus were soon spoken, and then merrily whirled round the wheels at the crack of the postilion's whip, and we left Silver Square behind us, greatly excited, no doubt, by the unwonted stir we had made. Soon, too, the city was in our rear, and in an hour we were gaily bowling over the smooth turnpike road, with green hedges and meadows on either side.

I have no intention of describing the day's journey along one of the pleasantest roads leading out of London: it is enough to say that, at three o'clock in the afternoon, we drove into the old-fashioned city of Canterbury, and drew up at one of the principal inns, where we alighted, and where Mr. Falconer ordered what seemed to me a sumptuous banquet. Not that he was an epicure, for his habits were particularly simple; nor that our eight or nine hours' journey had quickened his appetite; for, when the dinner had made its appearance, he contented himself almost entirely with vegetables and bread, washed down with a glass or two of wine. But it was characteristic of him to think a good deal for the comfort of others; and if he chose to starve himself, that was no reason why I and Alphonse should be starved too—so he said, as he pressed upon me with the kindest solicitude the choicest morsels from the various dishes set before us. This is a simple thing to relate, or even to remember, perhaps, after so many years; but I will not blot out what I have written, because it is indicative of the kindness which, in those early days, I constantly received from Mr. Falconer.

And I may as well say also, as another of my remembrances of that particular day, that our journey from London to Canterbury was a very silent one. In general, when at home by ourselves, Mr. Falconer was ready enough to enter into conversation with me, drawing me out, to use a common expression, to speak of my own scant attainments under the fostering care of Betsy Miller, and of my wishes and hopes for the future; then giving me interesting accounts of the foreign countries in which he had lived, and what pleased me almost better, lively anecdotes of his boyish days at school. But on the day of our long journey (it seemed long to me then) Mr. Falconer had spoken very few words from the time of his first stepping into the carriage, save to give necessary instructions to the post-boys, who were, of course, changed at every stage. It seemed to me that he was lost in some deep and solemn reverie, in which he almost forgot, not only my presence as I sat by his side, but also that he was travelling anywhere. Once or twice, when I ventured, with boyish freedom, to call his attention to any object which attracted mine, as we whirled rapidly along, he started up in a kind of bewilderment, and retorted to my exclamations, "Oh yes, Hurly; very curious, very curious indeed," and then immediately subsided into his silent state. I was not sorry, therefore, when our day's journey was broken by our arrival at Canterbury, and the necessity for

dining.   For it was but a break in the journey, in so far as one
more stage had to be passed over before it was ended.

Accordingly, when we had dined, and, like true Canterbury
pilgrims, had visited the shrine of St. Thomas-à-Becket, and
glanced at the other noted sights of the archiepiscopal city, we
resumed our seats in the carriage, and, after another hour's drive,
came to our resting-place at an old-fashioned inn, in the equally
old-fashioned, but pretty little town of Wingham, where the
kind-hearted landlady of the "Lion," compassionating my evident
fatigue, to say nothing of a terrible headache, induced, I am
afraid, by my over-generous dieting at Canterbury, insisted on
putting "the poor little fellow" to bed, which she did, and, with
her own hands, tucked me in comfortably between the sheets,
bestowing on me a motherly kiss as she bade me good-night, and
charged me to sleep soundly till morning—which I did.

CHAPTER XI.

A MORNING CALL IN THE COUNTRY.

OW, Hurly, for a good long walk this morning.   Can you
manage to stretch your legs, do you think?"
      We were at breakfast in a fine large room in the
"Lion" (which had once, as we were told, lodged a king, or
some royal personage), when Mr. Falconer thus addressed me.
He had been up, and had explored the town from one extremity
to the other, before my eyes were open, or my head removed from
its pillow; so he told me.   But he had good-naturedly waited
till I was ready to join him at the breakfast-table.

I was prepared to accompany him, of course; and before long we were on the road, being well stared at as we passed through the town, first because we were strangers, and next as being under suspicion as foreigners, a conclusion not unnaturally arrived at, in consequence of Mr. Falconer's luxuriant beard and rather fantastic costume.

It matters nothing to my story to what part of the surrounding country our steps were directed. For the gratification of the curious, however, I may briefly tell that we passed through a large and very pretty park soon after leaving the town, and afterwards through another before arriving at our destination. I may add, also, that Mr. Falconer had by this time recovered from his previous day's fit of taciturnity.

"Do you know, Hurly—no, you don't know, but can you guess what has brought us into Kent?" he asked, gaily, as we trudged along.

Now the truth is, I had guessed. I had retained in my mind the conversation Mr. Falconer had held with Mrs. Meredith, two or three weeks before, and the scrap of a dialogue which had passed between him and my grandfather still later; and I had had no great difficulty in arriving at the conclusion that his object was to visit the lady whom he had called Julia, and for whom he had advertised. So said I—

"You are going to see Julia, I think, sir?"

"Ha! and who told you about Julia?" he asked, with some evident amusement.

"Nobody, sir; only you mentioned that name to my grandfather when I was by; and I thought you seemed a little glad when you had that letter from her."

"Only a little glad, Hurly?"

"Glad and sorry too, sir," said I.

"You young rogue," rejoined the gentleman, laughing, and

pretending to threaten me with his walking cane: "I didn't know you were so sharp."

"You asked me if I could guess, sir," I said, apologetically.

"And you have guessed rightly. I *am* going to see an old friend (we may call her Julia here, when there is no one else present), whom I have not seen, nor even heard of, for more than thirty years. Do you think she will be glad to see me—as glad to see me as you fancied I was to hear from her?"

"Perhaps she will be sorry, sir—as sorry as you seemed to be," I retorted, saucily.

"Perhaps," said Mr. Falconer; but he did not seem to think so.

"Maybe she will not be glad to see *me*," I said.

"Ha! what makes you think so, Hurly?" he asked.

"You two may have so many things to talk about that she would not like me to hear," I replied.

"We must get out of ear-shot, then," he retorted, laughing one of his pleasant laughs. "At any rate, I dare say we shall manage to dispose of you somehow."

"Is she a nice lady?" I asked, presently—that is to say, when we had walked a quarter of a mile side by side, silently.

"She! Of whom are you talking, Hurly?" demanded Mr. Falconer, waking out of a brown study into which he had fallen.

"Julia, sir."

"How should I know, sir?" he rejoined. "Didn't I tell you I had not seen her for thirty years? People alter very much in thirty years, Hurly."

"Yes, sir; I dare say they do," I assented.

"Your grandfather was a handsome enough young fellow when I first knew him thirty years ago. And I——"

"You are very handsome now, sir," I interposed. Do me the justice, reader, of giving me credit for meaning to be respectful. The fact is that, in my two or three months' companionship with

Mr. Falconer, he had so far caused me to forget the fifty years' difference in age there was between us as to make familiarity in conversation a matter of course; indeed, I verily believe that he sometimes half fancied himself a boy like myself when we were together, or perhaps there was a little guile on his part to "draw me out," as I have before observed; at any rate, he took my interruption in good part.

"You are a young flatterer, Hurly," said he; "but it is not worth laying my stick about your back, either; and so I will tell you that thirty years ago the young person whom you heard me call Julia *was* a very nice lady—at least, I thought so. She had a very charming temper, as I believed, and I know she had a soft and gentle voice, brown hair, bright sparkling eyes of no particular colour that I can remember, teeth white as ivory or whiter, pretty pouting ruby lips—which you know nothing about at present, Hurly—a delightful little nose, not at all Roman, but rather the reverse, and dimpled cheeks and chin. You see how perfectly I recollect, eh?"

Poor Mr. Falconer! I did not suspect then how he was trifling with his own feelings to give me a little amusement; or was he grimly and resolutely holding up himself to himself in a ridiculous light, to keep himself from playing the fool in the approaching interview? I cannot tell.

"You have a very good memory, sir," said I, innocently.

"Oh, very. But what do you think of the portrait I have drawn, Hurly? Will it do for that of 'a very nice lady'?"

"Pretty well, sir," I returned, entering into the spirit of Mr. Falconer's present loquacity; adding "only——" but Mr. Falconer cut me short with—

"Without joking, Hurly, I was very fond of that young lady when she was young; and now she is so much older I feel sorry for her. She has had a good many troubles to bear, I find. She

F

has lost her husband—Frank Tozer, my cousin, of whom you have heard me speak—she has buried several children, and I am afraid she is not very well off. So we must do what we can to comfort her; eh, Hurly?"

"Yes, sir."

"She has a son—only one, I am told—and he is about your age; a little older, perhaps; and I have brought you with me partly that you may make his acquaintance. I cannot tell what sort of a boy he is; but, as it is possible that you may know something of each other as you grow older, I wish to see how you get on together. Do you understand me, Hurly?"

"I think I do, sir," said I; and I thought I did. I could not help knowing, for instance, that Mr. Falconer was a rich man, without any other relatives than these newly sought and found distant cousins. I was only a boy, to be sure, and not a very precocious one either, I hope; but I had heard something about heirship, and knew, at any rate, that when people die they do not take money, or houses, or lands with them into the grave, consequently that they leave their wealth to others. I had heard what Mrs. Meredith had said about the Silver estate not going a-begging, and Mr. Falconer's wanting an heir; and it required no great stretch of sagacity, even in me, to arrive at the conclusion that this boy whom he had never seen, and of whose existence he had till lately been ignorant, but who was the son of his cousin and of the lady of whom he had once been fond, was on the fair road for this heirship, if all things turned out well. I even had the boldness to wonder whether the gentleman had any intention of offering himself as a second husband to the widowed lady whose youthful charms he so distinctly remembered, and whom he was so anxious to comfort. All this passed through my mind as one branch of the subject; another branch was that Mr. Falconer had kindly feelings towards myself, and had promised to do something at the

appeared to be red and moist with recent crying, and who, after vainly endeavouring to extract from my leader his name and business, save that he desired to see her mistress, rather unwillingly as I thought, introduced us into one of the darkened rooms, and departed on her errand. I judged by this, therefore, that Mr. Falconer had not pre-announced his intended visit.

Some time elapsed before we were disturbed; but as we sat in silence I could not shut my ears against the penetrating sound of certain distant voices, one of which I believed to be that of the diminutive handmaiden, who seemed to be plaintively defending herself from the angry chidings of the other voice, which was remarkably sharp and high-pitched; nor could I avoid fancying that I presently heard the discussion, or conversation, suddenly closed by a smart concussion, very suspiciously like that caused by a box on the ear, which was succeeded by a subdued and smothered scream. Then ensued a few hysterical sobs, followed by a deep silence. Upon this, I ventured to glance at my companion, and was glad to observe that he apparently had not heard the ominous sounds which had struck me with a kind of boyish terror, but that he had gently drawn up one of the window-blinds, and was gazing out upon the road, evidently buried in his own thoughts. I could not help wondering, however, how a lady of so sweet a temper and so soft and gentle a voice as, according to Mr. Falconer's account, belonged to the Julia of his younger days, could endure the presence of such a termagant as the unseen female undoubtedly was.

While pondering this knotty problem, a gliding of female steps in the passage preceded the opening of the parlour-door, to admit a lady of whom I will endeavour to give a brief description from memory.

She was short in stature, and exceedingly thin. Her cheeks were hollow, partly owing, I suppose, to the loss of teeth; her complexion was sallow; her hair, such as could be seen of it from under the pent-house of—well, let me call it a morning cap, a large morning cap, composed of checked muslin—was of coarse texture and dark hue, streaked rather plentifully with gray. Her eyes, though partly concealed by green spectacles, yet seemed to me to sparkle angrily; while the more prominent feature in the lady's countenance was sharply pointed, rather turned up, as though in disgust at the follies of the world, for which, also, it deeply blushed—at the tip.

The lady whose portrait I have thus imperfectly drawn was attired, from neck to ankle, in a close-fitting morning robe of a yellowish material, which was dear to prudent and economical house-dames in those days, and which I have since learned is, or was, India nankeen; it having the excellent quality (so I have been told) of never wearing out. The lady's feet were encased in list slippers. Of her head-dress I have already spoken. Add to this costume that her hands were slipped into an old pair of dark kid gloves—for gentility's sake, I suppose—and the drawing is sufficiently complete.

It is not to be supposed that these particular observations were taken by me at the first entrance of the lady, but rather that the several details impressed themselves upon me in the interview which ensued. Indeed, she gave but little time for silent remarks of any kind, as she moved forward with a quick and angry step towards the unblinded window, from which Mr. Falconer had withdrawn, pulled down the blind with a fierce jerk, and said, in a voice which I recognised as that which I had previously heard —it being sharp and high—

"A very great liberty to meddle with my blinds, sir."

"This must be the lady Julia's housekeeper," thought I to myself, as Mr. Falconer made a low and silent bow; "and a very queer-tempered housekeeper she is, too."

CHAPTER XII.

AN UNEXPECTED MEETING, AN UNWILLING RECOGNITION, AND DIVERS EXPLANATIONS.

" VERY great liberty to meddle with my blinds, sir," was the first salutation of the female in nankeen, whom I took to be the lady Julia's housekeeper; and she glared angrily at my companion through her green spectacles, as she drew down the blind with a jerk.

Mr. Falconer bowed low, and remained silent, looking curiously, as I thought, at the speaker.

"I presume you are the person who sent in a handbill last week about pills, and powders, and salves," continued the lady, still speaking sharply: " now I may as well tell you at once that I don't want any of your foreign pills, or powders, or salves. I employ a regular surgeon and apothecary when I am unwell; and I never encourage quack medicine-venders—poisoners I might call them—either English or French."

I ventured to look up into Mr. Falconer's face as the supposed housekeeper brought this exordium to a close; but I speedily withdrew my glance. The expression on that gentleman's countenance was so irresistibly comic, that in another moment my gravity would have been entirely upset. The idea of his being mistaken for a travelling quack doctor was so preposterously funny, that it was as much as I could do to forbear laughing outright, though I bit my lips fiercely, and cast my eyes down on the carpet. Unfortunately, my internal merriment was not so completely subdued as to escape notice; for, before my companion could reply to the injurious suspicion, I felt that the green spectacles were turned upon me, and I heard myself addressed as "a very rude boy," and called upon to say whether it was a proper thing to come into a lady's house for the purpose of making game of her. Mr. Falconer saved me the trouble of answering the question.

"You must excuse and pardon my young friend for unintentionally offending you, madam," he said, very politely. "The truth is," added he, "the young gentleman is a little amused, I see, by a very natural mistake into which you have fallen; for I beg to assure you, madam, that I am not a quack doctor, nor have I any connection with pills, powders, and salves, of either home or foreign manufacture."

It might have been my fancy, but I certainly thought the lady seemed somewhat startled when Mr. Falconer spoke. She was, perhaps, struck with the proof that so outlandish a looking personage should speak English so perfectly. At any rate, for one moment she appeared to be taken aback; but she instantly recovered herself.

"Oh, indeed!" she said, in a slightly subdued tone. "I thought, from your appearance and dress, that you must be the Monsieur le Grand, or some such name——"

"Very far from it, I assure you, madam," returned Mr. Falconer, quickly, and bowing low again.

"Oh, indeed!" repeated the lady. "May I ask, then, who you are, and what has procured me the honour of a call? In general, sir," she added, "I do not admit strangers into my house."

This was not very sweetly spoken; but there was less acerbity in it than in her former manner, and there was also an air of rather severe dignity, which did not sit at all unbecomingly on the elderly lady. But I was rather puzzled. I had been so certain that this person was merely the housekeeper of the lady we had travelled so far to see, that it surprised me to hear her speak of *her* house, and the honour of a call upon *her*. I had not exactly forgotten what Mr. Falconer had said about the lady being not very well off; but I certainly imagined that a housekeeper and the small servant I had seen formed a sufficiently limited establishment for the rather genteel house in which I found myself. Wondering, therefore, that a housekeeper should be permitted to speak of her mistress's house as her own, I looked once more towards Mr. Falconer, watching for his reply. It was long in coming, for he was evidently embarrassed; and when at length he spoke, it was in so altered a tone that I should not have believed it to be his, if I had not seen the movement of his lips.

"Am I so much a stranger, then?" he asked. "Am I so changed that you do not recognise me, Julia?"

A faint, involuntary cry escaped from the lady, as though she were suddenly and wonderfully astonished. Yet, however great her surprise, it could not surpass mine. This, then, was the lady whose fancy-portrait I had not long since heard described, and who was so fondly remembered by her old friend of thirty years ago! But where was the soft and gentle voice? where the engaging manner? Where were the ruby lips, and dimpled chin, and dove-like eyes, and auburn locks? And where, oh, where was the sweet temper of which I had heard? Had they ever been? Or had they existed only in the fervent imagination of the former admirer?

I looked again at the lady. Evidently a strong effort was required, but it had been made; and she now stood very firm, though her face was rather turned away from her visitor, and a pale blush mantled on her cheeks.

"May I beg you to explain, sir?" she said, not angrily, nor severely, but still with sufficient energy, which seemed to imply, "Here I am, on my own ground, and beneath my own roof; and

I can hold my own against all comers, and I will." Bear in mind, the lady expressed this only by her looks and bearing; she said, "May I beg you to explain, sir?" and added, more hesitatingly, "You will, perhaps, be kind enough to be seated."

"Not while you stand, dear madam," returned Mr. Falconer; and then, with an old-fashioned, formal politeness, which very well became him, he moved forward a step or two, and led the lady to a chair; to which act of courtesy she yielded as though under some powerful constraint. Then the gentleman seated himself. I noticed, however, that, whether by accident or design, he placed himself with his back to the darkened window, so that his countenance was almost lost in the shade, while the obscure light which entered the room was cast full upon the lady's face.

"You ask me to explain, madam. Is it needful?" Mr. Falconer put the question rather tenderly, as I now remember.

"Yes, it is, sir," she replied. "I—I do not even know who you are. You refused to send in your name, sir; and, until you enlighten me on that point, you are a stranger. I may guess, but I do not know."

I could not see whether or not Mr. Falconer smiled; I fancy he did, however, as he replied, "I see, I should have told your servant that my name is Falconer—the Jack Falconer whom you once knew."

"It is so, then," said the lady, apparently but little moved. ("She never was fond of him, however fond he was of her," was my inward thought.) "It is so, then. I fancied as much, not when I first saw you, but afterwards. You must excuse my not instantly recognising you, Mr. Falconer: you are much changed."

"Time, and thought, and experience, and——"

"Say trouble and sorrow, if you were thinking so," interposed the lady, when she found that her visitor hesitated. "Or, as I

am used to plain truths, shall I say the words for you? Yes;
time, and thought, and experience, and trouble, and sorrow change
us all.   I am changed from what I once was.   Do not hesitate to
say so, Mr. Falconer: it will be honest."

"My dear cousin——"

"Thank you, Mr. Falconer, for that word," said the lady,
quickly; "at least it sounds better than the 'Julia,' as between
us two.   And without any further compliments, which would
sound strangely from my lips, at least, let me apologise for the
unhappy mistake I made just now.   My very stupid maid—the
only servant I have, cousin—told me that my visitor was a Jew,
or a foreigner, and I jumped at the conclusion which betrayed me
into my hasty expressions.   Pray, forgive me."

"There is no need to urge even an excuse.   If a man will set
nature against fashion," said he, passing his hand lightly over his
flowing beard, "he must be prepared to put up with the results.
At all events, it would have been strange if you had at first
known me in this disguise, as I suppose I must call it.   But you
ask me to explain; is there anything further that needs my
explanation, my dear cousin?"

"Yes, there is," said the lady, almost repeating her former
words, and in the same tone.   "I think you ought to explain
why, after so many years, you have thought it worth your trouble
to seek me out.   It is not like you, Mr. Falconer, and I can
scarcely believe that your object is to see, with your own eyes, the
consequences of my former folly and credulity, and to exult over
my downfall; and yet——"

The lady paused here.   The strong restraint she had placed
upon her feelings was probably in danger of giving way; and she
would not yield.   It was plain to me then, boy as I was, that she
was acting a part, unnaturally, as in some extraordinary drama,
which in her heart she scorned.   Knowing what I now know, I

am convinced that, but for her stern pride, she would have been glad to have bent down before the man she had so long ago injured, and bathed the hand she longed to clasp with her tears. As it was, however, her eyes were dry, and her voice was hard and resolute.

"Is it not enough, cousin Julia," asked Mr. Falconer, reverting to her demand for an explanation, "that I am here by your own express invitation?   Be assured, when I determined to advertise for my poor cousin Frank, not knowing whether he were living or dead, I had no intention of personally intruding myself upon you till your reply opened the way, as I hoped, for our—our reconciliation, or at least for our obliteration of so much of the past as is painful for us, or painful for me to remember.   You surely will accept this as my explanation for this visit, which I fear is less welcome than I trusted it would be?"

"You speak enigmas, Mr. Falconer," returned the lady, with more agitation than she had hitherto shown; and as she spoke she passed her hand wearily over her brow.   "I know nothing of the advertisement of which you speak; it is impossible, therefore, that I could have replied to it.   There must be some strange mistake."

Mr. Falconer hastily unclasped his pocket-book, and handed to the lady the letter he had received in the previous week.

"And you believed that I wrote this?" she exclaimed sorrowfully, and with a flushed countenance, when she had glanced at its contents.   "But of course you did—why should I ask?   Oh, Mr. Falconer, what must you have thought of me?"

"You did not write it, then?" said he, eagerly, and avoiding her closing question.

"I did not write it.   I could not have written it.   I have seen no advertisement.   How could I?   I never see a newspaper, Mr. Falconer."

"I am heartily glad you did not write it, Julia," said the gentleman. "I am more pleased than I can express to know that you disavow it. May I hope that the statements it contains are as untrue as the sentiments are feigned, as untrue as that the signature is a forgery?"

"I do not say that, sir. The letter is evidently that of a gossiping mischief-maker, or of a practical joker, who knows enough of my past history and present circumstances to give a colouring of truth and candour to the whole. The statements are, for the most part, true, Mr. Falconer. My husband has been nearly ten years dead: my elder children are dead; they were daughters, and they all died in infancy, as the letter states. I have one son living: he was an infant when his father died. All this is correctly written, as though I had dictated it."

"But the other statements are malicious slanders? Tell me that they are so, cousin, and it will make me happier than I have been for many a day," said Mr. Falconer, very earnestly, and bending forward as though the welcome reply would reach him the sooner for this attitude.

The lady hesitated a moment; and I may remark here that during the latter portion of this singular interview her manner had considerably softened. I do not mean that it manifested much cordiality; at any rate it was constrained; but it was no longer defiant. Evidently, too, her feelings were touched, especially when she referred to the deaths of her infants; and she had taken off and laid aside her green spectacles, very much to the improvement of her countenance, which, but for the odious head-dress she wore, would not have seemed uncomely for an elderly female. All this I had time to note before she spoke again, to the following effect:—

"There is a great deal of truth in all that is set down in this extraordinary letter. I spoke just now of my former folly and credulity, and of my present downfall; and I do not recall the words. Oh, Mr. Falconer, I was cruelly deceived! I was made to believe, by your own friend, that you were unworthy of any woman who had a regard for her own character and happiness: that you were a libertine, that your property had been squandered in vice, and that you were on the brink of ruin——"

"Stay! Did Frank Tozer, my cousin Frank, tell you this?" Mr. Falconer asked.

"He told me this and more; but I will not pain you and humble myself by repeating all his falsehoods, which he followed up by offering to deliver me from the snare into which I had fallen."

A deep groan burst from Mr. Falconer. "Do not say more on this subject, I entreat you. Oh, Frank, Frank! And yet I loved him!"

"I will not say more than is necessary, now that we have met," said the lady sorrowfully, yet still preserving a composure so great as to prove how severely she had trained herself to endure. "I will only add to this part of my explanation—for it is I who must now explain—that I was bewitched, I think, by the man who made me his dupe. He was clever, you know, and plausible; and I was fickle. It is an old story, Mr. Falconer: it has been told over and over again before you and I were born, and will be repeated after we are dead. 'The heart is deceitful above all things, and desperately wicked.' Well, I was deceived by my own heart; and that man (your friend, mind) persuaded me that he loved me. You know what followed."

"Yes, I know what followed." The words escaped mechanically and dreamily from my poor friend's lips.

"After we were married," continued the lady, "and my husband had secured to himself the miserable fortune which had lured him on, and we had left London, and I was so bound to him that I was helpless for myself, then he came out in his true colours. He told me how he had deceived me, not humbly and penitently—if he had done this, I could have forgiven him—but he told me of it boastingly, and said that my money was all he cared for. Then my misery began."

"Do not say more, my poor Julia," exclaimed Mr. Falconer, in a broken voice, while tears ran down his cheeks unchecked. "If I had known—if I had only known this!"

"What could you have done? What could any one do? As I had made my bed, so must I have lain on it to the bitter end. It was best that my misery should be unknown; best that our new neighbours around should look upon me with contempt, as they soon learned to do, because he who should have vindicated my fair fame traduced me, and he who should have protected me broke down my spirits by his brute violence."

"Did he dare—— ?"

"He dared more than I have the heart to tell," she replied; "judge, then, whether I could have written with the wicked levity that letter betrays."

"You could not. I ask your forgiveness, dear cousin, for believing, for one moment, that it was written by you. But there are other circumstances mentioned: have they a foundation for truth?"

"That my husband's purchase of a practice in the country was a false report which he himself set about? Yes, that is true. That we came to this place, and that, having bought this house with a part of my money, we lived on the interest of the remainder, one half of which he squandered? Yes, this is true. That my husband sank into habits of intemperance as well as of idleness? Yes, this also is true. And it is true that I bore this, as I best might, for twenty years. What more would you have, or need I tell, Mr. Falconer?"

"Nothing; nothing. My poor Julia!"

"You ought not to pity me, sir: I ask no pity," continued the strange lady. "It is written that 'whatsoever a man sows, that shall he also reap;' and this is as true of woman as of man. I have sown, and have reaped. I hope this will be remembered at last."

I did not then know what the poor lady meant by being "remembered at last." I fear now, however, that she intended to express a hope that her sufferings in this life, and her proud submission under them, would be accepted by God as a sufficient compensation for the misdeeds of a whole life. She meant, I think, "If I have sinned, have I not been punished here? And what more can the righteous Judge demand?" And so the unhappy woman would have discarded the thought of "repentance towards God, and faith in the Lord Jesus Christ," as Methodistical and absurd; forgetting, or being wilfully ignorant of the fact, that there is no remedy for sin but that which is to be found in the bleeding wounds of a dying, and implicit trust in a risen, exalted, and pleading Saviour; no escape from eternal ruin for sinners but that which is indicated to us by a tender, compassionate, and fatherly, yet a just and righteous God, when he proclaims, "Look unto me, and be ye saved, all the ends of the earth: for I am God, and there is none else;" no comfort and happiness to be found like that which Christ promises when he says, "Come unto me, all ye that labour and are heavy laden, and I will give you rest. Take my yoke upon you, and learn of me. . . . For my yoke is easy, and my burden is light."

No, I did not know then what was meant by being "remembered at last." But I do know now that this is one of the manifold delusions with which the great enemy ensnares and ruins human souls: and that men and women are daily entering an eternal world, laying the flattering unction to their souls that all

G

will be well with them *there* because so much has gone badly with them *here.*   I do know that there are those who would keep a running account with the Almighty, and bring him in as debtor to them for heaven and happiness at last, because their life on earth has been one of disappointment and care.   Dear reader,— there is not one word in the entire Scriptures that can give countenance to such a thought.   There *is* "a calm for those who weep; a rest for weary pilgrims found;" and the weeping and weariness may be intended to lead onward to the calm and rest; but only when they lead first of all to the Cross of Christ; not otherwise.

> " Take His easy yoke, and wear it;
>   Love will make obedience sweet:
> Christ will give you strength to bear it;
>   While *his* wisdom guides your feet
>   Safe to glory,
>   Where his ransomed captives meet.
>
> " Sweet as home to pilgrims weary,
>   Light to newly-opened eyes;
> Or full springs in deserts dreary,
>   Is the rest the Cross supplies:
>   All who taste it,
>   Shall to rest immortal rise."

For such as these, doubtless, the afflictions of the present world "work a far more exceeding and eternal weight of glory;" but for such only.

CHAPTER XIII.

I AM INTRODUCED TO MASTER MARMADUKE TOZER, AND MAKE HIS ACQUAINTANCE.

IT is indicative of the absorbing interest felt by the two interlocutors of the preceding dialogue in the subject-matter of their communications, that the presence of a third person had so long been overlooked. On arriving, however, at the part of the conversation where I have broken off, the lady, attracted, perhaps, by some involuntary movement on my part, turned sharply, as I thought, towards me, and, after fixing her keen eyes on me (for they were keen when detached from her green spectacles, which I afterwards learned she wore as "pre-servers," and not because of any positive defect in her vision), spoke a few words to Mr. Falconer, in so low a tone that their import escaped me.

"No, no," he said, quickly; "I am not so happy. Even you have the advantage of me there. The grandson of a very good friend of mine—an orphan."

"Is it needful that he should have heard the story of my degradation?" she asked, more angrily than she had spoken since the commencement of the interview.

"I forgot that he was here," said my friend, humbly and deprecatingly; adding, "but George Burley is discreet, and will not betray confidence.* And I had a reason for making him the

---

* I hope I shall not be accused of betraying confidence now. So many, many years have passed since the events I am now recording took place, and all of whom I have so far written have been so long dead, that no interests can be injured nor feelings wounded by these late disclosures.

companion of my visit.   Referring to the forged letter which I took to be genuine, I expected a warmer welcome than otherwise I should have dared hope for ——"

"And you wished to have a check against imprudence, in the presence of a witness," interposed the lady, with a bitter smile. "Well, you have found out your error, Mr. Falconer, and I trust your heart will not be quite broken."

"You mistake me, my dear cousin," rejoined the gentleman. "The truth is, I have taken an interest in this boy ; and there are few left for me to love.   You also have one dear tie, at least, to bind you down to earthly affections ——"

"What do you mean, Mr. Falconer?" demanded the lady, impatiently.

"You have a son."

"Oh, true : yes, Marmaduke is my son, of course ; and he is, as you say, dear to me.   Well?"

"And I hoped, and do hope, that he will be dear to me also. Not to the diminution of my affection for this young friend ;" and he laid his broad hand with much kindness on my head, for I had ventured to steal to his side ; "but I think my heart is large enough yet to contain two friends, at least."

"I think it is ; I am sure it is, Mr. Falconer."   This was spoken with more cordiality than the lady had before shown, and with some softened feelings too ; for I saw that, for the first time in this extraordinary scene, her eyes were moistened with tears.

"And therefore," continued Mr. Falconer, "I wish to unite, if possible, these two friends of mine in one common bond of union. At least, I hoped it might be so ; and I ask now that they may be made known to each other.   It may be that a friendship thus formed may be useful to them both hereafter.   Have I your consent, Julia?"

"It is a strange request ; stranger than all to come from you," replied the lady. "How do we know that a friendship thus formed may not be anything rather than useful? You have had experience enough of boy-friendships, I should have thought. But it shall be as you please," she presently added, after once more fixing her eyes on me, and scanning me very closely, as I thought.

She rang a small hand-bell which she reached from the mantel-piece; and, at the summons, the little servant made her appearance. Her eyes were still red; I noticed that; and I observed also that a broad red mark extended from her left cheek, and culminated on the ear on that side of her face. She was quite composed, however.

"Tell Marmaduke that I wish to see him here," said Marmaduke's mother; and the servant retired. A minute or two afterwards the door again opened, and admitted a very handsome boy, somewhat taller than myself, with a fair complexion and light-brown hair which curled naturally over his forehead. He seemed amazingly shy; for he halted at the threshold, and looked down upon the floor.

"Come here, Marmaduke." There was not much fondness in the mother's tone, I thought.

The boy obeyed; slowly, however, and not lifting his eyes.

"This gentleman," said the lady, making a gesture towards Mr. Falconer, "wishes to see you. You may speak to him."

"I am glad to see you, sir," said the boy, in a subdued whisper. He might have been glad, but he did not seem so. He was neither glad nor sorry, I dare say; but he cast a furtive glance at the door, I thought, as though anxious to assure himself that a way of escape was left open for him. He advanced, however, to Mr. Falconer, and offered his hand.

I have never forgotten the look of peculiar benevolence, combined with penetrating examination, with which the gentleman regarded the shy boy as he held his hand, nor the soft and gentle tones in which he said—

" And I am glad to see you, Marmaduke—dear Marmaduke."

I do not know that the lady was jealous of this loving-kindness ; I do not see how she could have been, seeing how she had, throughout the previous interview, repressed as far as she could all Mr. Falconer's manifestations of tenderness towards herself. She was evidently impatient, however, and interposed between her son and her visitor.

" You see Marmaduke," she said : " do you wish now that any acquaintance should be made between the two boys ? I do not see why there should," she added ; " but it shall be as you please."

" I do still wish it, the more now that I have seen your son," he replied.

" Marmaduke," continued the lady, turning to her boy, " you may take this young gentleman with you into the garden ; but remember——"

What Marmaduke was to remember was not said, nor does it signify. I have only to report that my new acquaintance walked out of the room with a downcast countenance, and that I followed him on receiving a silent hint from Mr. Falconer.

I had not known much of children at any period of my life. The seclusion of the large old house in Silver Square, and my grandfather's solitary life, together with Betsy Miller's objection to my making friends with London boys, had shut me out, in a great measure, from juvenile companionship. At the same time, there were two or three boys in the square of whom I had some knowledge, and with whom I was permitted occasionally to consort. I knew something of their ways, therefore, and (by observation) of the ways of London boys in general. But, of all the boys I had ever seen or of whom I had ever heard, Marmaduke was surely

MR. FALCONER'S INTRODUCTION TO MARMADUKE.

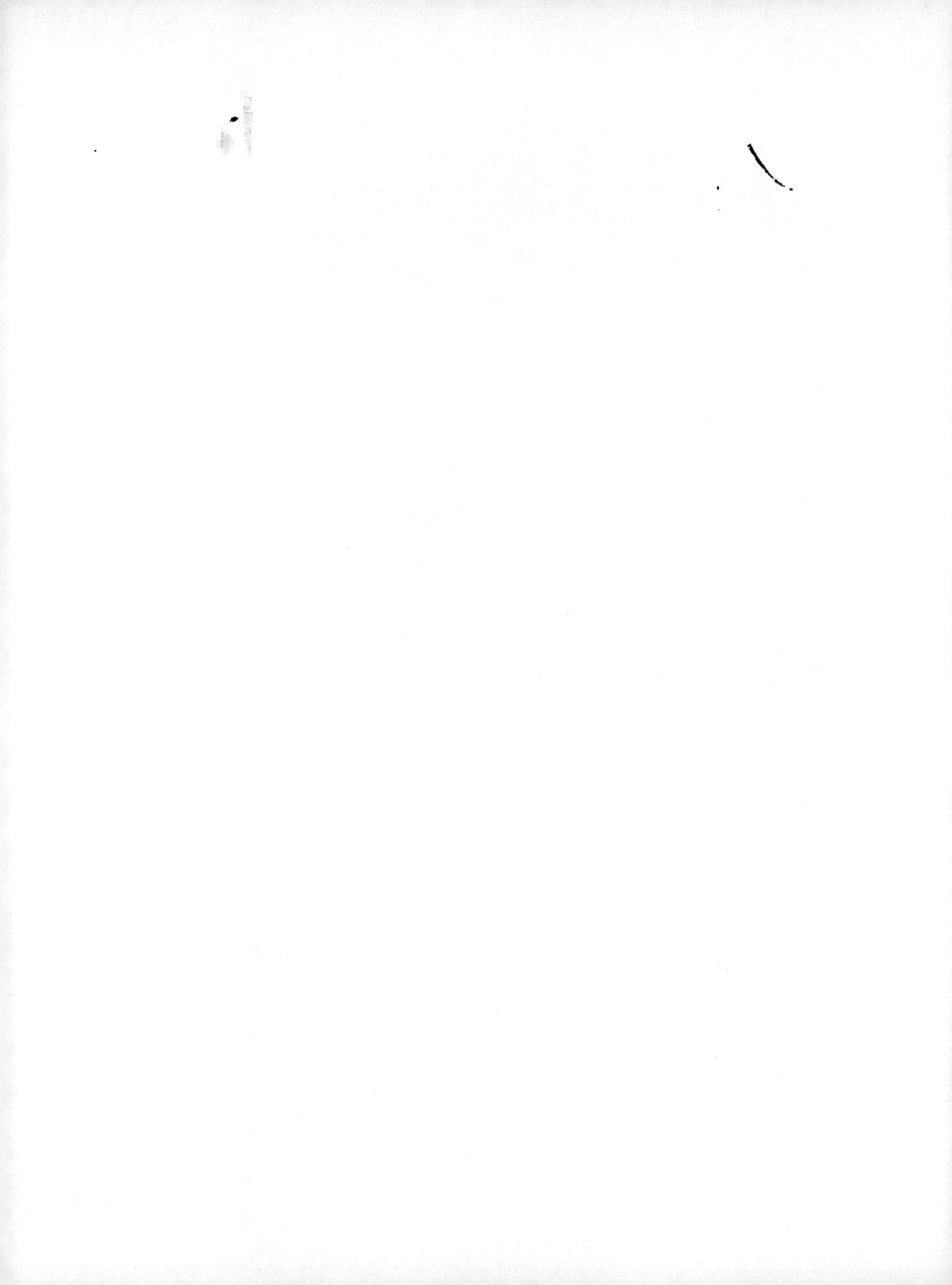

the most strange. With a slow, solemn, and mournful step, he conducted, or rather preceded me through a long passage which led to a small parlour, opening by glass doors into a moderate-sized garden. He spoke no word to me, scarcely looked at me, certainly did not once look me in the face, but walked gloomily to the end of a broad gravel path which extended the whole length of the garden ; then he turned and paced back again to the glass doors, I keeping close to his side, and waiting to be spoken to, as a point of politeness, as I thought. In the same melancholy fashion we retraced our steps, only varying the monotony by branching off into two or three cross-paths which separated one garden bed from its neighbour. At length, tired of this dumb companionship, I plucked up courage to speak ; and the following dialogue ensued :—

" Your name is Marmaduke, isn't it ?"

" Yes."

" Marmaduke Tozer, isn't it ? " I knew this, for I had heard the name mentioned by Mr. Falconer at the blacksmith's shop, when he asked directions to the lady's house.

" Yes."

" Isn't it a funny name ? " I asked, forgetting politeness.

" Yes, I suppose it is."

" My name is George Burley, but they call me Hurly Burly as often as the other," said I, volunteering information which my new acquaintance had not sought.

" Oh ! "

" That's a funny name, too ; isn't it ? "

" Yes—no, not that I know of," said Marmaduke, reddening.

" What's your servant's name ? " I asked, seeing that, like one of the cross-paths we were traversing, my former inquiries led to nowhere.

" Marianne."

"What else?"

"Bolster."

"Marianne Bolster! Why, that's the funniest name of all. I say, Marmaduke——"

"What do you say, George?"

"Come," thought I, "this is a little improvement."

"Do you ever play at anything?" I asked.

"Not much."

"Perhaps you have not got anybody to play with?"

"Nobody but Marianne. I play with her sometimes, when my mother lets me."

"Oh, dear!" thought I again, "what shall I say next? Oh, I know."

"This is a nice garden."

"I hate it!" exclaimed Marmaduke, so energetically that I turned on him with surprise, and saw that he was very near crying.

"Hate it! Why, that's the funniest thing of all," said I. "Now, if my grandfather had a garden like this in London, I should love it, I know. Wouldn't I have some of those nice-looking apples!" I added, as we were passing a dwarf apple-tree laden with nearly ripe fruit.

"Not if you got paid out for meddling with them," said Marmaduke, reddening, and walking quickly on.

"Paid out?"

"Like this," said he; and he pulled off his jacket, passionately, and bared his arm to the shoulder.

I understood it all now. Those marks that I saw there let me into the secret of my new companion's timidity. The moving, guiding principle in the boy's training had been fear—not love. I shall have something more to say on this subject hereafter.

CHAPTER XIV.

THE QUACK DOCTOR.

THE remaining half-hour I spent with Marmaduke in his mother's garden was neither enlivening nor instructive, and I was not sorry when I received a summons, by the mouth of Marianne Bolster, to rejoin Mr. Falconer, who was ready to leave. I was proportionately surprised, therefore, when Marmaduke (on my receiving the summons) turned round upon me, and expressed a hope that I would come and see him again, because he had so much enjoyed my society.

Departing from the garden, I found Mr. Falconer in the passage. He was indulging, I suppose, in a few last words with the lady, the purport of which, as far as it reached my ear, was that he was invited, and accepted the invitation, to spend a day with her before his return to London. As a matter of necessity, I was included in this invitation.

Our return walk was a very silent one. We almost lost our way once or twice, I remember, when we got into the parks of which I have made mention, and should have done so altogether if I had not had my wits about me. Set right by these, however, we reached the Wingham "Lion" in safety, much to the satisfaction of the landlady, who began to fear that the dinner she had provided for her guests would be spoiled by over-cooking; much also to mine, for I was tired by the double walk, and hungry from long fasting; and much to that of Alphonse, who, being a stranger in a strange land, began to have dismal apprehensions respecting the barbarians by whom he was surrounded.

I shall pass over the other events of that day, until the evening, when I witnessed an amusing scene which I shall endeavour to describe.

I had been out in the town, with Alphonse as my silent companion, and had just re-entered the inn, when loud shouts of laughter, from the large kitchen or tap-room of the "Lion," attracted our attention; the laughter being occasioned, as it seemed, by the utterances of a sharp and quick, but monotonous voice, which was evidently addressing a risible and amused, if not derisive audience. The room being immediately on our left hand as we entered the house, and the door being partly open, it being also a public room, there was no particular reason (so I thought, at least) why I and Alphonse should not share in the fun which seemed to be going on.

There were a score or more townsmen, of a rather low class apparently, seated at benches with their ale-pots before them, and some of them were smoking tobacco. All of them were listening to a strange-looking fellow, who, standing by a small table near the middle of the room, which was spread over with a number of pill-boxes, gallipots, phials, and small paper packets, was loudly vaunting the virtue of his medicines, and urging the company to buy, and thus ensure to themselves the means of long life, perfect health, and entire ease from all the pains incident to humanity. I have said that the quack doctor (for this, no doubt, was his vocation) was a strange-looking fellow. And so he was. His countenance—so much as could be seen of it—was thin and remarkably sallow. His eyes, which were dark and sparkling, were overshadowed by enormous and very bushy brows, black as jet; these corresponded in colour with a beard and moustache of large dimensions, which almost concealed his mouth, and added to the pallid appearance of the cheeks which they left uncovered. The hair on the charlatan's head did not match in texture, however, nor quite in colour, with that on the lower part of the face.

THE TRAVELLING QUACK DOCTOR.

It was thin, and limp, and rusty, and, being combed smoothly back from the margin of a rather low forehead, gave to that feature as much length and breadth as could be spared to it by the encroaching eyebrows below. The costume of the gentleman was, as I could not help remarking, particularly shabby, proving that he had a soul above buttons, or that the pressing ardour of his lofty and liberal pursuit of the healing art gave him no time to attend to the fopperies of dress, or, lastly, that his benevolent designs towards suffering humanity brought but scant supplies to his purse. My readers must pardon this rather prolix description of a personage of whom I shall have to write more before my story is ended, and whom I at once concluded to be the Monsieur le Grand who had so offended the lady I had that day visited, with his handbill, the more so that he spoke with a decidedly foreign accent, which denoted him to be a Frenchman. I must also be permitted to give as faithful and literal report as I am able, of some portion of his address.

"See here," he was saying as I entered the room, and he held up a small pill-box between his finger and thumb—"in this leetle box is von, two, t'ree, vat you call pill. Do you take too much rosbif for your dinner? Var good! or drink too much of the strong beer of my friend in this hotel, and the 'Lion' mount up into your brain? Var good too! Then you say, 'This will not never do: my head swim, my vat you call rebel at being so put upon. I must put end to this business: I must leave off to eat and drink.' I say no, you shall not do not'ing of the sort. Here is von leetle pill; you shall put it in your mouth, and you shall never see it no more; but, hey! in von leetle half-hour you shall feel as you nevare vas, and you shall go again to your rosbif and plum-pooden' and your good beer; and it shall do you no more hurt than not'ing at all.

"Here, again," continued the quack, putting down the pill-box and taking up a packet, "is von leetle dust of poudre. You have child, poor leetle infant, and he say 'Veek, veek, veek-a-veek.' Then you pat him on the back, and cuddle him, and sing-song. All no use : he go on cry, 'Veek, veek-a-veek.' Then you try another plan : you give him von good shake, and von slap, and two slap and two shake ; and this make him 'Veek, veek-a-veek' all the more. Then you say, 'Oh, there is that fine leetle poudre I bought of von French doctor : I try him.' So you mix him up vid some nice sugare, and pop him in the leetle child's mouth. Then you shall see he vill never cry no more, but vill sleep like vat you call von top, and vake up in five, six hours, altogezzer von 'nother thing."

In the same fashion, with a wonderful amount of grimace, and with a considerable admixture of dry, droll humour which was the more quaint by being spoken in a broken dialect which I have only partially imitated, Monsieur le Grand praised his ointments and salves for cuts, wounds, and bruises, the materials for which he had obtained, without regard to expense, from the distant lands in which he had travelled. I omit altogether the apochryphal tales he told of wonderful cures wrought on princes and potentates in foreign courts by each and all of the medicines whose efficacy he proclaimed ; and of the equally wonderful hair-breadth escapes he had experienced from the malice of his enemies (the regular doctors) in almost every country in the world, who were jealous of his superior skill. I omit, also, the interruptions he met with from the company in the tap-room, which sometimes took the form of a civil banter, sometimes of an impertinent question, and still oftener of peals of merry laughter elicited by the impudent pretensions of the charlatan. Whether eventually he succeeded in disposing of his stock of pills, powders, and salves, or at what price he dispensed them, I am unable to say, as I soon got tired of the scene, as well as half-choked with the fumes of strong tobacco, and withdrew, leaving Alphonse, however, to profit (if he would) by the skill of the charlatan, who, if not his own countryman, was, like himself, a foreigner.

I afterwards learned that the quack doctor, having exhausted his panegyrics on his medicines, condescended to amuse the company in the tap-room by various tricks of legerdemain, which, as they were represented to me as being remarkably clever and surprising, I regretted I had not stayed to witness.

CHAPTER XV.

I WITNESS A CURIOUS TRANSFORMATION.

N the following morning, while we were at breakfast, Mr. Falconer told me that he should be busily occupied in writing for two or three hours in the forenoon, and recommended me to take a morning walk into the country, attended by Alphonse. Accordingly, when our meal was finished, I sought the Frenchified Swiss, but not immediately finding him, and also not particularly desiring his company, I put on my hat and went out alone.

The little town itself did not need much exploring; and, being soon tired of staring in at the windows of the few shops it boasted, I struck into the country, in a direction opposite to that of our walk of the previous day; and, after following some distance the windings of a small river or stream, I crossed a meadow by a footpath which apparently led to a neighbouring village, the church spire of which was to be seen in the horizon. Arriving, by means of this footpath, at a narrow bridge which crossed the little river, I sat down and watched the water as it rippled along the weedy banks.

H

How long I sat there in the strange dreamy mood which flowing water is apt to engender in the mind, I cannot say. I know only that I was suddenly roused from my solitary thoughts and air-built castles by a hand laid rather heavily on my shoulder; and, on turning quickly round, I encountered the visage of Monsieur le Grand, who was looking down upon me, over his black moustache and beard, with a grim sort of smile.

"So, young fellow, you are here, are you?" said he, not at all in a foreign accent, however, which would, no doubt, have surprised me if I had given the circumstance a thought; but I did not.

"Yes, sir," said I.

"And if I were to pitch you into the river, what would you do then?" he asked.

"Get out again, on the other side," I answered, springing on to my feet, and putting myself on my guard; for I did not know how far the Frenchman might be in earnest.

I had a better opportunity now than on the previous evening of scanning the quack doctor's countenance, especially as he did not seem immediately disposed to put his implied threat into execution. My examination, as I stood looking him steadily in the face, led to no result, however, save that of a confused, dreamy idea that I had somewhere or other seen him, or some one exceedingly like him, at no distant period of my life. I rather think that he enjoyed my inquisitive looks and my evident perplexity, for he stood patiently under my scrutiny, only carelessly swinging to and fro a largish green baize bag he carried in his hand, which, I suppose, contained part of his stock of medicines.

"Well?" said he, when I had had my stare.

"Well?" said I.

"You will know me again the next time we meet, I suppose?" he continued.

"Yes, sir."

"Don't make too sure of that, Mr. Hurly Burly," said he, grinning.

"How came you to know me?" I asked, in some surprise that he had my nickname so pat upon his tongue.

"Because I am a conjurer, and know everything. How did you enjoy your walk yesterday?"

"I don't know what business that is of yours, sir," said I, rather chafing under his keen gaze, and resenting his unsought familiarity. "But if you know everything," I added, "you need not ask me any more questions."

"Ho, ho! Sharp, too, I protest! But don't be too saucy, young gentleman. Remember, the river is close by, and it wouldn't cost me much to give you a good sousing. And as to questions, I shall ask you as many as I please; and you will please to answer them. To begin at the beginning, what has brought you all this way from London?"

"You know as well as I do, I dare say," I replied; "but, if you must be told, I came because—because I was told to."

"Good boy!" he said this sneeringly, and then added; "and the old lady in green barnacles, she was very pleased to see you yesterday, I suppose?"

"Better pleased than she will be to see you, sir," I answered, laughing at my remembrance of Madam Tozer's indignant mention of the "pills, powders, and salves," and at her mistaking Mr. Falconer for the foreign quack.

"You are merry, are you, young fellow?" remarked the charlatan: "what are you grinning at?"

"I beg your pardon, sir," I responded: "I was not laughing at you. I was only thinking of a mistake the lady made. She thought Mr.——somebody else was you; and it made her angry."

"Mr. Somebody Else means Mr. Falconer, of course. I told

and should have made a good thing of it if I hadn't been too fond of lifting my little finger—so :" he made a gesture with his hand, raising it over his mouth with his head thrown back, which explained his meaning ; namely, that he had ruined his temporary success as a pedlar by overmuch drinking.

"It was then," he went on, "that I made acquaintance with the lady you and old Falconer went to see yesterday."

"How did you know we went to see anybody?" I asked, interrupting William Bix.

"I saw you go into her house."

"But I did not see anything of you," said I.

"No, I dare say you did not; and I did not mean that you should. Not that it would have mattered much if you had, for you would not have been any the wiser for it, nor would Mr. Falconer either; at least, I don't think he would have known me. But I did not choose to try the experiment, so I snugly ensconced myself in the 'Four Horseshoes,' and looked out of the window."

I remembered, when my uncle mentioned the "Four Horse-shoes," that a public-house with that sign stood on the opposite side of the road, over against Mrs. Tozer's house.

"But how is it you are in this neighbourhood just at this time? And why should you be watching Mr. Falconer? Or how should you know that he would be going into that house?" I asked.

"Ho, ho! So you can ask questions as well as I," said the profligate. "Very good: you may ask as many as you please, and I shall answer as few as I please. I shall not answer these, for instance. I told you just now that I am a conjurer, and that accounts for my knowing all that I want to know, doesn't it?"

"No," I replied, bluntly ; and, before I proceed any further with the dialogue which ensued, I may say that, if my readers are surprised that I, a boy of ten years old, fell in so readily with the strange humour of my companion, and conversed so freely with him, in spite of the warning I had received to have nothing to do with him, I also was equally surprised at myself. There was a sort of evil fascination about the man, I believe, which led me on. Perhaps, also, there was a natural facility in myself in being at ease with those into whose society I was thrown, which, while dangerous to me in some respects, was useful to me in others. I suppose that, in the cultivation of this adaptability (if I may so call it), the medium way is the best, if one can but hit upon it.

"Well, at any rate," continued my uncle Bix, "I did see you both go into Madam Tozer's house; and that is enough. I was telling you that I made her acquaintance when I was a travelling optician, and persuaded her that, if she did not keep in the shade and wear green glasses, she would lose her sight. It was all nonsense, of course: her eyes are as good as yours or mine; but I had got spectacles to sell, and I meant to sell them. I found out, too, at that time, a thing or two in her ladyship's history which I dare say you know something about too—eh?"

"I am not going to say what I know or don't know," said I, both shocked at his falsehood and warned into prudent caution by the inquisitive and eager looks of my companion, as much as by his words.

"Good boy!" he said again, sneeringly as before. "But there's a truce between us, so I shall not pitch you into the river; besides, it does not matter to me whether you know or don't know," he added, repeating my words; "so we will change the subject. I suppose you are wondering now, if the truth were known, how I came to change my trade?"

"I was wondering more," said I, "why you should dress yourself up in that beard and those eyebrows."

"I'll tell you, Hurly Burly. There are two good reasons for it. The first is that, unfortunately, when I was this way before, I ran up a longish bill at my good friend's expense—the keeper of the 'Lion,' I mean—which it was not convenient to me to pay, and I was obliged to give leg-bail. Do you know what that is?"

"You ran away without paying, I suppose, uncle."

"Right. Well, it is no more convenient to me to pay it now than it was then. So, you see, I was obliged to disguise myself lest I should be too affectionately received."

"You said you were reformed, uncle," I remarked, rather scandalised at the cool manner in which he referred to his unliquidated debt.

"Don't interrupt me," he returned, "or I shall forget my second reason, which is, that the people who will buy my medicines when they fancy I am a Frenchman or a Jew, would not have them at a gift if they knew me to be an Englishman."

"All the better for them if they didn't buy them," I blurted out.

"You are wrong, Hurly," said my uncle, laughing. "My medicines will do no one any harm. You shall try them yourself;" and he added something in Latin, I supposed, which I did not understand then, but now believe to have been "*Experimentum fiat in corpore vili.*"

"No, thank you," said I, hastily, and in some slight alarm.

Uncle William did not press the point. "I shall save my pills, then," he said; "but, as to your injurious surmise, I'll give you to know that my medicines are compounded *secundum artem*, and of very harmless drugs. You may have heard that I was a doctor once, Hurly, or very near being one. At any rate, I picked up enough science to keep me from unconsciously poisoning my patients; and, as it would answer no good purpose to commit manslaughter, I don't commit it. Do you see that, Hurly?"

"How came you to know that they call me Hurly?" I asked, without answering my uncle's question.

"Hem! Well, I'll tell you. I took the liberty of making an

inquiry or two of the grocer's wife round the corner, near Silver Square, and she told me."

"Well, I must go now, sir," I said, rising to my feet; for Mr. William Bix's talk began to weary me.

"No, not just yet," he rejoined, rising also. "You don't think that I have let you into my secrets for nothing, do you?"

Remembering the scene I had witnessed in Mr. Filby's shop, and the eagerness with which, afterwards, my uncle held out his hand to clutch Mr. Falconer's charitable gift, seeing, too, the present seedy plight of my ne'er-do-well relative, it was natural enough for me to say—

"I have only got five shillings" (which sum, by the way, Mr. Falconer had given me on the morning of our leaving London)—"I have only got five shillings, uncle; you can have half if you like."

"You little——" (well, never mind what he called me)—"You little something," said he, "do you think I am going to beg of *you?* But it is handsome of you, too, to offer it. I don't want your money, however. The three guineas old Falconer gave me set me up in my present trade; and I have given over drinking. Didn't I tell you I was reformed? No, no; I don't want your money," he continued; "so put it up before I am tempted to take it" (it was in my hand by that time). "I want information. When are you and Mr. Falconer going back to London?"

"If you are a conjurer, uncle——" I began; but he stopped me sternly, and repeated the question.

"We are going back to London on Saturday," I said.

"And to-day is Wednesday. What are you going to do between now and then? Are you going to see my friend Mrs. Tozer again? and when?"

I did not think there could be any harm in my saying that Mr. Falconer had been invited to spend the following day with the lady, and had accepted the invitation; also, that I was to accompany him.

He muttered to himself something that I did not hear, for he was fixing on his false beard and moustache, which he drew from his pocket. When this was done, and he was busy with his eyebrows, he turned to me again.

"Now you must give me a promise, on your word and honour: say so."

"Say what, sir?"

"On my word and honour——"

"What am I to promise?" I asked, cautiously.

"That you will tell no one that you have seen me and spoken to me."

"Not Mr. Falconer, uncle?"

"No; neither Mr. Falconer nor the old man in Silver Square, nor Betty Miller, nor any one else. Do you hear?"

Hesitatingly, I gave the required promise.

"On your word and honour you won't tell: say so."

"On my word and honour, uncle."

And so we parted, not to meet again till after many days.

The unexpected meeting and interview with William Bix gave me, however, not only a fresh insight into his character, but a subject for grave reflection. Here was one, who so evidently, that even a boy could see it, had superior talents, which, if combined with perseverance and good principle, would almost have secured success in any honourable calling; but who had been reduced to dishonourable shifts and schemes for a bare subsistence, and, like the prodigal in the divine parable, had been "fain to have filled his belly with the husks that the swine did eat." Unhappily, he had not shared in the prodigal's penitential resolve,—"I will return unto my father, and will say unto him, Father, I have sinned." And while I thought on this, as I returned to my quarters at the "Lion," I remembered what Betsy Miller had once said to me when she was speaking of my profligate relative, namely, that education (even when combined with talent) is only good when good use is made of it,—but otherwise that it makes the possessor only the more wicked and mischievous. I remembered also how, at the same time, she had told me, in warning tones, that such men as William Bix pass for a time, in the crowd, without being found out: but only for a time, for that sooner or later there comes a *finding-out time*. Remembering this, I could but see how very true was the warning; and at least one effect of the scene in which I had just borne an involuntary part, was to strengthen my boyish resolution to adhere to the Bible maxim, which, under Betsy Miller's tuition, I had, with much besides, committed to a pretty retentive memory :—" Enter not into the path of the wicked, and go not in the way of evil men. Avoid it, pass not by it, turn from it, and pass away. For they sleep not, except they have done mischief; and their sleep is taken from them, unless they cause some to fall."

CHAPTER XVII.

SOPHY.

T is well for biographers and all other historians that they are under no express obligation to account for the strange contradictions and inconsistencies in human conduct which they have to record. If they were compelled to do this, they would often be forced to lay down their pens in desperation. As a case in point, I am not able to declare the motives which induced Mrs. Tozer to invite her old admirer to spend a day with her in her own home, when it was evident that his first visit had been so provocative of mental anguish.

There are persons, no doubt—such as middle-aged, or more than middle-aged, bachelors and widowers—who suspect a snare, a trap, a baited hook, or a pitfall (to use their own expressive similes), in every friendly smile which greets them, and every polite attention offered to them on the part of kind-hearted and compassionate spinsters or widows. Probably this feeling arises from pure vanity: and the ladies thus accused of deep-laid plots are perfectly innocent in thought and intention. Certain I am that no such preposterous a design entered the head or heart of Frank Tozer's widow, whatever other motive she might have had in offering her hospitality to her former friend; nor did Mr. Falconer believe that, at sixty years old, he was still deemed worth reclaiming by the lover of thirty years ago. If for a few days he was led to entertain this notion, and was amused at its absurdity, he must have been disabused of it by the lady's earnest and indignant disavowal of the forged letter he had received, as well as by her bearing towards himself in the interview I have described. He was not sorry for this, I am sure; and quite satisfied with leaving his old love fathoms below the tide of time and circumstances which had rolled over it, he, no doubt, felt himself more untrammelled in carrying out his original intention, that of taking his cousin's orphan boy, young Marmaduke, under his protection, and making him his heir by testament, as he really was by law. In accepting the lady's invitation, therefore, *his* motives, at any rate, were near enough to the surface of his conduct.

Having said this much by explication, I proceed with my story.

Another walk through the two pleasant parks and along the village road, on the appointed day, brought us to the widow's door, which was opened to us by the much-enduring Marianne Bolster, whose countenance, I was glad to observe, was radiant with smiles, and who, without questioning, introduced us once more into the gloomy parlour. Here we were speedily joined by the widow, and presently by her son also, who, in the very timid way I had previously noticed, silently offered his hand to his newly-found relative, and then slunk into a dark corner of the room.

Apart from this indication of a settled dread of his mother, on the part of Marmaduke, our reception was more encouraging than on the former occasion. If Mrs. Tozer was cold and formal, she was polite and courteous; and the introduction of the lunch-tray gave me no small joy, for I had been reckoning up with some dismay that three hours at least must elapse before dinner-time.

I was not so occupied, however, with the important business of eating and drinking as not to notice that our hostess was much improved in her outward appearance, having exchanged her extraordinary ugly morning cap for a handsome turban trimmed with lace—a sort of head-dress fashionable enough in the year 18—, though antiquated now; and replaced her nankeen *robe de chambre* by a rich silk grown. And, though no art or change of costume could altogether conceal the ravages which time and trouble had wrought on a countenance that had once been pretty, I was surprised into thinking the lady much more interesting, in spite of her green spectacles, than she had appeared to be on the former visit. She was very gracious to me too; and when Mr. Falconer presently proposed that the two boys—meaning Marmaduke and myself—should be permitted to amuse ourselves as we pleased, she signified her assent to our taking a walk till dinner-time. Accordingly, I found myself demurely marching with my silent companion away from his mother's door.

Demurely and silent, that is to say, as long as we were within possible sight and hearing; after this Marmaduke relaxed. He had lived all his life in the village, had been almost secluded from society, was inspired with a terrible dread of his mother, who had hitherto been his sole teacher, and evidently a very severe teacher too ; and he ardently longed to be delivered from the bondage of home, and meant, when he was a little older, to run away and go to sea as a sailor.   This, as far as I can recollect, is a fair summary of our confidential communications, until we came to the announcement of the desperate determination last mentioned, when Marmaduke broke out passionately—

"And I would run away to-morrow, if it wasn't for Sophy."

"Who is Sophy?" I wanted to know.

"She lives with her grandmother and grandfather.   He is the Squire's gamekeeper ; and Sophy is—never mind what she is ; you shall see her, Hurly."

Saying this, Marmaduke took my hand and dragged me along. We were, I suppose, a mile or more from the boy's home ; and, as I remember it now, every step he had taken had increased his hilarity.

"I tell you," he said, as we hurried on, "if it hadn't been for Sophy, I should have run away ever so long ago ; but it wouldn't have done to leave her behind, you know."

"Why not, Marmaduke?"

"Why not!   Why, how stupid you are!"

I *was* very stupid, no doubt, and the more proved myself to be so by not understanding Marmaduke's further assertion that he liked Sophy Tindall better than anybody else in the whole world, and all the more because his mother couldn't bear old Storks the gamekeeper, nor the gamekeeper's old wife, nor anybody belonging to them.

"But it isn't good of you, Marmaduke, to like people that your mother dislikes, is it?" I asked.

"Oh, isn't it though?" said he, scornfully.   "I wonder who

there would be for me to like if I were to wait for her liking. But come along if you are coming."

Presently we turned down a green lane, bounded on one side by the palings of the park through which I had passed that morning, and presently came upon a pretty cottage, built in an ornamental style, and having a high thatched roof. It stood back from the green lane by the width of a moderately-sized garden, which was fenced in with rustic rails. This, as I presently found, was the back of the cottage ; the front facing the park, to which its inhabitants had free access.

"Here's where Sophy lives ;" said my companion ; and then, without further ceremony, he threw open the garden-gate, dashed up the path, shouting to me to " come along ;" and in another minute I found myself in a good-sized kitchen, floored with red bricks, and in the presence of a neat little elderly woman, whom Marmaduke familiarly addressed as " granny."

"This is George Burley, granny," said he, after the first salutation, and laying his hand condescendingly on my arm. " I told you about him yesterday, you know, and said I would bring him to see you if I could. Where's Sophy ?"

Sophy was gone to the " great house," but would be back presently, we were informed ; and then Mrs. Storks, who was really a very pleasant, good-tempered, bustling, homely sort of housewife, bade us be seated, telling me at the same time that she was quite proud to have a visit paid her by a live Londoner.

"And I reckon," added Mrs. Storks, "you won't be any the worse for a slice of plum-cake and a glass of wine. Boys are always hungry, you know." And then, disregarding my assurance that I had eaten one lunch already, she bustled to her pantry and brought forward a huge cake, and a black bottle which contained currant wine of her own make, as she assured me, and therefore couldn't do any harm to anybody.

Meanwhile I had time to cast my eyes round the room. It was superlatively clean and bright, from the tin candlesticks on the mantelshelf to the pewter plates on the dresser, which shone almost like looking-glasses. Over the fire-place, resting on a rack, were two or three formidable-looking guns ; and suspended against the opposite wall were as many glass cases, containing stuffed birds and small quadrupeds, being trophies of the old gamekeeper's skill, no doubt.

"Now, then, Hurly, make haste : we musn't be wasting time, you know," Marmaduke urged, as I was delicately nibbling my slice of cake and sipping the currant wine, which I thought delicious then, but which I remember brought tears into my eyes by its peculiar tartness. "Why, how long you are about it ! " he added, as he crammed the last morsel of *his* slice into his mouth. "No, I won't have any more, thankee, granny" (this to our entertainer) ; "I shan't be able to eat any dinner else, and then I shall be found out. Have you done, Hurly ? "

"Deary me, what a hurry you are in, Master Duke ! " said the gamekeeper's wife.

"I shouldn't wonder if I am, granny. I want to see Sophy, you know, and "—looking out at the window, which opened on the park—"here she comes, and I am off. You stop here, Hurly, till I come back." And, without any further ceremony, my companion opened the door and was gone.

I do not think that my astonishment on finding William Bix under the disguise of a quack doctor was greater than that which I now experienced at the change which had passed over Marmaduke Tozer. It was not so much his precocious manliness which surprised me—though this was startling enough—as the ease with which he appeared to cast off the restraints of home when removed only by a short distance from its influences. It was the old saying of "two faces under one hood" exemplified. Within reach of his

mother's eye and voice, Marmaduke was evidently under a spell of
terror ; escaped from these, his animal spirits rose, and his wild
nature exulted in its momentary freedom. I was wonderstruck
then, but I do not wonder now while I recall these passages in my
early experience. It was quite natural, and very common also.
Later observation has taught me this—shown me that the unrea-
soning and unreasonable severity of home discipline is the readiest
way, first to deception, then to hypocrisy, and then to uncurbed
license. Tell me that a child has been brought up *very strictly*, so
that love is almost banished from his heart, and there needs no
great prescience to guess what will follow.

CHAPTER XVIII.

I HAVE ANOTHER SECRET THRUST UPON ME.

REMAINED staring out of the window after Marmaduke
left, and watched him as he scampered over the green-
sward of the park towards the child whom he "liked
better than anybody else in the whole world." Judging from
what followed, the liking was mutual, for the next thing I
noticed was little Sophy running to meet the boy, and throwing
her arms round his neck in an apparent ecstasy of delight ; and
then, forgetful of his previous hurry, and of his promise to introduce me to the gamekeeper's little daughter, Marmaduke drew
her aside, and quietly seated himself by her on the grass, under a
broad spreading tree.

" A pretty pair of them, aren't they, now ?" said Mrs. Storks,
who was looking out at the window, over my head.

They were a pretty pair, certainly, and would have made an

ĭ

interesting painting. Marmaduke was a remarkably handsome boy; and I was near enough to see that his child-companion was a very lovely little girl, with blooming cheeks and bright auburn locks, which waved gently in the warm autumn air. Presently, when we were yet nearer together, and she shyly turned away from me, as from a stranger, I could not help thinking her the prettiest little damsel I had ever seen, with her deep blue sparkling eyes, and rosy lips, and dimpled chin, and laughing glances. She was not more than seven years old at this time, and she looked as though sorrow could scarcely find a lodgment in her light and happy heart.

Sophy Tindall had known one sorrow, however; for, like myself, she was motherless; and the shadow of another was yet hanging over her, for she was almost worse than fatherless—so Dame Storks mysteriously and confidentially informed me as I still stood watching the "pretty pair" from the kitchen window. It was not till long afterwards that I knew so much of her history as that the mother had been deserted by her husband in the early infancy of the child, and had sought refuge in her father's house, soon to die, broken-hearted. I shall not dwell upon this story now.

Marmaduke lingered some time with his little playfellow in the park, and when they came in together he was in haste to leave the cottage; so I had little opportunity for making acquaintance with the pretty child, if I had wished to do so.

"We'll go home now," said Marmaduke, gloomily, as we left the gamekeeper's door; and then he relapsed into his chronic taciturnity, which was not broken till we were fairly out of the green lane. Then he spoke.

"I say, Hurly—honour, you know."

"What do you mean, Marmaduke?"

"Don't you let out where we have been."

"Why not?" I asked, innocently.

"Why not, stupid? Didn't I tell you that my mother can't bear the Storkses?"

"Why can't she bear them?"

"How should I know? 'Twas something about my father, I reckon, before I was born. But what does that matter? You are not to tell about having been there, mind."

"Doesn't your mother know that you go to see them?" I asked, fencingly. For, though I had no intention of betraying Marmaduke, I rather winced at being made the depositary of another dark secret. There were two burdening my mind already; for, first, as my readers may remember, I had been charged by Mr. Falconer not to tell my grandfather of William Bix's visit to Silver Square; and, next, I had been commanded by William Bix not to mention to Mr. Falconer our meeting and conference near Wingham. And now to have another perilous secret added to these was more than I could very well bear. *I* had not asked to be taken into anybody's confidence, and why should that confidence be thrust upon me? All these thoughts, or something like them, passed through my mind when I asked my last question, to which Marmaduke replied, curtly enough—

"*She* know! No, she don't know. *I* should think not. So mind, you are not to say anything about it."

"But suppose your mother asks me where we have been?" I objected.

"How can you tell anybody where we have been, when you don't know a place about here?" argued Marmaduke.

"But she may ask me if we have been in anywhere," said I.

"And can't you say we haven't, stupid?" said he.

Very reluctantly I replied that I could say so, of course, but I didn't like to tell a lie.

"You would do it for yourself, I reckon, Hurly," rejoined

Marmaduke, with an air of great innocence. "But I dare say you won't be asked anything. I shall tell my mother that we have been as far as the windmills; and if she asks you, mind you tell her the same."

I agreed at last to do this; and with a guilty conscience I walked on by Marmaduke's side, glad enough, when we reached his home, to hear no questions asked. How Mr. Falconer and Mrs. Tozer had passed the two or three hours of our absence I never knew—more agreeably I suspect, however, than on our former visit, as they appeared to be on tolerably good terms with each other; and I have nothing more to say on this score, save that the dinner-hour passed away pleasantly enough, and that Marmaduke shrunk within his shell, like a frightened snail, as usual.

But a new surprise was in store for me. In pursuance of his design of making his two *protégés*, namely, Marmaduke and myself, better acquainted with each other, Mr. Falconer had contrived, while we were absent in the morning, that I should be invited to spend a week at the widow's house, while he extended his journey to the coast towns, which he wished to visit. I am not sure that this arrangement was altogether agreeable to me, for I had strange misgivings respecting the treatment I might receive. As, however, the lady gave me the invitation with some degree of cordiality, and the gentleman willed that it should be so, I had only to submit.

"You will be very happy, I have no doubt, Hurly," said Mr. Falconer, as he parted from me that evening; and he heaved a sigh as he spoke.

CHAPTER XIX.

ON THE LAST DAY OF MY VISIT I MEET WITH AN ADVENTURE.

NOW the week of my visit was spent in Mrs. Tozer's house is not at all worth recording. It is enough to say that, though I was not quite so happy as Mr. Falconer evidently expected me to be, I was not very miserable. The lady did not take much notice of me, certainly; but she was neither unkind, nor uncivil; and she gave her son more liberty than usual, in order that we might amuse ourselves together. That Marmaduke made use of this unwonted liberty in paying daily stolen visits to the gamekeeper's cottage, and that, on our return from these visits, he accounted to his mother for the time of our absence, so as to conceal his disobedience, may be understood. I pass over all this to arrive as quickly as possible at the last day of my sojourn in that lady's house.

As usual, Marmaduke and I started off on our after-breakfast walk, and proceeded towards his favourite place of resort, not, however, by the road I have already mentioned, but in an opposite direction, which took us first of all into the park, and then by a circuitous route conducted us to the park front of the cottage.

"It isn't so safe to go always the same way," said Marmaduke, who seemed so long to have practised deception upon his mother that it had become a second nature. "If I was to go always the same way," he added, "she would be asking me all sorts of questions, you see."

"Hadn't we better not go there at all, to-day?" I said, feebly. I had learned by this time how deep was Mrs. Tozer's dislike to the gamekeeper and his wife : whether this dislike were reasonable or unreasonable it was not for me to judge ; but I was able to guess what the consequences would be to Marmaduke, at any rate, if our visits to the cottage should be discovered. At the same time I had begun to share in my companion's liking for little Sophy and her chatty, good-humoured grandmother, and should have missed this last opportunity of bidding them good-bye.

"You needn't go if you don't want to go," said my friend ; "you can wait here, and I will come back to you when I have been ; only you told granny you would see her again before going away."

"Oh, if you go, I'll go too," said I ; and so we walked on. Before we reached the cottage, however, we were startled by hearing our names shouted from behind, in a childish voice ; and on looking round we perceived little Sophy running after us with all her might, and beckoning for us to stop.

She had been so frightened, she said. She had been up to the great house (by the way, Sophy's journeys to the " great house " were very frequent, for she was a favourite with the ladies there) —she had been to the great house, and was returning through " that corvet " (*Anglicè*, covert), and she pointed to a tolerably extensive belt of thicket through which a pathway to the house ran, when she was stopped by a man—oh, such a big, ugly man— who caught her up in his arms and kissed her twenty times. "Twenty times and more," said she, in a paroxysm of disgust and fear combined, " he did ! "

"What sort of man was he ? " I asked. But the little damsel could give no better description of him than that he was big and ugly, and had black hair all over his mouth and chin.

"I'll go and find him," I said, starting up and running towards the " corvet," which was distant about a couple of hundred yards, probably. And, though Sophy called me back in terror, and

AT THE OLD GAMEKEEPER'S COTTAGE.

Marmaduke bade me not be silly, I was soon out of their hearing.

"Black hair all over his mouth and chin, had he?" thought I to myself. "That's my wicked uncle, William Bix; and I'll ask him what he means by frightening Sophy like that." The resolution was a doughty one, certainly; but I had no opportunity of proving to myself how brave I could be; for, though I arrived at the "corvet," and penetrated through it, no person was to be seen; and, as my courage soon cooled down, I was not sorry to return to Sophy and Marmaduke with a report that the man had disappeared.

This adventure had taken up some time, however; and some extra time was taken up as well, when we arrived at the gamekeeper's cottage, in telling Dame Storks how shamefully little Sophy had been frightened. And then, as the old gamekeeper himself happened to come in while we were there, we had to repeat our story to him. I was not sorry to see that he did not think much of it when we had finished our tale, for he said, "Is that all?" and laughed; adding that he supposed the ruffian (as Marmaduke, in his indignation, had termed the invader of Sophy's pretty cheeks) could not resist the temptation presented by them, and didn't mean anything more than friendliness; but that he (old Storks) would blackbeard him, if he ever caught him in the park or out of it. I was, on the whole, I repeat, rather glad that the adventure had taken this turn; for, as my indignation blew off, I did not want my uncle William (supposing him to have been the stranger) to be exposed: and I determined also to keep my own counsel. So, here I was, with another secret—one of my own—on my mind, in addition to the three which already burdened it.

But what with these lengthened explanations, and the time it took to laugh off Sophy's terrors, it was nearly an hour beyond the usual time of our return from these morning strolls before we reached home. And, by reason of this delay, I found that I had narrowly missed meeting Mr. William Bix in his disguise; for we were informed by Marianne Bolster—with whom, by the way, I had become tolerably familiar—that in our absence the quack doctor had called, and that her mistress had bought a lot of physic of him, thus proving his previous prediction to me to be true. It was quite as well, perhaps, that I escaped the rencontre, especially as Marmaduke, directly he heard the small servant's description of Mr. Le Grand, jumped to the conclusion that he and Sophy's persecutor were one and the same. This was whispered to me secretly, of course, with a trembling caution, which I did not need, to "keep my mouth shut about Sophy and all the rest of it." One good result of the quack's call seemed to be that we were not to be interrogated by Marmaduke's mother respecting our morning's peregrinations. But in this we were mistaken.

"Where did you walk this morning, Marmaduke?" asked the lady, in the course of the afternoon.

"In the park," said the boy, in the boldest tone in which he ever addressed his mother, which was anything but bold.

"And whom did you see there?" she wished to know.

"Nobody, ma'am."

"Indeed!"

"Oh, yes, ma'am; we saw old Storks, the gamekeeper, didn't we, George? He was going home across the park. He had been shooting, I should think; for he had his gun over his shoulder."

"And you went to the windmills yesterday, I think you told me. You have been to the windmills a good many times since George Burley has been here, have you not? You wretched boy," she added, sternly, turning to Marmaduke, "it is not enough for you to try to deceive, but you must try to teach others to do so too. Do you think I do not know where you have been every day this last week?   Do not answer me, sir, but go to your own room."

The boy did not move.   He seemed positively paralysed by dread.

"Go," she repeated, yet more sternly, and stamping her little foot on the floor.   "You are your father's own son," she went on, speaking bitterly; "and you give me cause to be thankful that you are my only living child."

How uneasily I sat on my chair when I found myself alone with Mrs. Tozer, I need not say.   Apparently, however, she did not share in my uneasiness; she took no notice of me, but replaced her green spectacles, and resumed some needlework she had previously laid down.

I could bear it no longer.   I timidly stole up to her, and begged her, very pathetically I have no doubt, very earnestly and sincerely I am sure, to forgive Marmaduke "this once, just this once."

The lady went on quietly with her work, and I ventured to look into her face.   No gleam of relenting reached me through the green spectacles.

"I shall punish him," she said, in a cold, measured tone.   "I shall flog him to-morrow, after you are gone."

I slunk away in despair.   After that I knew no pleading would avail.

"You had better go and amuse yourself in the garden," she said to me presently; and I went, glad to escape from her presence.

I shall not prolong this part of my story.   I have only to say that I saw no more of Marmaduke that day, till I went to bed and crept in by his side, when I found him sobbing and bemoaning his hard fate, and repeating his threat of running away; that the domestic atmosphere was not at all cleared in the morning; that, soon after breakfast, the welcome face and voice of Mr. Falconer came to deliver me from that terrible house; that my last glance at Mrs. Tozer's imperturbable countenance showed her determination to be unmoved; and that, in our walk towards the pleasant Wingham "Lion," after our farewells were spoken, I fancied I could almost hear the shrieks of the guilty boy undergoing his punishment.

I dared not venture to tell my good friend Mr. Falconer the cause of my dulness, which he was fain to attribute to regret at leaving such kind friends behind; and he good-naturedly strove to raise my spirits, as we walked on, by describing the places he had seen since we parted. In due time we arrived at Wingham, where I found post-horses ready to be put to our carriage, which presently whisked us off to Canterbury, and thence to London. We reached Silver Square late that night; and after another busy week spent in London, Mr. Falconer and Alphonse started off to their Continental home. From this time, nothing material to my history occurred for nearly three years, at the end of which time I was thirteen years of age.

CHAPTER XX.

AFTER THREE YEARS.

WAS thirteen years old; and, save that I was nearly three years older than at the close of my last chapter, no great changes had taken place in my history. My relations with the small household in Silver Square remained on the same footing. My grandfather was getting rather more infirm than when I first knew him, for he was fast approaching the threescore and ten years which the Psalmist places as the ordinary boundary of human life; but he bore the burden of years bravely. He was methodical and temperate; and we know that these habits are favourable to hale old age and long life.

Betsy Miller was still my grandfather's housekeeper; and, only that she had more frequent recourse to extraneous assistance on her high days of bustle and cleaning, she remained pretty much the same as when I first introduced her to my readers. She was, perhaps, a trifle more gaunt and bony; and her hair was becoming undeniably gray, for she was near upon fifty years old. But both her energy and her devotedness to my grandfather's interests were unabated; while her motherly kindness towards me, if there were any difference, was augmented.

It is, perhaps, scarcely necessary to say that I had, long ere this, passed from under Betsy Miller's sway in the matter of education. One of the results of Mr. Falconer's lengthened sojourn in Silver Square, as recorded in my former chapters, was that I was sent to a good day-school in the city, where, for three years, I had had my irregularities pretty well rubbed down by constant contact with some fourscore boys, and had imbibed a good deal of scholastic lore which would have been quite beyond Betsy Miller's power to impart. And, without saying more than is becoming on this score, I may add that, not being naturally stupid or perverse, I had escaped punishment in general, and was reckoned, I believe, by the masters, as rather a promising pupil.

In the three years which had thus passed away, Mr. Falconer had remained abroad. We often heard from him, however, in Silver Square, and his letters to my grandfather were never concluded without some kind messages to me.

In all this time I had heard nothing of Mrs. Tozer and Marmaduke. Once, indeed, when suffering for a time from ill-health— or rather from the delicacy which sometimes attends rapid growth, especially in closely pent-in cities—the question was mooted by my grandfather, whether it would not be prudent to send me into the country for a season; and he proposed writing to Mrs. Tozer to ask her to receive me.   But I recoiled from this intimation with so much horror, and begged so earnestly of Betsy Miller to frustrate so dire a consignment, that the idea came to nothing.   Probably Mrs. Tozer would not have received me; but I was very glad not to have to risk her consent to my visit.

I was thirteen years old then, and was still looked upon as being frail and delicate in constitution, when another era in my history was opened.

My grandfather called me one day into his office, and gave me a letter to read.   It had come by post that morning, and was from Mr. Falconer.   It was to the effect that, when he was last in England, and spent a few days in exploring the south-eastern coast, he had made acquaintance with Mr. T. (to avoid the awkwardness of a mere initial, I will write down Thompson), who was the proprietor of a large boarding-school, at about a mile from a very romantic spot on the coast, which I may as well call St. Judith's Bay.   The letter went on to say that the writer had lately renewed this acquaintance by happening to fall in with Mr. Thompson, who was spending his midsummer vacation in a Continental tour, and that he was very much pleased with that gentleman, whom, indeed, he praised in high terms.   The latter went on to state, further, that this meeting had resulted in a plan respecting the two boys, meaning Marmaduke and myself; that he (Mr. Falconer) had made arrangements with Mr. Thompson for our being received into his establishment; that I might go to St. Judith's as soon as it suited my grandfather's convenience to send me; and that I should no doubt find my friend Marmaduke already there.

This letter—of which my memory has preserved the above abstract—was written in very affectionate terms, and spoke of the concern Mr. Falconer felt at the reports of my grandfather about my weakly state, which he hoped fresh country air and sea-bathing would remedy. As a matter of course, Mr. Falconer added, all charges were already arranged for, to be put to his account; but he further desired that twenty pounds should be applied, out of funds in my grandfather's hand, to fitting me out for school; also that, from the same funds, I was to receive ten pounds a-year as pocket-money.

"You see what Mr. Falconer writes, Hurly," said my grandfather, in rather a tremulous voice. "What do you think of it, my dear boy?"

"It is very good of Mr. Falconer, grandfather," said I.

"Yes, yes; Mr. Falconer is generous and open-handed in all he does. But what do you think of this plan of his? How do you like his proposal?"

"I shall like to go to the school, sir," I replied.

"Ah, it will be a change for you, Hurly; and the young are fond of changes. I dare say you have found things very dull and humdrum in Silver Square since you left off being quite a child." My dear grandfather said this rather sorrowfully, I thought— more sorrowfully than reproachfully—and his eyes moistened a little.

"I have not been dull, indeed and indeed," I said, earnestly and truly; "and I do not want to leave you, grandfather; I shall never be happier anywhere else, I am sure."

"I am *not* sure, Hurly," returned my grandfather, with unusual solemnity and feeling. "The world is young to you, and new to you; and pleasure is easily to be found. You have a contented disposition, I know; and I know, too, that you are one of the comparatively small number who have a way, without designing it, of making friends wherever they go. I have no doubt you will be happy at school—as happy, at any rate, as you have been in this gloomy house."

"It has never been gloomy to me, grandfather," I said, a good deal moved by the old man's kindness. "You have always been so good to me—so very good. How could I help being happy?"

"To whom could I have felt and shown affection, if not to you, my dear boy?" asked my grandfather, with a heavy sigh. "You are all that is left to me of my own, to love. I am like a half-dead and decayed tree, Hurly. The trunk remains, though the heart is eaten out of it; but the branches—the branches! Oh, Hurly! they were very flourishing once: so the poor trunk thought, in his foolish pride. But God has smitten them; and now——"

My poor grandfather did not complete his lamentation, but he turned away, and leaned his head for a moment or two on his hand, while his elbow rested on the desk. I saw his lips move, as in prayer. I think he *was* praying; and I also turned away reverently.

And self-reproachfully, too. My grandfather knew that, by this time, I knew a great deal about his son, William Bix. He knew that I knew what a trouble that son had been to him, and had brought shame upon him as well. He knew that I knew how, in spite of all bygones, he loved that wicked son, with a long-tried and enduring love. He knew that I knew how he mourned over the memory of past days, when William was a child, and how he longed for the time, which never would come—no, never—when the poor prodigal should penitently return, to be received with warm embraces, and compassion and forgiveness. All this my grandfather knew that I knew; but he did not know that I had ever seen this wicked uncle of mine; that I had held communication with him three times since his shadow had crossed the sorrowing father's path; that I knew what place he had haunted only three years ago, and something of his mode of life; that I knew this as a secret I had been forbidden to reveal; and that I guessed at another secret concerning William Bix which I would not have ventured to reveal, and which I will not reveal at this part of my story. Well, there was nothing really wrong in my keeping this knowledge, any part of it or all of it, from my grandfather. It would have done him no good to know it: it might even have made him more unhappy about his William than he was already. I was bound in honour to Mr. Falconer, and to Betsy Miller, to keep silence about my first introduction to my uncle, and, in a kind of honour to my uncle himself, to keep silence about my later intercourse with him. I repeat, therefore, that I was not wrong in keeping my knowledge to myself. But I was sorry that I had it in my keeping, and when I saw my grandfather, in his unwonted manifestations of anguish, mourning over his poor, wayward, wandering boy—ah, yes, I wished I could comfort him (which I could not do) by saying, "This thy son, which was dead, shall live again; and, though lost, he shall be found." No, the secret knowledge I had of my uncle would have brought no comfort to my grandfather, but to hold that knowledge without sharing it with him made me feel as though I were guilty.

Some such thoughts as these passed in a muddling sort of way through my mind as my grandfather sat with his face half covered, and his lips still silently moving, until, presently, he turned to me, and said, in a livelier air—

"But about this going to school, Hurly. It is, as you say, very kind of Mr. Falconer; and we must, Betsy and I, submit to losing you for a time. There is only one thing that puzzles me."

"What is that, grandfather?" I asked. But my grandfather did not answer me quite directly. He put another question instead.

"What sort of a boy is Marmaduke Tozer?"

K

"I like him very much, grandfather."

"Yes, yes, you have told me that before. But is he a *good* boy?"—my grandfather laid great emphasis on the *good*—"is he honest, truthful? Tell me that, Hurly."

"I was there only a week, you know, grandfather," said I, unable to answer the question so satisfactorily as I could have wished, and unwilling to speak of the dark traits of the boy's character which I had observed. For I may as well say here that I had, in the three years which had passed away, been very silent about the deception Marmaduke had endeavoured to practise on his mother, and the consequence of its discovery.

"Well, well, I hope he is open and honest, and then all will be well, I dare say. But what puzzles me," he added, musingly, "is why, with his experience, Mr. Falconer should wish you two boys to be thrown together. However, he knows what he is about, I have no doubt, and I dare say you and Marmaduke will be very good friends. If he is honest and true, I hope you will; not else, Hurly."

A good deal more passed at this time between my grandfather and myself; but I need not repeat it, as it consisted mostly of good advice, which, whatever impression was made on me by it, as falling from his generally taciturn lips, would, perhaps, read dull if written down. So I will only say that Betsy Miller received *carte blanche* orders that day to furnish me with all requisites in the way of new clothing; and that during the next month the old house in Silver Square was in as great commotion as though I had been going on some foreign embassage.

Before closing this chapter, however, I may again remark that authors might well despair if they had to account for or explain all the inconsistencies they have to record. What puzzled my grandfather has always puzzled me; and I can only faintly suppose that Mr. Falconer believed it would be to my future advantage to make the friendship of his intended principal legatee, either forgetting how dearly he himself had paid for schoolboy friendship, or else believing that what had once happened was out of the ordinary course of events, and was not likely to be repeated, on the same argument that the safest spot in a thunderstorm is where a thunderbolt has once fallen.

CHAPTER XXI.

AT ST. JUDITH'S; WHERE I AGAIN MEET WITH MARMADUKE.

A MONTH passed away, and then I was travelling once more into Kent, not this time in a grand carriage, however, but on the outside of a stage-coach. To reach my destination on the same day, I had to rise very early in the morning, and take the earliest coach to Dover, whence I was to be transmitted by a carrier's luggage-cart to St. Judith's. I was unaccompanied by any protector, but my grandfather gave the guard of the coach a handsome fee to take care of me during the journey, and to see me and my boxes safely delivered into the charge of old Hanmer, the St. Judith's carrier.

There is no need for me to describe this second journey of mine. It is enough to say that, late in the evening, I arrived safely at my destination.

That I was received with a good deal of grave kindness by the principal of St. Judith's, and with an equal amount of good-humoured, sensible alacrity by his bustling housekeeper, does not take long to tell. And another line or two may be spared for me to say that, in the three years I remained beneath Mr. Thompson's roof and under his care, I experienced no change in this demeanour. This is saying much, but not more than is due to the memory of my kind old preceptor, and of the methodical lady who managed the domestic affairs of the large and flourishing establishment.

Having paid this tribute of gratitude, I have only to add here that, in consideration of my fatigue after a day's travelling, I was presently conducted to a large dormitory containing eight or nine beds, double beds too; for those were not the days in which schoolmasters advertised single beds and separate rooms for each pupil. My bed was pointed out to me; indeed, my name was already written on a card and tacked over it, and on another card alongside of it was written the name of Marmaduke Tozer.

So Marmaduke had already arrived, and he was to be my bed-fellow. I thought I would keep awake till he came to bed, then.

But I didn't. I was soon asleep, and so soundly asleep that I did not wake when the other boys came to bed, nor even when Marmaduke lay down by my side.

The sound that greeted my ears and roused me from my first refreshing slumber was the loud ringing of a large bell very near to our dormitory; and I opened and rubbed my eyes and then sat upright in bed, in that sort of stupid wonderment which most persons are apt to experience on being suddenly awakened, especially in a strange bedroom. I soon knew where I was, however, my memory being enlivened by the sight of a number of nightcapped heads starting from under the bedclothes on the opposite side of the dormitory, as well as by a gentle touch on the back which caused me to turn to my bedfellow.

"How are you, Hurly?" and "How are you, Marmaduke?" and "I am so glad you are come," and "I am so glad you are here." Imagine all this spoken.

"There's twenty minutes allowed for dressing and prayers, Hurly; and then we are off down to the bay for a dip in the sea : this is one of our bathing mornings, you must know. But

ON THE WAY TO SCHOOL.

I was told to tell you that you needn't get up unless you like. Perhaps you would rather rest after your journey."

" No ; I'll get up and go with you, Marmaduke. I'm so glad to see you ;" and then I sprang out of bed.

Twenty minutes later, and I found myself in a spacious playground with nearly a hundred boys of all ages from eight to sixteen, who had descended from the various dormitories, each with a towel in hand, and who were being marshalled in due order by five or six teachers, for the march to the bay. A little later, and we were out in the village, which we soon left behind us after passing a fine old Norman church. Then we reached the brow of a hill, beneath and beyond which the bay spread before us in tranquil beauty. How the whole troop scampered down the hill, scattered themselves on the beach, and were soon splashing in among the green waves, scarcely need be told ; nor need I dwell upon the effect produced by my first plunge into salt water. Let it pass.

" Now, Hurly, give me your arm, and let us have a confab," said Marmaduke, when we were mounting the hill on our return.

I complied.

" How long have you been here, Marmaduke ?" I asked.

" Call me Duke, if you love me, Hurly—Duke for short—as Sophy always does."

" Duke, then," and I repeated my question.

" About a month. Almost as soon as my mother got Mr. Falconer's letter. And I was as glad to get away from home as she was to get rid of me. Very shocking, is it not, now, for me to say so ?"

I thought it was.

" It can't be helped, I suppose," said Duke, sullenly ; " at least, I know I can't help it. You never heard what happened after you left, I dare say."

"No ; but I can guess. Don't say anything about it, Duke," said I, fancying that he referred to the threatened punishment.

"Oh, I may as well tell you. I ran away, that was all."

"Ran away! Oh, Marmaduke!"

"Yes, I did, that same night, after I got flogged—it was my last flogging, Hurly. I got out of my bedroom window—it isn't far to drop, you know—and got among the gipsies—was with them two months. What do you think of that?"

I did not know what to think; I was so sorry to hear Marmaduke talk in that way; and I said so.

"What's the use of being sorry? It wasn't bad altogether, for they behaved very well to me, the gipsies did; and I should have turned one myself, and been with them to this day, if it hadn't been for thinking of Sophy."

"Ah! but what had that to do with it, Duke?"

"Everything. Sophy would never have turned gipsy, would she? So I thought I had best give it up; and I did."

"But did not your mother know where you were?" I asked.

"Not she. She had me hunted for, sharp enough; but she wouldn't have found me ever if I hadn't given myself up."

"Why not?"

"Have you never heard the song, Hurly, 'Stain your cheeks with nut and berry; for the gipsy's life is merry, merry'? That's how it was. They stained my face and altered me so that nobody would be likely to know me."

"You gave yourself up, then?"

"Yes : or one of the gipsy fellows did it for me ; only he made my mother promise, first, to treat me better if I came back again. There, now, you know all about that, Hurly," continued the boy ; "haven't you anything else to ask?"

I had a question or two to ask, certainly. First, did Marianne Bolster still live with Marmaduke's mother?

"Oh, dear, no. Mother never keeps her servants very long. She has had two or three since Bolster left."

I did not wonder at this when I remembered the red mark I had once seen on the girl's cheek. That question being disposed of, therefore, I asked another.

"Is Sophy grown much?"

"Isn't she?" said Marmaduke. "And she is more beautiful than ever," he added.

"Do you often see her?" I asked.

"How can I, while I am here, miles and miles away?"

"I mean did you often see her before you came here, and after you got back from being a gipsy?" I explained.

"I should think I did, too. Do you think I would have gone home again without making sure of that? I go to old Storks's house whenever I like, now, when I am at home."

"Perhaps your mother and Mr. Storks have made up their quarrel?" I suggested.

"No, they haven't; at least, mother has not. *He* never had a quarrel."

"But you don't keep on doing what she does not like, do you, Duke?"

"Oh, come, if you are going to preach, you may cut it short, Hurly," said he. "And, as to doing or not doing, she just told me I might do as I liked: she should not try to interfere any more. If I would have low company, I might; and all that sort of thing, Hurly."

He said this in a tone of deep defiance which proved, I thought, how deeply seated was his disobedience and rebellion; and I was sorry for him, for, boy as I was, I felt sure that these feelings would end badly. I suppose Marmaduke saw that I was shocked, for he said, carelessly—

"There, you needn't look so blue, Hurly; that won't do any good, you know."

I did not think it would, so I put another question :—one, indeed, which I had asked once before.

"Why does not your mother like the Storkses?"

"Oh, only some nonsense of hers about old Storks drawing my father into bad company, and being his pot-house companion. All stuff, Hurly. From all I have ever heard, my father was much more likely to have drawn Storks in."

And this was all I ever heard by way of explanation of Mrs. Tozer's bitter enmity against the gamekeeper and his wife. If there were any deeper reasons, the lady kept them secret.

The conversation I have recorded lasted till we reached the breakfast-room, and there it ended.

CHAPTER XXII.

FRIENDSHIP NOT PROMOTED BY FURTHER ACQUAINTANCE.

MARMADUKE TOZER was not improved. I did not see then—boy as I was—how sadly deficient he was in those qualities which *must* appear in youth if they are to shine out brightly in manhood; but I saw enough to cause me to remember what my grandfather had said ; namely, that, if honest and true, he hoped Marmaduke and I should be good friends, but *not else.*

Marmaduke was *not* honest and true. I do not mean by this that he was habitually given to cheating and falsehood, but he was undeniably selfish ; and no person can be this, and at the same time, in the full sense of the words, either honest or true. He was crafty also. I am persuaded that the severity of his early training had taught him this ; that the constant fear of his mother's anger had made deception a second nature with him. He was given to boasting—to bragging we used to call it. By some means or other, he had come to the knowledge of Mr. Falconer's intentions towards himself; and I believe that I, unwittingly, enlarged his ideas of that gentleman's great wealth, which I spoke of as I had heard, principally from Betsy Miller. It was astonishing the airs he gave himself after this revelation, and the patronising manner he adopted towards me, telling me what great things he would do for me when he came into his property. I should not have minded this if the matter had passed only between ourselves, but he took care to show, in the face of the whole school, that he already considered himself vastly my superior in respect of fortune, and this troubled me. It annoyed me the more because he really was very far from generous with the money he had at his command, which, I may say, was just what Mr. Falconer allowed him, as in my case; namely, ten pounds a year.

Yet, notwithstanding these drawbacks in Marmaduke's essential character—and which, probably, I now see much clearer by the light of subsequent events than I could then have done—he had qualities which made him rather popular in the school. He was bold, even to recklessness, in all games of strength and agility; and he had an outward show of good-nature and frankness, which concealed the cunning which lay beneath, and which only occasionally betrayed itself.

Let it be understood, also, that I never had any decisive quarrel with Marmaduke. On the contrary, we were on tolerably good terms with each other; but our acquaintance did not ripen into friendship. I was sorry for this at that time: I am glad of it now.

In a school of a hundred boys, it would be strange if any one unit of that number should be entirely dependent on some other particular unit for support, and consolation, and sympathy.

Marmaduke did not depend on me, nor I on him. He very soon found congenial associates in two brothers—Quercus and Philander Brown by name—whose home was at Blackheath; while I picked up a friend in a little fellow, younger than myself, who came from London, and who excited my sympathy, first of all, by the suit of mourning which he wore, and which he accounted for by telling me, in mournful tones, and with tears in his eyes, that his mother was dead—had been dead only a few months. He was a gentle little fellow, with very strong affections and feelings, very ill-prepared to cope with the rough companionship of a large boarding-school. He was very glad to have a friend, so he told me, and I was very glad to have him for my friend. His name was Edwin Millman.

It came to pass, therefore, that, though Marmaduke and I kept on good terms with each other, we were each content to see the friendship of the other running in another channel. It may be that this comparative distance was rather promoted by our being in different classes. Marmaduke's home education (notwithstanding its stringency) had not produced fruits of learning very plentifully, and he was low down in the school.

I must pass rapidly over this part of my history, and shall only say here, that weeks and months rolled on without any occurrences needful to be noted down. We were a tolerably happy and harmonious community, very well governed by genuine kindness, at a time when kindness in teaching was an exception—harshness the rule. At Christmas I went home to Silver Square for the holidays, and my grandfather and Betsy Miller were pleased to see how much healthier and stronger I had become : and when the holidays were over I returned to St. Judith's not broken-hearted.

CHAPTER XXIII.

THE NEW TEACHER.

N the second half-year of my pupilage at St. Judith's a new teacher made his appearance, as second classical tutor and writing-master.

"Such a queer-looking man," remarked Edwin Millman, who had caught sight of the new arrival, in the hall, the evening before his introduction to the school.

"In what way queer, Edwin?" I asked.

"Oh, he is so old-looking—forty years old or more, I'll be bound—almost as old as the dominie himself."

"Is that all?"

"No; he has an odd face, and wears great blue goggles, with blinkers like carriage horses; and his hair is brushed down smooth over his forehead, I suppose because he hasn't enough of it for a Brutus."

"Anything else, Edwin?"

"Yes; he is dressed just like a parson, with a white cravat, and no collar, and a waistcoat that buttons up close under his chin, and a long coat, like a great coat, reaching pretty nearly down to his heels—all in black, he is, only it seems precious rusty. I say, George," the boy added, after a pause, and speaking confidentially, "I don't like his looks."

"Because he looks old, and has thin hair, and wears blue spectacles, and dresses like a parson? Is that why you don't like his looks, Edwin?" I asked, laughing at the solemnity of his tone.

"No, of course not, George; but he has got a nasty-looking

mouth—spiteful. He looks as if he could *bite* any one he takes a dislike to, and bite hard."

Here our conference ended. To tell the truth, I was not much taken with my companion's description of the new teacher—whose name we learned was Smithers—and I regretted more than ever having lost Mr. Smithers's predecessor, a kind-hearted, gentlemanly young man, who had been at one of the Universities, and was now entering into holy orders.

We were to hear more of Mr. Smithers, however, before seeing him; for that night, after prayers had been read to us in school according to custom, Mr. Thompson called attention, and in a brief speech informed the assembled boys that he should have the pleasure on the following day of introducing to the school a gentleman with whom he had received the most flattering testimonials from the principal of a large school in the neighbourhood of London, as being an exceedingly conscientious and painstaking teacher, as well as a thorough student; that this gentleman (Mr. Smithers by name) had been seven years in the establishment he had just left, and that therefore Mr. Thompson's correspondent had the greatest confidence in speaking of his character and acquirements.

"I tell you this, boys," continued our master, "that you may be prepared to treat Mr. Smithers with proper respect. Unfortunately," he went on to say, "the gentleman is somewhat peculiar in his manner, and rather eccentric in his costume, which is to be attributed, no doubt, to his studious habits. But you know, some of you, what the poet says :—

> "'Worth makes the MAN; the want of it, the *fellow*;
> While all the rest is leather and prunello.'"

With this pithy quotation, Mr. Thompson descended from his rostrum, and he left us in much wonderment respecting our new teacher.

On the following morning Mr. Smithers entered the large school-room arm-in-arm with the principal. Of course all eyes were turned towards the door, and I dare say not a few "Oh, my's!" were softly breathed. For he was a strange-looking personage, this new teacher, much as Edwin Millman had described him to me, but with greater exaggerations in the reality than in the description. He was tall and gaunt; and this characteristic was increased in appearance by the extraordinary coat of rusty black which, buttoned closely from the top to the lowermost button, and fitting tightly to his spare frame, reached almost to his shoe-ties. This, with the straightly-combed hair and whiskerless face, and especially with the large blue-blinkered spectacles in addition, which gave an awfully cadaverous hue to his colourless countenance, raised a titter in the school, which, however, was speedily hushed by a stern glance of our master's eye.

"What a guy he is, though! isn't he?" whispered my right-hand desk-fellow in my ear: "only wants a dark lantern and matchbox, eh?"

"Keep quiet," I said, bending over my books with strange perturbation; for, in spite of the new disguise in which I saw him, and the new name he bore, I had fancied I recognised in the new teacher my uncle, William Bix.

And yet it could not be. I knew enough of my uncle's history to know that he could not have been seven years, if he had been one, a teacher in a school. How, then, could he have obtained the testimonials of which Mr. Thompson had told us? I argued this in my mind until I began to smile at the freak of imagination, and to set myself in earnest to the morning's work.

Presently a class was called. I was at the head of it, and marched boldly up to the new teacher. I cannot say that our eyes met, for his were so completely hidden by his coloured glasses that not a sparkle could be seen. But I did not need to look into his eyes.   It was enough to see, in the sallow cheeks, the rather strongly-developed nose, the massive under-jaw, and the thin-lipped, closely-compressed mouth, the unmistakable features of the quack doctor of three or four years ago.

He knew me, too.   In one moment his countenance became ghastly pale, and his white upper-lip trembled.   So did his hand when he held it out for my Latin grammar.   The emotion did not last long, however, and it was unnoticed by any save myself.   It evidently required a strong effort to overcome his surprise, but William Bix was equal to it: before one could have counted twenty, the natural sallowness had returned to his cheeks, the thread of pale vermillion to his narrow lips, and firmness to his quivering nostrils, and the class was proceeding with its rehearsal.

I have elsewhere recorded that my uncle, in his youth, had received a good education.   I do not suppose that he was very well "read up," as students say, in the classics, and I apprehend that his knowledge was somewhat rusted by disuse.   But he was equal, at least, to the requirements of a private boarding-school in the country, at a time when a little Latinity in general went a long way; and in the opinion of the class, our new teacher acquitted himself satisfactorily.   Better than I did, certainly; for I lost two places in the class by stupid mistakes in parsing, owing to the strange confusion of mind into which I was plunged by this unexpected apparition.

Presently the class was dismissed, but not before Mr. Smithers (my uncle for the present must bear this *alias*), under pretence of wiping his glasses, removed them for a moment from his eyes, and darted at me a glance so full of dire threatening, and set his teeth at me so houndlike, that I felt my blood run cold.   Edwin Millman was right enough when he said that the new teacher looked as if he could bite, and bite hard, too.

CHAPTER XXIV.

MR. SMITHERS.

"YOU did not get on very well with your parsing this morning, my lad. I am afraid you are not very industrious. Come this way: I should like to have a little chat with you about the irregular verbs."

This readily-prepared and quietly uttered speech was addressed to me after school-hours, while I was strolling with Edwin Millman in the large playground, and looking on at groups of our schoolfellows, who were engaged in various games.

Obeying the mandate, I followed Mr. Smithers to a secluded corner of the ground, where, hidden by a clump of trees, was a rustic arbour, then unoccupied. Here he sat down, and motioned me to his side.

"Can we be overheard here?" he asked, in a guarded tone.

"No uncle."

"Not that word again—never again while I am here, nor afterwards in speaking of me if I should be the first to leave," he said, fiercely. "Do you understand?"

"Yes, I do."

"Now, then, before we begin business"—this he said more mildly—"have you spoken about me to any one, since you recognised me this morning? I mean, have you spoken about me in any other way than as Mr. Smithers—the new teacher—quite unknown to you, of course?"

"I have not spoken about you at all," I said. And this was true; for, undecided what course to take, and mindful, too, of the threatening looks of my uncle that morning in class, I had deter-

L

mined for that day, at least, to observe a prudent silence altogether about him.

"Not spoken about me at all," he said, suspiciously—"not even
to that boy you were walking with?"

"No, I have not."

"That's well. I commend your discretion," returned Mr.
Smithers. "And now, how came you to be here? Tell me."

I told him that I was sent to school by my grandfather, at the
request and expense of Mr. Falconer.

"I might have thought of that when I knew the other boy was
sent here by that lunatic; but I didn't," he muttered to himself.
"But it is of no consequence," he added; and then he again
addressed me.

"Look you, Hurly; you have no enmity against me, I suppose:
you don't want to injure me?"

"No, certainly not," I replied.

"And you can keep a secret?"

Secrets again! Oh, how I loathed the very word! I had
hoped I had done with other people's secrets. However, I
answered him, sullenly I dare say, that I had kept one secret of
his, at any rate.

"Oh, you mean about our meeting at Wingham, and so on.
You never told anybody about that, then?"

"No; nor who it was that frightened little Sophy Tindall in
the park a day or two afterwards," I said, as boldly as I could.

I saw that this reference took Mr. Smithers unexpectedly; for
he seemed annoyed, though he said, mildly enough, "And if I
did speak a few pretty flattering words to the child, what harm
was there in that, Hurly?"

"No harm in speaking; but—but you frightened her, you
know," I said.

"Very well, I frightened her, then, if you like; and there's an end of it. But you have not answered my question, whether you can and will keep another secret."

"I don't want any more secrets," I answered, passionately; "and I shan't prom——"

"Stop!" said Mr. Smithers. "Don't be rash. I suppose you don't want any harm to come to the old man at Silver Square?"

I looked at the speaker, and saw in his face the same set expression of merciless threatening which I had before noticed that day. No wonder, then, that my boyish courage quailed, and that I replied, in a trembling voice, that he—Mr. Smithers, Mr. Le Grand, or William Bix, or whatever other name he might go by—knew, or ought to know, that I loved my grandfather too well to wish him harm.

"Yes, of course," said he, drawing his hand over his face, and so, as it seemed, removing or rather replacing the mask. "Very well, then; you will consult that old man's safety by keeping silent and quiet about me. Breathe but a syllable of your previous knowledge of me, and look for news of mischief in London."

This attempt to alarm my fears succeeded, and he perceived the advantage he had gained.

"I see a promise in your eyes," he said, smiling. "And now let us talk quietly over matters. I suppose it rather struck you as singular to see me walking into the school-room this morning, as the new teacher, Hurly?"

"Yes, it did. I did not know that you ever had been a teacher in a school."

"I never have been before now," said he, calmly.

"Mr. Thompson said you had. He said you had been seven years in a school near London, and that he had received good testimonials about you from the master."

"Upon my word, I am much obliged to Mr. Thompson,"

rejoined Mr. Smithers, laughing; but it was a harsh, grating laugh, without music or gladness in it. "I did not know that our friend had been so communicative; and it makes it necessary for you to be rather deeper in with my secret than I intended."

"Were those testimonials false ones?" I said, fearfully.

"Exactly so; they were. I wrote them myself, Hurly; and they were not altogether false, either. There's nobody in the world knows my good qualities as well as I know them myself; and I am quite sure I shall make a good teacher—as long as it suits my purpose; and, seeing that no one else would take the trouble to say so, I was obliged, you see, to lay aside my modesty, for once, for the good of society. As to the little embellishments of my seven years' experience, and the school near London, and so on, they were necessary to me, and harmless, Hurly; harmless."

I have written down the words, but it would be impossible to describe the look of boastful cunning, combined with assumed innocence, by which they were accompanied. I do not think that my unprincipled relative really imagined that he could deceive me by his flimsy and impudent arguments, but he certainly looked, or pretended to look, as though he thought I ought to be satisfied with them. This roused my indignation.

"You are a bad man, sir," I exclaimed, "and you are trying to make me as bad as yourself; but you won't. Your deception isn't harmless, and you know it is not."

Mr. Smithers turned rather pale, and his eyes gleamed fiercely—by the way, I may mention that he had removed his unneeded spectacles during this conversation—his eyes gleamed upon me fiercely then, but he maintained his composure.

"The deception is harmless," he said. "Whom does it injure?"

"Some better man than you, who might have been in this situation if you were not here," I answered.

"Pho, pho!" he replied, scornfully; "we none of us know what might have been. But say that I am a bad man (and I have never set up for goodness)——"

"Yes, you are setting up for it now," I said, hastily.

"Don't interrupt me, Hurly: that's rude and ill-mannered. And, now I think of it, do they call you by that silly name—Hurly—here?"

"Yes, sometimes they do—some of the boys.

"Well, after this private conference, I shall not: you will be George Burley to me, nothing else. There's to be no familiarity between us, mind. But keep your own counsel about me, and you shall have no cause to complain. So we understand one another."

The crafty fellow! He was binding me over, body and soul, to serve him.

"But say that I have been a bad man, Hurly," he continued; " is there not the greater reason why I should change my course? I was a drunkard once, and I left off that badness by turning water-drinker; and why should I not leave off other badnesses, my boy?"

"I wish you would, unc—Mr. Smithers, I mean," said I.

"Well, am I not leaving them off?" he resumed. "Is not my endeavouring to get an honest living by the drudgery of teaching a parcel of stupid boys, a proof that I wish to reform and amend? Come, now, what do you make of that?"

I made nothing of it, and answered nothing.

"What was I to do, Hurly? Nobody would give me a character, as I said before; therefore, why should I not give myself one?"

"You had better have kept to selling spectacles or physic," I said.

Mr. Smithers laughed again, as before.

"Come, come," he rejoined: "we shall get no further by

sparring, I see. To arrive at the point, here I am, and here I mean to stop as long as it suits my purpose. Leave me alone, and I will leave you alone. But, if you turn against me, it may be unpleasantly fruitful to yourself, and to the old man in Silver Square. I did not dream of meeting you here, but we have met, and let us both be wise and make the best of it. There, now I think my lecture on the irregular verbs is finished," he said, putting on his blinkered spectacles and rising. "You had better go and join your schoolfellows, and leave me here," he added. And I did as he bade me.

What was I to do? Here was another secret thrust upon me without my seeking or consent. And this secret committed me to conniving at a gross and criminal deception. It was my duty, no doubt, to go at once to Mr. Thompson, and make a clean breast of it by exposing the impostor. But I dared not do this. The knowledge of my uncle's baseness, the remembrance of his threatening looks, the recollection of the scene which had once transpired in my presence in London, and the absolute necessity there seemed to be for keeping my grandfather in ignorance of his unhappy son—all these considerations deterred me from the course I ought, otherwise, to have taken. "Unpleasantly fruitful," he could make it, he had said, to myself and my grandfather. Yes, no doubt he could, and would if offence should be given. I quite believed that.

Moreover, I felt some compassion for the wretched man. Was it not true that, if he would reform and really wished to amend his life, there was no one to lend him a helping hand out of the slough of wickedness and low vice, and (probably) many crimes into which he was deeply plunged—no one, at any rate, but his father? And he, poor old man, had not much power to help, save such as he derived from Mr. Falconer; and Mr. Falconer, with all his excellent qualities, had no faith in William Bix, never again would have faith in him, and was, moreover, a hearty and persistent hater where he had once taken a rooted dislike. No, my uncle had no one to appeal to for help who would believe in his repentance, supposing it to be sincere.

He was like the dog of the proverb, who, having an ill name, may as well be hanged at once. I pitied him for this, and asked myself who I was, to stand in the way of his intended reformation and return to virtuous respectability.

It was a boy's sophistry, this, no doubt; for I might justly have known that there can be no return to virtue through crooked and devious ways of sin. If William Bix had been out of love with his sinful self, he would not have committed a forgery for the benefit of that sinful self. Some such thought as this struck me, I suppose; for after a few seconds of compunctious feeling, I instinctively knew that my uncle was no penitent.

What was I to do, then?

I made a sort of compromise with my sense of duty. For the reasons given, I was afraid immediately to betray the trust Mr. Smithers, or William Bix, had been compelled to repose in me, and I determined not to do so. But I would wait a little while. Perhaps some unexpected occurrence might prevent the necessity for my speaking out. The discovery of the imposture practised on him might be made by Mr. Thompson without my help, or the impostor might himself soon get tired of the drudgery to which he was self-condemned. From my heart I hoped he would.

It was a mystery to me, indeed, why my uncle had forsaken the roving vagabondish life, in the enjoyment of which I had last seen him, and in which I fancy he levied sufficient contributions from the public to keep him in tolerable condition, to chain himself down to an usher's desk. Calling to mind that, though he was evidently surprised to find me, he was aware that Marmaduke was at Mr. Thompson's school, I came to the conclusion that he had some plot to carry out with regard to young Tozer, or perhaps his mother. This was too deep a subject for me to dwell upon, however, and it was soon dismissed from my mind. But I could not so soon dismiss the sense of humiliation and self-reproach which hung about me, that I was conniving, though against my will, at a gross and criminal fraud. Talk about Marmaduke's not being honest and true, indeed ! Where were my honesty and truth ?

Time passed on, and no discovery was made. Mr. Smithers gave satisfaction to his employer. He was assiduous, quiet, unobtrusive. He proved, also, to be quite equal to his work, and, strange to say, became (notwithstanding he was a strict disciplinarian) rather a favourite with the boys. It may be assumed that I watched him narrowly ; but I did not see that he attempted to open communications with Marmaduke. This puzzled me.

I have just said that no discovery was made. This is wrong : I made one. The reader will bear in mind that Mr. Smithers was writing-master, as well as classical teacher. One day, in the course of his instruction, he spoke of the advantage of facility and versatility in penmanship. Every good penman, he said, ought to write several different hands ; such as a business hand, a gentleman's hand—

"And a lady's hand, too, perhaps, Mr. Smithers ?" said one of the listeners.

"Yes—well, yes ; a lady's hand : no objection to that ; though a gentleman would rarely, perhaps, have to put it to use. But it is well to know how to do everything ; so, for instance——" He took a sheet of paper, and, with great facility, wrote a few lines, as exactly like the current handwriting taught in ladies' schools in those days as it was entirely unlike his ordinary round-hand style.

"There," he said—handing the paper to the boy who had

spoken—" you would not think that to be a man's writing, would you? What do you think of it, George Burley?" he asked, as the paper was passed on to me.

I looked up in his face, thinking of the forged letter Mr. Falconer had received in the name of Julia Tozer. I am sure that Mr. Smithers read what was unconsciously expressed in my face. He stroked his own softly.

" Yes, I wrote it, George," he said, with a half-smile, softly. The other hearers supposed that he referred to the paper in my hand. I knew better what he meant.

A strange, incomprehensible man, this Mr. Smithers!

CHAPTER XXV.

EXPLANATIONS.

THE morning after making the discovery mentioned in my last chapter was one of our sea-bathing mornings, and I was joined by Mr. Smithers (for so it will still be convenient to call William Bix) as we were marching to St. Judith's Bay.

" You are a sharp lad, George Burley," said he, when, under some pretext or other, he had drawn me a little apart from the rest of the boys, so as to be out of earshot.

" Am I, sir?"

" Yes; why you know you are, and I don't like you the worse for it. *I* was reckoned sharp and clever when I was your age."

I knew this; I had heard it from other lips than his; but it gave me no gratification to be told that I bore any resemblance to him. Sharp and clever! Well, I had no objection to being sharp and clever, but better be dull and stupid all my life than turn sharpness and cleverness to such base purposes as he had turned them.

Some such thoughts came into my mind, and rested there with a heavy weight long afterwards; and it was not till I reflected that cleverness and vice are not necessarily associated in any person's character, that I got rid of the uncomfortable feeling.

"I think we may as well understand one another better than we have done," continued Mr. Smithers. "Confess, now; you do not know what to make of me, do you?"

If I had replied exactly as I thought, I might have said that I made a great rascal of him. But this would not have been polite, nor very wise either; so I said that I supposed I did not altogether know what to make of him.

"You have behaved very well to me," he said. "You have kept my secret admirably. No one can possibly guess from your manner towards me that we have ever met before, still less that we are such near and dear relations" (this was spoken half-sneeringly); "and I am persuaded that you intend to keep close concerning me, not only here, but in Silver Square. Now this is what I like, and I have a mind to take you further into my confidence. What do you say?"

"If you please, sir, I had rather you didn't," said I, in desperation.

"But how can you help yourself?" he demanded, with a grim smile. "If I choose to place confidence in you, I may, I suppose. And there is no harm in it either, is there?"

I told Mr. Smithers that I was much obliged to him for his good opinion of me, and that I did not know of there being any harm in it; but that what I meant was, if it was all the same to him, I did not wish to have any more secrets to keep for anybody.

He laughed, not loudly—for that would have attracted notice, which he wished to avoid—but sardonically. "You have told me as much as this before," said he, "and I give you credit for immense prudence. But yet you know as well as I do that you are burning with curiosity about me. Come, now, don't you want to know why I wrote that forged letter to your white-bearded friend, Jack Falconer?"

"I dare say you did it out of mischief, or spite, or something of that sort," I replied.

"You are wrong, then," said he, with another disagreeable laugh. "I have found out that it is very bad policy to be mischievous and spiteful, at any rate without an adequate motive. By the way, you know that I drink nothing stronger than water now?"

Yes, I knew it; I said so, and might have added that one of the boys had made a doggrel song about him for this strange peculiarity, for so it was then considered.

"Now listen, George Burley. When you first saw me, years ago, in old Filby's shop, you know what I was?"

"Yes, you were——" I stopped short of saying something uncomplimentary.

"You need not hesitate," said my uncle. "You may say what you please: you won't offend me. I was a beast, was I not?"

"You were too fond of strong drink, sir," said I.

"Just so. And at that time, when I was putting an enemy into my mouth to steal away my brains, I should have been foolish enough to do anything for mischief and spite, even for the fun of it. But I saw my error, and am reformed, you see.'

"Yes, sir; and a very good thing, I think," said I.

"A very good thing; yes, I am inclined to think so; at any rate, it has answered my purpose hitherto. Perhaps you would like to know how, and when, and why I altered my habits?"

As there could be no dangerous secret in this information, but as, on the contrary, this conversation seemed to be leading us away from such matters, I said I should like to know.

"Good," said he; "so you shall. You remember that day

when I called at Silver Square, and, instead of finding the old man at home, as I expected, fell in with Mr. Falconer, whom I did not at all expect nor wish to meet?"

"Yes, I remember."

"You remember, too, that I then for the first time made your acquaintance, with the knowledge that you were not only my nephew, but had been adopted by your grandfather to step into my shoes?"

"I don't know what you mean by stepping into your shoes, sir," said I.

"Never mind; *I* understand it; and it is rather creditable to me, *I* think, to have kept on such very good terms with you. But I am running away from my story, and I must not make it too long. I began to tell you about my reformation. You know, I dare say, that Jack Falconer gave me some money that day in Silver Square—threw it to me as he would have thrown a bone to a dog. Three guineas he gave me, and I would have thrown them back if I could have afforded the loss; but I couldn't, and so I pocketed the affront. Now you may suppose, perhaps, that the first thing I did after that was to go and get drunk. But I didn't. I had a pretty considerable battle with myself, however; but prudence conquered, and I made a vow that day that I would never wet my lips again with anything stronger than water till I had taken my revenge on Falconer. You may stare, boy; I'll give you leave to disbelieve me if you like; but it is true for all that; and what is more, I have kept my vow, and mean to keep it. If the fellow had given me only three shillings, I should have given way to my propensity. But three guineas! why I hadn't handled gold, I don't know when; and I began, all at once, to feel like a miser. Three guineas was a rich capital for me; and why shouldn't I trade upon it? Thanks to Betsy Miller and you, I had had a good meal of bread-and-cheese, and was not hungry; and before hunger had time to come round again I had spent thirty shillings on sufficient drugs to set me up as a travelling quack doctor. My medical education helped me out there, you see. And, now I have told you the how, and the when, and the why of my reforming my drinking habits, let us go back to what we first started with—my writing that letter."

Mr. Smithers stopped here to take breath, and left me for a moment or two, while he stepped forward to call order in his troop of pupils, who were becoming boisterous. Having accomplished this, he returned to my side, and resumed the conversation, we being now about half-way between the school and our bathing-place.

"Now, then, for that letter in which I personated our dear friend Mrs. Tozer. You said that I probably wrote it out of spite or mischief: what would you think if I were to say that you were the cause of it ?"

"I, sir !"

"Yes, you. I can make it clear to you in a few words. But, first of all, I must tell you that I happened to see the advertisement (Mr. Falconer's I mean) in a newspaper while I was hawking my medicines in the neighbourhood of London. I understood it all at a glance. It was evident to me, who was pretty well up in the history of Master Falconer and his precious friend Frank Tozer, that Jack was getting soft-hearted towards his cousins, and was beating about for a reconciliation, and after that, of course, was to come an alteration in his will. Now it did not, and does not, signify a straw to me what becomes of Mr. Falconer's money when he dies, for he will take good care that I get none of it if he can help it. But it might signify to you, George; and, from two or three things I heard, I fancied it might signify to you whether or not Jack found his friends. Do you follow me now ?"

"I don't understand you, sir," said I.

" You are not quite so sharp as I thought you to be, then ; but I'll try to make myself clearer. It was currently reported round Silver Square that your white-bearded friend was so fond of you that you were likely to be his heir when he died. Did he never give you a hint of this intention ?"

" No, he never did ; and I didn't want him to," I replied. " And, another thing, I am not to be his heir whether I want to be or not."

" Well, well, don't be too warm. If you talk so loud, you will be overheard, and that isn't worth while. To go on with what I was saying, I believe you stood a good chance of a fortune, unless some one else should be found to supersede you. But I saw in that advertisement some danger of your having a rival; for I happened, as you are aware, to have a previous knowledge of Mrs. Tozer, and I felt pretty sure that, if Falconer found her out, and became acquainted with her circumstances, and should take a fancy to Marmaduke, as was not unlikely, your chance would be gone. Now do you see why I wrote that letter ?"

" No, sir," I said.

" I'll tell you, then. I knew Jack to be fastidious, and I fancied that I could give him the alarm, and even drive him away from England, if I were to personate Mrs. Tozer, and, while giving a true account of herself and of her husband's death, should write in such a style as would make him believe that she was seeking to entrap him into marriage."

" It was very mischievous and wicked in you to do such a thing," I interposed.

" Granted, my little mentor ; but I did it for your sake, you see. For why should Jack Falconer's money go out of our family, I thought to myself, even though I should not have any share of it ?"

" But your letter did not do what you wanted."

"No; it seemed that I reckoned without my host. At any rate, my plans miscarried for that time. Either I did not write plainly enough, or Falconer was more obtuse than I supposed: whichever way it was, the bait attracted instead of repelled, and all I could do was to be upon the spot, as you know, and watch for results. But the game is not over yet; and you may find out, by-and-by, that I have been a better friend to you than you suppose. And now we may as well end our talk for this time. I need not remind you that all I have said has been in confidence." Saying this, Mr. Smithers walked away, and left me in a maze of wonderment, with another secret thrust upon me to burden my mind.

I have said before, and I repeat it now, that, if a writer were expected to explain and lay bare, or even to understand, the hidden springs and motives of all the strange actions of those of whom his story treats, he might well lay down his pen in despair. Let the reader think for a moment of the many unaccountable and contradictory and paradoxical characters to be met with in everyday life, and he will understand what I mean. Especially let him remember what is said in the Bible about the human unrenewed heart, that it is "deceitful above all things, and desperately wicked," and he will admit the difficulty to which I have referred. Nevertheless, a partial key may be suggested for the apparent frankness of my unprincipled relative, in the fact that he felt assured of my being pretty well provided for by Mr. Falconer, even though I should not eventually be his principal legatee, and that it answered my uncle's purpose to impress me with a sense of obligation towards himself, and so, like the unjust steward in the Divine parable, "make to himself friends of the mammon of unrighteousness." Moreover, whether he would or not, I knew too much about him to render it safe for him, should I choose to reveal what I knew; and, by putting on a show of frankness and friendliness, and further confidence, he hoped to secure my continued silence.   All this is clear to me now, though I did not think of it then.   I had wit enough, however, to perceive that he had some selfish end to answer by his pretended openness; and it struck me, as it has since done still more forcibly, that in the reformation of which he had made a boast he was much like the man in another of our Saviour's parables whose heart was the home of one unclean spirit, which, being expelled, made way for seven other spirits more wicked than himself.

But after all, my dangerous uncle, with all his professed frankness, had cleared up but a very little of the mystery which surrounded him.   Even if it were true that he had forged the letter for my benefit (having an eye to his own ultimate advantage), this was no explanation of his previous knowledge of Mrs. Tozer, nor of his reasons for following Marmaduke to St. Judith's School, where he did not expect to find me; above all, it did not give me any insight into his past history in relation to a matter which dwelt very much on my mind.

CHAPTER XXVI.

A NARROW ESCAPE.

WAS puzzling myself with various conjectures, and very sincerely wishing that Mr. Smithers had kept his confidential communications to himself, when we reached the beach, and then a circumstance occurred which effectually, for that time, put them out of my thoughts.

I have said that there were nearly or quite a hundred boys in the school. Of course they were of various ages and different temperaments—some dull and stupid, others sharp and clever, as

Mr. Smithers had pronounced me to be ; some good-natured and generous, others ill-tempered and avaricious; some timid and meek, others bold and boisterous. This is nothing to my present purpose, however, except that it leads me to say that some of the characteristics I have mentioned seemed to be lost to their owners in the act of putting off their clothes for the purpose of bathing. Some of the dullest and stupidest of the boys were the most famous swimmers in the whole school, while the sharp and clever ones, with all their efforts, could never learn to strike a single stroke in the water effectually. So with the timid and meek on land—they were, some of them, the boldest and most adventurous in the sea ; while the bold and daring spirits were effectually cowed by the sight of salt water, and were in the habit of standing shivering on the beach long before they could summon courage to wet even the soles of their feet.

One of the best swimmers in the school was my particular friend and chosen companion, Edwin Millman, who, with his clothes on, was one of the quietest and gentlest boys I ever knew. As for myself, I was a very fair hand at splashing about on the margin of the water, but I had an invincible dislike to the process of plunging beneath the surface, as was expected of us, and also rigidly enforced on recusants ; and, as to hazarding my life in venturing to swim out of my depth, I should have considered it a tempting of Providence, and I would none of it.

There were general instructions given, indeed, to our monitors and teachers, on no account to allow the bathers to go beyond a buoy which duly marked the line where shallow water ended. But this regulation, like many old laws in all codes of juris- prudence, had become almost a dead letter. At any rate, the few good and bold swimmers in the school—unmindful of the warning conveyed in the tragic history of Smith, Brown, Jones, and Robinson, as set forth by Mr. Daniel Fenning, and so dear to

M

schoolboys of fifty years ago—scorned the buoy, and were never so happy as when disporting themselves in the deep water beyond.

On the particular morning of which I am treating, and while I was cautiously advancing, step by step, into the bay, and three or four score of boys were lining the beach in various stages of picturesque disarray, a loud and piercing cry was heard from the surface of the deeper sea, followed instantly by loud shouts of alarm from the few bathers who were already in the water, and who, at the same time, were seen strenuously scrambling towards the beach in sore dismay. Another cry, which sounded like "Help, help me!" uttered in a despairing tone, roused me from a sort of stupified trance. By this time the water was deserted, and very hurried questions were put by the startled multitude who were yet dry-foot: "Who is it?" "What is it?" "What is the matter?" and so forth.

I heard the answers, too; at least, I heard parts of them, and they were enough.

"It is Millman—Edwin Millman—cramp. Oh, he'll be drowned!—told him not to go beyond the buoy. Oh-o-o!"

All this was but the affair of a few seconds, and, on casting my eyes seaward, I saw, some distance beyond the buoy, my poor friend, sinking deeper and deeper, until, in spite of his impotent struggles, his head was almost entirely submerged, and then one arm was thrown up, frantically beating the water. Then I turned my head and looked to the shore. One glance was enough to show me that there was little hope of Edwin being rescued. A crowd of eager, blanched, and frightened faces were, indeed, gazing towards their cramp-seized schoolfellow, and two or three of the teachers (Mr. Smithers among them) were hastily throwing off their garments; but I knew that only one of these could swim, and I suspected that he was a coward.

"I can never get out so far as that," I heard him say; "and if I could," he added, in a tremulous voice, "I should get pulled under water; for I never have saved anybody from drowning, and I don't know how. We had better send to the fishermen's huts, Mr. Smithers, and get them to push off in a boat."

There was little hope, therefore, for my poor friend, from that or any quarter, and, when I turned my agonized glance towards the spot where I had last seen him, he had disappeared, and only a slight ruffle disturbed the smooth water that had closed over him.

I did not hesitate any longer. Edwin himself, poor boy, had given me a few lessons in swimming, and I knew how to keep myself for a little while on the surface; so I struck out as well as I could, my very desperation giving me momentary strength and courage, I think.

"Come back, Burley!" and "Don't be a stupid, George!" and "Hurly, Hurly, mind what you are about!" sounded faintly in my ears as I tried to keep my head above water, and continued to struggle on. It was marvellous to me at that time, and it is almost as marvellous now, that from the moment of my first striking out I felt no fear whatever; it is equally marvellous that I positively made progress. How long it took me to reach the buoy I have not the slightest idea; but I did reach it, and it occurred to me then, for the first time, that I might have saved myself the trouble of swimming to that spot, where the water would have been about up to my shoulders when standing. I did not stop, however, to consider how much strength I had wasted, but still pushed on, excited by seeing my hapless companion, at only a few yards' distance, rising to the surface, and still faintly and ineffectually struggling. By this time I was aware that the temporary panic on shore had subsided, and that a score at least of stout swimmers had splashed into the water, and were hasten-ing to the rescue.

Of what followed I have only an imperfect remembrance. I think I recollect, as one painfully recalls a last night's dream, reaching young Millman as he was in the act of sinking for the second time, and grasping him by the arms ; then of our sinking together, and of my struggling to get free from his convulsive clasp ; then of a horrid sound in my ears like the rushing of many waters, combined with the booming of a funeral bell ; then of a painful choking when my little breath was gone, or rather, as I suppose, when my lungs refused any longer to remain inactive ; and then all thought and sense left me.

When I came to myself, I found that I was stretched on the beach, undergoing a considerable amount of friction at the hands of three or four eager schoolfellows, who, taking their instructions from Mr. Smithers, as I was afterwards told, were doing all that lay in their power to restore me to life, *secundum artem.*

But this dim consciousness did not last long. I sank into a sort of dream, in which, though my mind was active, I lost all know-ledge of my own identity, and had strange visions of beautiful green fields and brilliant sunshine ; and, before I once more regained my waking senses, I was being conveyed schoolwards, partly clothed, by two stout fishermen, who had volunteered this service. Then I was laid in bed, covered with warm blankets, and supplied with powerful restoratives, till I sank into a deep healthy sleep, to awake, some hours afterwards, somewhat weak and languid, but otherwise none the worse for my immersion.

My first thought on waking was to ask, of a nurse whom I found by my bedside, what had become of Edwin Millman ; also how I was got out of the water. But she was stupid, and the only reply I could obtain from her was that the other young

A NARROW ESCAPE FROM DROWNING.

gentleman was "doing us well as could be expected, considering."

"He wasn't drowned, then?" I said, eagerly.

"No, he wasn't drowned, which is a great mercy; for he was a terrible while a-coming to," she replied, adding that I should hear all about it by-and-by, but that I had better not talk now. I obeyed her injunctions; and, "by-and-by," I heard, from one of the boys who was permitted to see me, that Edwin had had a very narrow escape; that if it had not been for Mr. Smithers, who persevered, for an hour or more after I was restored, in using the ordinary means in such cases provided, before any apparent success attended them, the poor boy would have been dead. Eventually, however, his suspended animation returned, and he was brought home as I had been; but he was still so weak that two doctors were in attendance on him.

"Will he get better?" I asked.

"Oh, no fear, Hurly. He'll be all right before long; so the doctors say."

This was better than I had feared; and, for the first time, I was thankful that my uncle, with his *alias*, had made his appearance at St. Judith's; for undoubtedly his knowledge and skill had contributed to the saving of my poor friend's life.

"You don't ask how you were got out of the water," said my schoolfellow.

"No; how was it?"

It was thus: five minutes or more after Edwin and I had sunk in each other's grasp, and when half-a-dozen hardy swimmers were diving for us ineffectually, the tide carried us in towards shore, and we were seen and picked up by Mr. Smithers and another of the teachers who had ventured out no farther than the buoy. And I may just remark that the only one of the teachers who could swim, and had proclaimed his cowardice at the first alarm, directly afterwards took to his heels, leaving half his garments behind, and claimed credit for being the first to convey tidings of the disaster to the school. I may also add that Mr. Thompson was so insensible to this good service as to call him a poltroon, and to dismiss him the same day from his situation.

CHAPTER XXVII.

VISITORS AT ST. JUDITH'S—MR. SMITHERS HAS A SUDDEN ATTACK
OF TIC-DOULOUREUX.

TWO days after the rescue from drowning, I was sufficiently well to take my place in class again; but young Millman was yet under the hands of doctors and nurses. His constitution had received a shock, and some care would be required to avert further bad consequences. I had been permitted (at his urgent request) to see him; and, poor fellow! he seemed very glad to see me. He was pale, and trembled exceedingly when he threw his arms round my neck, and called himself a variety of ill-names for having nearly caused my death, while he thanked me for having saved his life.

"It was Mr. Smithers who did that," said I; "for if he had not gone on working away at you as he did, you wouldn't have been brought to—so everybody says."

"Ah, but Mr. Smithers didn't venture his life to save me, as you did, Hurly," said the grateful boy.

"All I did was to pull you under when I got up to you," said I; "but it doesn't matter how it was, does it? Here we are, both of us safe and sound, and that's the principal thing."

"Is it, Hurly?"

"Why, yes; isn't it?"

"No, I don't think it is, quite," said Edwin, thoughtfully. "There's something worse than dying, you know; and something better than living."

"Oh, ah, yes; I know what you mean," I rejoined; "you are thinking of that hymn you copied down the other day."

"Yes," said he; and then, with a slight effort of memory, he repeated the following lines :—

> "' The world can never give
>   The bliss for which we sigh;
> *'Tis not the whole of life to live,*
>   *Nor all of death to die.*
>
> "' Beyond this vale of tears
>   There is a life above,
> Unmeasured by the flight of years,
>   And all that life is love.
>
> "' There is a death whose pang
>   Outlasts the fleeting breath;
> Oh, what eternal horrors hang
>   Around *the second death!*'

"Think of that, Hurly," added my schoolfellow, in a solemn tone; and tears came to his eyes. And all I had to say, in reply, was,—

"Never mind about that now, Edwin. You'll soon get well and strong again."

"But, Hurly, suppose we had both been drowned?"

"There's no occasion to suppose anything of the sort, is there?" I asked. "We weren't drowned, you know."

"It would have been very shocking," said he, musingly.

"For you, who have a father and sister, and all sorts of relations, it would have been," I said; "but there's nobody much to care for me." My conscience smote me directly I had said this;

for I thought of my dear grandfather and Betsy Miller; but the bolt was shot.

"I did not mean that," said the boy. "I was thinking that, if we were not fit to die, it would have been very shocking for us."

Not fit to die! I did not quite enter into this view of the case. To be sure, I had never thought much of death, with its dread solemnities and after-consequences; but when, on any particular occasion, the subject had come into my mind, I was pretty well satisfied that matters had been so arranged for me soon after my first entrance into the world, that when I could live no longer I was in a fair way for what was to follow. I do not plead that my ignorance and unconcern were excusable; but I may say that it had never entered into any of the instructions I had received, at Silver Square or elsewhere, to strive to enter in at the strait gate and the narrow pathway of eternal life. And though, as I have before said, I had been in the habit of reading the Bible, it was more as a school lesson-book than to have its vital truths brought home to my heart.

My conversation with Edwin Millman ended here for this time; but the substance of it was recalled to my mind a day or two afterwards, when I was summoned into the visitors' room of the school-house.

On entering, I found myself in the presence of a gentleman whom I had never before seen. He was alone, and was seated in an easy attitude near the window, with a book in his hand which he seemed to be reading. Considerably past middle-age, he looked even older than his years warranted, by reason of the hue of his hair, which was blanched almost to snowy whiteness, while in other respects he was evidently in the firm vigour of life. My readers must pardon my dwelling on this description, as I am speaking now of my first introduction to one who afterwards proved himself to be a kind and valuable friend. Moreover, I had time to notice all that I have mentioned, and also that he was clothed in a full suit of black, before he was aware that he was being observed.

I suppose I entered the room with the due deliberation and noiselessness which had been impressed upon me as a point of good breeding, for I had been some little time standing near the door before the gentleman looked up. Then he laid down his book, and motioned me nearer.

"I did not know you were in the room, young gentleman," he said. "You are George Burley, I suppose?"

"That is my name," I said.

"And mine is Millman," returned the stranger, taking me kindly by the hand.

"Edwin's father, sir?"

"Yes, Edwin's father. I have just been with him, and he has confirmed what I before heard from Mr. Thompson, that you bravely ventured your own life to save his. I shall not attempt to tell you how much I thank you. Some day, if you should ever be a father, you will understand it better." Tears stood in Mr. Millman's eyes as he said this.

What I said in reply is no great matter. I think it was to the effect that I was very glad I had tried to be of service to Edwin; that we had always been such good friends; and that if I did not save his life—which I earnestly disclaimed—it was some pleasure to me to think that I had made the attempt.

The gentleman smiled, and invited me to sit down by him. "You speak with the generous enthusiasm of youth," he said, when I was seated; "and I am very pleased that my son has such good taste in the choice of his friends. I wonder," added Mr. Millman, after a short silence, "whether you or he have ever thought much of another friend?"

As he seemed to expect a reply, I said that we were both friendly enough with all the boys at our desk; but that I did not care so much for any of them as I did for Edwin.

"You do not quite understand me, I see," said Edwin's father. "I mean, have you, either of you, sought the friendship of the Lord Jesus Christ? I am not a preacher," he added, with a pleasant smile, "and, if I were, I hope I should take care not to tire any one with long sermons; but, do you know, the first thought that struck me, when I received the letter which told me of my son's and your narrow escape, was this: 'How would it have fared with the poor boys if they had not been rescued?' And the first thing I did was to pray that this deliverance from an early death might be but the type of your more blessed rescue from the wild waves of human passions and follies by Him who is revealed to us as 'mighty to save.'"

This, as far as I now recollect, was the sum and substance of Mr. Millman's short and serious sermon; and I should not refer to it now only for this reason, that it was the first time in my remembrance that religion had been placed before me as a personal matter, with which I had something to do, and much to do, apart from the machinery of general forms, and rites, and ceremonies. And though at the time I thought little of the few words thus spoken, and lived long afterwards in foolish neglect of the matter thus commended to my notice, neither words nor matter passed entirely away from my mind.

Mr. Millman remained some days at St. Judith's; and, on Edwin's regaining sufficient strength, he and I were frequently in his company, as he took short excursions in the neighbourhood. I fancied, at first, that I should find him an *awfully* good man; but I was mistaken: there was nothing awful, or dull, or repulsive about his goodness. On the contrary, he was as attractive as my old friend Mr. Falconer, but in a somewhat different way; and when, on taking leave of St. Judith's and of his son, he told me that, if I did not find out Edwin when I returned to London, Edwin should find me, I was glad to feel assured that Mr. Millman's house would be open to me.

Mr. Millman was not Mr. Thompson's only visitor that half-year. A few weeks after the accident in bathing, and when it had almost ceased to be talked about, I, one day, when busy at my desk, felt a heavy hand laid on my shoulder, and, looking round, whom should I see but Mr. Falconer, with his venerable beard, and genial smile, and bright, pleasant eyes looking down upon me?

That I sprang from my seat, and clasped the hand outstretched to me, does not need many words to tell.

"So, Hurly, you thought I was never coming to see you again, I suppose? And where is Marmaduke?"

Marmaduke was soon found, and we were released from school for that day by Mr. Thompson, who had introduced the visitor. And not only we two, for, with his usual good-nature, and a just appreciation of what is very acceptable to schoolboys in general, Mr. Falconer, before he retired with us, begged a half-holiday for all the boys.

"Mr. Smithers, will you have the kindness ——" the principal began, and turned to the writing-master's desk, to find it vacant.

I knew that it was vacant, for almost my first thought, after the surprise of seeing Mr. Falconer was over, was, "Here will be a pretty exposure when he finds out that William Bix is a teacher in this school," and I turned my head just in time to see my uncle hastily leaving the school-room with a handkerchief up to his face.

He—that is to say, Mr. Smithers—did not make his appearance again that day. It was soon understood that he had retired to his room, pleading a sudden and violent attack of tic-douloureux as an excuse for his absence; and it was not until the next day (when Mr. Falconer was gone) that the pain ceased. Tic-douloureux, indeed! Of course I knew what occasioned Mr. Smithers's absence, and so, once more, I became a silent party to a deception.

I was not sorry that no exposure had taken place; for, to say nothing of the share of blame which might have fallen upon me, I really had no ill-will towards my unhappy relative. No doubt it was discreditable to him to have been obliged to have recourse to an *alias*, and utterly unwarrantable in him to have obtained a good situation by false representations and forgery; besides, he was certainly thoroughly unprincipled and rotten at the core. All this I knew; but yet I, in some sort, pitied him, and should have been sorry to have seen him brought to fresh disgrace while apparently striving to regain a respectable position in the world by self-denial and industry. Moreover, had he not saved Edwin Millman's life by his skill? I repeat, therefore, that I was glad of his escape, though under cover of another cheating pretence.

To return to Mr. Falconer's short visit. He had landed at Dover—so he told Marmaduke and me—only a day or two before, and was on his way to London to see my grandfather on business, but could not deny himself the gratification of stepping out of his road to see how we were getting on. What further we said and did on that half-holiday; how our foreign-looking patron won the hearts of all the boys in the school by his genial disposition; how, on leaving, he lavishly "tipped" us, his two *protégés*; how, a few days afterwards, came, direct from London, a large case for the boys of St. Judith's School, containing three such sets of cricketing tools as had never before been seen there, as a present from Mr. Falconer—all this may be passed over lightly as too trivial for this present history. I cannot pass over so lightly, however, the remembrance that, even to my boyish apprehension, our kind and generous friend was evidently much broken in health and spirits, and that he himself appeared to be aware that old age and infirmities were creeping on him apace.

"I may never see you again, Hurly, nor you me," he said to me, in an unusually sombre tone, when he said "Good-bye," and added a fervent "God bless you." The vaticination was fulfilled. We never saw each other again. I have often thought since then how wisely and mercifully future events are hidden from us! We are sometimes inclined to murmur or repine that "here we see through a glass, darkly," and to think that, if we could but foresee what is to happen to us or to others in the course of Providence, we should be so much better prepared to meet what may be called the accidents of human life, or to avert their consequences. This is a great mistake. The only effects of such a terrible gift of foreknowledge would be to destroy our energies, and to make unhappiness universal and perpetual. It is better, infinitely better, to be placed in such a position, with regard to God our Maker and Christ our Saviour, as to be enabled to say, with humble confidence, firm reliance, and undying love, "My times, O my God and Father, are in thy hands: thou shalt guide me with thy counsel, and afterwards receive me to glory."

I have no more to set down respecting my schoolboy days; but I must add that, the day after Mr. Falconer's visit, the pseudo Mr. Smithers, who had for some time previously seemed to avoid me, took me aside and questioned me as to whether I had betrayed him. Finding by my answers that I had not, he once and again called me a good fellow, for which I did not thank him.

I may also say that, in proportion as Mr. Smithers had shunned me, he had attached himself to Marmaduke. This no doubt was natural enough, for Marmaduke had great expectations.

CHAPTER XXVIII.

I PAY ANOTHER VISIT TO MRS. TOZER, AND HAVE ANOTHER SECRET COMMITTED TO MY KEEPING.

WAS about three years at St. Judith's School. At the expiration of that term both Marmaduke and I, and also Edwin Millman, left it "for good," to use a common, though not always a strictly correct expression. Before returning to London and Silver Square, I was invited by Mrs. Tozer, and strongly pressed by Marmaduke, to spend a week or two at their home. My grandfather consenting, I accepted the invitation, and arrived there at the close of a pleasant summer's day, not anticipating, however, much gratification from the visit.

I found Mrs. Tozer much changed. The poor lady's unhappy temper had brought on a kind of perpetual nervous irritability, rather trying to two lads of sixteen, full of animal spirits, and disposed to give scope to them. She was deficient in health also —was thin, and weakly, and faded; and her complaints of her sufferings, whether imaginary or real, were almost incessant, if not loud.

The altered character of the relationship between herself and her son must also have been a source of great grief and mortification to Mrs. Tozer. I have recorded Marmaduke's own account of the decided means he adopted for delivering himself from the severity of his mother, and now I witnessed their success. She never spoke to him—she seemed as though she dared not speak to him—save in tones of almost abject submission and entreaty; and he, instead of shrinking from her in fear and trembling, exercised over her an unfeeling and cruel tyranny. I will not say that there was no love lost between them, for I firmly believe that the mother loved Marmaduke with increasing strength as her influence over him diminished; but it was a love more akin to pain than pleasure. I will give an instance of the alteration I witnessed.

"What are you going to do this morning, Marmaduke?" asked Mrs. Tozer, submissively, the day after our arrival, as we sat at breakfast.

"Don't know, mother:" said Marmaduke, carelessly.

"Would you mind staying indoors, as you have no particular engagement? I want to have a little talk with you, my dear. It seems so long since you were at home last."

"I *should* mind it a precious lot," he replied, laughing. "And, now I think of it," he added, "I have an engagement; haven't I, Hurly; and you too?"

I did not know of any particular engagement, save that he had told me on the previous evening that we must go and see old Dame Storks and Sophy Tindall. So, when he said, "I have an engagement, and you too," I replied, *sotto voce*—

"You can put that off, can you not?"

"Can I, though? No, I can't; and so, mother, you must put up with my absence, if you please. I will bestow myself upon you the first wet day instead."

The poor mother sighed.

"There you are again, mother, sighing like a furnace, as Jacques has it in the play," exclaimed Marmaduke, impatiently. "It is enough to make one melancholy to hear you. Why can you not be cheerful and jolly? I never saw anything like it," added he, with the air of an injured person. "Here, directly I come home from school, and want to have a little fun and liberty, you must be trying to keep me indoors as if I were a great girl, and putting on a doleful face because I won't do it. And Hurly here,

N

too! What is he to do with himself if I were stupid enough to box myself up with you all the morning?"

"Well, well, Marmaduke," said the lady, meekly—oh, how meekly, compared with her former harsh manner of dealing with the wayward boy!—"well, I do not wish to interfere with your pleasures, my dear boy——"

"If you didn't, mother, you wouldn't have these everlasting blinds pulled down all day long," said Marmaduke, interrupting her, and at the same time rising and drawing up the blinds with a rapid and determined hand; adding, "So here goes. I can't think what pleasure you can have, mother, in making every room in the house as gloomy as a prison."

"You may have the blinds up if you like, Marmaduke," said the submissive mother: "you can do anything you please with me, you know."

"Yes, mother, I know that, and mean to. It didn't use to be so, by a precious way, though." He muttered this last sentence in my ear, in a sort of aside.

"And if you go for a walk, which way shall you go?" asked Mrs. Tozer, presently, when she had exposed herself to another burst of impatience by sighing again and complaining of the bad headache from which she was suffering as the result of a sleepless night.

"What should you say if I were to tell you we are going to the windmills, mother?" And this he asked with a voice of such deep resentment as showed to me how the remembrance of an old offence and of his last severe punishment rankled in his breast, though inflicted six years before.

Mrs. Tozer reddened, looked angry for a minute, penitent for five minutes, and humbled for the rest of the day. Meanwhile, breakfast being over, Marmaduke called me out and said——

"We may as well get our hats and start at once: I am dying to see that darling little Sophy."

"You won't go out this morning, though, really; will you, Marmaduke?" I asked.

"Not go out! Why not?"

"Because your mother asked you to stay at home."

"What does that signify?" he asked, sharply.

"A good deal, I should think; this first day of being at home, and all. Do, now, please her."

"I shall do nothing of the kind, unless she is pleased with what pleases me," said my companion. "No, no; I had enough of petticoat government when I couldn't help myself; I am not going to submit to it now when I am not obliged to do so; so here's your hat," taking it from its peg and tossing it to me: "let us be off."

There would have been no use in my saying more, for Marmaduke was determined to have his way—the more determined, I am afraid, because his having his way would thwart his mother. Neither would it have availed anything if I had refused to accompany him and stayed at home, for I should have been no substitute for him in Mrs. Tozer's eyes.

So we went away from the house and strolled along the well-remembered road to the shady green lane which led to the gamekeeper's cottage. There was little alteration there. The flower-garden was blooming just as it had bloomed six years before, and the same objects of attraction in natural history hung up in their glass cases against the kitchen wall; also, as I have no doubt, the same fowling-pieces and shooting requisites. The cottage outside and inside was as neat and clean as ever, and old Mrs. Storks, who received us with open arms and a hearty welcome, was as garrulous. Neither was she much changed. The six years which had passed over her head had dealt gently and kindly with her: her hair, to be sure—or such of it as could be seen under her mob-cap of sprigged muslin—was a little whiter than of yore, and her steps had some appearance of feebleness; but her voice was hearty, and her countenance was blooming, and her eyes were bright.

There was the old invitation to eat plum-cake and drink currant wine which had greeted me in that older time; and there was the same impetuous inquiry from Marmaduke, "Where is Sophy?"

And presently Sophy made her appearance. An alteration had taken place in her, most assuredly. The pretty child of seven years old had bloomed into a sweet lovely flower of youthful maidenhood, more shy than of yore, to me, who had grown almost or quite out of her remembrance; but affectionate and confiding to her old playmate, who had evidently improved his opportunities of acquaintance afforded by our school vacations.

We soon found ourselves—or rather I soon found myself— drawn out into the park by Marmaduke, to whom Sophy attached herself with the innocent confidence of a sister; and we strolled on together till the girl's shyness towards me was partly worn off. Presently we came to the spot where she had last appeared to me in alarm at the rudeness and roughness of the black-bearded stranger. I had my own reasons for asking her if she had since then experienced any repetition of such insulting familiarity from the same or any other man.

No, she never had, she said; though, for a long time, she was so afraid of it that she did not venture out of sight of home without the escort of her grandfather.

"And you never saw the man again, nor found out who he was?"

No, she never saw him again, she said; but she knew who he was. He was a nasty physic man, who went about the country

OLD SCENES REVISITED.

selling pills and powders.   But he had never been near the place since then; and he was wise in keeping away, for her grandfather —oh, she didn't know what her grandfather would do to him if he caught him, she said, laughing.

There was no more to be said on this score, therefore; and presently, feeling that I was somewhat in the way, or fancying that I might be, I left Marmaduke and Sophy to continue their walk, and, stretching myself on the grass, in the warm sunshine, waited their return.

I waited a full hour; and presently, after that, Marmaduke and I bade good-bye to the lassie, and took a longer walk through the park.

"Hurly, do you know what I mean to do?" said my companion, abruptly, as we were going along.

"No.   What?"

"I mean to have Sophy for my wife."

"Oh—umph!"

"What does 'oh—umph' mean?" asked he, suspiciously. "You don't want her, do you?"

"No," said I, laughing; "and you had better mind what you are about.   It was all very well when you were children together to be playing at love-making——"

"We never did play at it," said he, sharply.

"Oh, I beg your pardon.   I thought perhaps you did."

"You thought wrong, then, Hurly.   It was not play at all: it was always right-down earnest; and I am more earnest about it than ever."

"Isn't it a little too soon to be thinking of such things?"   I suggested.

"Too soon!"

"I mean, are you not too young yet? and Sophy, why, she is only a little girl."

"What nonsense you are talking!" Marmaduke exclaimed, impatiently. "What's the use of putting off 'such things,' as you say, till one gets too old to care about them?"

"Oh, very well; but do you think that Sophy Tindall is just the sort of girl your mother would like you to—to——"

"To fall in love with, you mean. I tell you what, Hurly: my mother pleased herself when she married my father; and I intend to please myself too whenever I marry."

Of course this was all very ridiculous in both of us, to be seriously discussing such a subject at all. But boys sometimes say and do ridiculous things. I shall not further hold up this folly to light, however; but the end of our conversation was that I had another secret thrust upon me.

CHAPTER XXIX.

AT THE GAMEKEEPER'S COTTAGE, WHERE I HEAR THE HISTORY OF
SOPHY'S MOTHER.

AFTER what I have stated in the last chapter, it will be no matter of surprise to my readers that, during the whole of my visit, Marmaduke and I were almost daily at the gamekeeper's cottage. I believe that Mrs. Tozer was aware of this, and inwardly fretted a good deal at the perversity of her son, but that, knowing how useless her opposition would be, she held her peace.

For my own part, I was thoughtless about consequences, and felt so much sympathy with Marmaduke's folly as to yield willingly enough to his guidance in the matter. Besides which, the peculiar artlessness and attractiveness of Old Storks's granddaughter won upon me. I saw that she was pleased whenever Marmaduke made his appearance; and why should I stand in the way of her gratification? I had another motive, which will presently appear, that warranted me, as I then thought, in cultivating her acquaintance.

Whether Dame Storks had ever had any especial design in permitting or encouraging the familiarity which existed between Marmaduke and Sophy—whether she suspected that it would, or desired that it should, lead to serious love-making, or whether she were simply elated by the honour showed to herself in these constant visits to her cottage, I am not able to say with any degree of certainty. I fancy, however, that she did sometimes think how nice and fortunate it would be if, by-and-by, her little Sophy should become the wife of Marmaduke Tozer.

And really there was nothing so very absurd in the thought. The difference in position between the son of a half-ruined man, of no especial rank or profession, and the adopted child of a head gamekeeper on a large estate, was not so great as to place an insuperable obstacle in the way of eventual marriage. There are worse-sorted matches than this made every day. Added to this, little Sophy was not deficient in manners and education. I have already said that, when a child, the ladies of the "great house" took notice of her; and, during the six years which had elapsed between the childhood of seven and the maidenhood of thirteen, these same ladies had bestowed upon Sophy so much pains as to raise her, educationally, far above the ordinary level of village girls. There was nothing preposterous then in the idea that Sophy might, at some future time, make a very suitable wife for Marmaduke. The folly of it was, that they set about thinking of it and planning for it so early. I am aware, however, that I am treading on difficult and dangerous ground here, and I had better get once more on to the *terra firma* of my story.

One evening, when Marmaduke and Sophy were sauntering

together in the park, without any fixed purpose but the delight of being in each other's company, and I, being somewhat tired of the dumb show, had returned to the gamekeeper's cottage to wait, as patiently as I might, my friend's pleasure to accompany me homeward, Dame Storks (who was seated in her easy-chair knitting a stocking) let fall a few words which aroused my interest, and subsequently arose a conversation which led to the following disclosures :—

"You do not think that Sophy's father is dead then, Mrs. Storks?" I said, promptly taking up her words.

"Nobody knows whether the man is dead or alive, Master George; leastwise *I* don't. And another thing, I don't want to know. All I want is never to set eyes on him again."

"Was he so bad a man, Mrs. Storks?"

"He was a base wretch, Master George; that's what he was," said the old lady, rapidly and nervously working away with her knitting-needles. "He was a *villain* to marry my poor girl and then to go away from her after he had married her, and leave her to die broken-hearted."

"Why did he do that?" I asked.

"Why do people do wicked things, my dear?" returned Dame Storks; "because they *are* wicked, I reckon; and the Bible tells us that a bad tree will bring forth bad fruit. We don't expect to get grapes from thistles, do we? But as to that man Tindall, he neither feared God nor regarded man. Poor Sophy! poor dear Sophy!" she ejaculated, laying down her work for a moment to wipe her eyes.

"Was Sophy, our little Sophy, named after her mother?" I asked presently.

"Yes, sir; and if you don't mind hearing a sorrowful story, I'll tell you all about it."

"It will give you pain, I am afraid," I said. Nevertheless my curiosity was easily roused on this subject, and I was not sorry when the dame replied—

"It gives me pain, anyhow, when I think of my poor girl; but talking about her sometimes relieves me."

Had I been older and wiser than I then was, I might have anticipated this answer, for I have since observed that to persons of a certain mental calibre there is a sort of mournful pleasure in being able to pour into the ears of a willing listener the tale of their own personal and private griefs. Visit yon poor widow, for instance, in her affliction, and talk to her on any subject but her heavy bereavement, and she will turn a listless ear to your well-meant attempts to divert her thoughts from their natural channel. But encourage her to speak of her departed husband and her interest is excited, the floodgates of her feelings are opened, her voice—in broken sobs it may be—has found a subject on which it gives expression to the thoughts of her heart; and when you depart, you leave her comforted, and invoking blessing on you for your ready sympathy. Or mark that downcast man who "hath had losses." Your cheerful chat oppresses him. You attempt to raise his spirits by relating some passing news, and he sets you down in his soul as unfeeling; tell him of his mercies, and he thinks—"Ah, the heart knoweth its own bitterness." But draw him out to tell you the history of his disappointments, and vexations, and difficulties—of the treachery of professed friends, the enmity of open foes, and the lukewarmness of his nearest of kin, and he esteems you a real right-hearted counsellor. He will then be more ready to listen to other topics. But to return to Dame Storks's story.

Her daughter Sophy was the village belle, so celebrated for her charms, indeed, in the little world around, that, by common consent, she was known as "the fair maid of N——" when comparatively only a child.

"I do not wonder at that," I said, interrupting the story at the commencement; "for if *our* little Sophy resembles her mother, she had a claim to the title."

"It may be so," continued the dame, with a degree of gratified pride, I dare say; "but my poor girl's beauty, whatever it might be, did not spoil her temper. It may be that she was a little vain of her prettiness; it was scarcely to be expected that she shouldn't be, considering how often she heard it praised; and if she had never heard a word, her looking-glass would have told her of it. But she was never anyways flighty; and a better daughter than Sophy was couldn't have been anywhere."

The poor mother wiped her moistened eyes as she said this, and paused a moment or two before she went on with her history, which it will be convenient perhaps for me to give for the most part in my own words, as a brief narration.

Up to fifteen or sixteen years of age Sophy Storks lived at home with her parents, receiving such an education as could be acquired at a village school, and perhaps a little more, because her father's connexion with the "great house" probably brought with it some indirect advantages to herself, as it afterwards did in a greater degree to her daughter. Be this as it might, the fair maiden had improved herself by that which lay within her reach, and aspired, as is usual and natural in such cases, to a position above that of household drudgery, or ordinary domestic servitude, which, had she been plain in person and obtuse in mind, would probably have been her lowlier but happier lot.

Her aspirations were not very ambitious, however, since they were satisfied by a short apprenticeship to a respectable and fashionable milliner in the good old cathedral town not many miles away. Having passed through this term creditably, and wishing for further improvement, she was advised to take a situation offered her in London.

I shall pass over Dame Storks's account of her parting with her daughter, which, though touching in its way, has no particular bearing upon her story. It is enough, therefore, to say that the young woman arrived safely in London, and that for some time her letters gave a satisfactory account of herself and her position. To be sure, those letters were not very frequent, for in the times of which I am writing, correspondence was not carried on with the frequency of these present penny postage days. It was not considered alarming, therefore, when, after the first few months had passed away, the daughter's letters became, "like angels' visits, few and far between."

But at length, when a year had almost elapsed, came a letter which brought with it sore dismay and trouble. The writer begged forgiveness of her parents for the grief she was sure she should cause them when she stated that she had changed her condition, and was married. They would be glad to hear, however, that her husband, whose name was William Tindall, besides being very fond of her and kind to her (they had been married three weeks when the letter was written), was quite a gentleman in his manners, and had expectations of being, some day, a rich man. The letter stated further that the writer remained in her situation, as her husband was unemployed, and her earnings were desirable for their present maintenance, but that he had promised to look out at once for some situation, and as he had such a good education there was no doubt of his success. Lastly, the parents were informed that their daughter and her husband were living in lodgings, somewhere near the Edgware Road, and that, as soon as she could, Sophy would visit them, and, if they would consent, would, on that occasion, be accompanied by her husband, whom, she was sure, they would like very much indeed, when they came to know him.

"Here was a pretty piece of business!" exclaimed Dame

Storks, when she came to this part of her story. "It was plain to us, as soon as we had read the letter, that our poor thoughtless girl had thrown herself away on a good-for-nothing fellow who wouldn't work for his living, but was mean enough to take her earnings to support him in his idleness."

"Very like what numbers besides would do, if they had the chance, I am afraid," thought I to myself; I did not say so, however, but asked the old lady what she and her husband did after the letter reached their hands.

"What should we do, Master George, but make up our minds to go to London ourselves, and find out the truth of the story, and see what could be done for the poor child?" Accordingly (to continue the narrative) the gamekeeper obtained leave of absence, and, two or three days afterwards, he and his wife commenced their painful pilgrimage to the great and terrible city, not forgetting to take with them part of the contents of an old leather purse, which held the results of many years' economy and self-denial.

In due time they reached London, and, without much difficulty, found their way to the locality of their son-in-law's abode, which was in one of those mean and poverty-stricken streets with which the suburbs of the metropolis abound, and very frequently in close juxtaposition with the homes of rank and wealth. The lodgings themselves were of a character with the neighbourhood—two small rooms, scantily furnished, over a greengrocer's shop kept by a grim and dirty woman surrounded by a brood of equally dirty children.

It would be easy to lengthen out Dame Storks's story by repeating in her own words every detail of the interview which followed; but I must restrain my pen. It is sufficient to say that the gloomiest forebodings of the distressed parents were confirmed. Their daughter, indeed, strove to put a bright face on the affair, and protested that she was very happy; but it was with a tear in her eye, and a faltering tongue; for the short experience of the honeymoon of her married life, not yet quite expired, had evidently convinced her that she had made a fatal mistake.

This impression of the parents was still further confirmed when the husband made his appearance, late at night, in a state of semi-intoxication, but full of boasting of his ample resources in the distance, and of the great things he was going to do for his darling little wife when he had obtained the situation his friend in the City had undertaken to procure for him. "It made me sick to hear him," said Dame Storks—"the nasty man! with his big swelling words of vanity, as the Bible says."

"What sort of looking man was he?" I asked, with some interest; my readers know why.

"Oh, he was good-looking enough, if he hadn't been so rakish-looking; a many years older than our poor girl, though."

"Um. How did your daughter first make his acquaintance?" I asked further.

"Ah, that was one of the worst things about it," replied Mrs. Storks; "our poor girl had been warned never to go to them wicked play-houses, and had promised us, before we let her go to London, that she would keep away from them. But she forgot her word, and went, and there she met with that man."

The result of their visit to the daughter convinced the game-keeper and his wife that nothing effectual could be done to qualify their daughter's unhappy lot. Unsuspicious and inexperienced as they were, it was not difficult for them to arrive at the conclusion that William Tindall was an unprincipled fellow who, driven to extremity by want of immediate resources, had thought it worth his while to marry a light-hearted and industrious girl to whose person he had taken a fancy, with the view of making her industry subservient to his idleness and extravagance. It is a stale and almost worn-out story, subject to many variations, but always tending towards the same end. And it is worth the consideration of those kind-hearted persons who desire to make woman independent of man, whether they are not attempting to invert the order of nature, and providing for heavier burdens being laid upon their *protégées* than those which they now have to bear. It is to be greatly feared, at any rate, that there are too many men in the world who, in such a state of things as is desired, would be very willing to take an unfair advantage of it. It is among savages that the woman is the working and food-providing power, while the "lords of creation" idly look on and consume the fruit of their labour.

In spite of my endeavours to curtail the story of my loquacious friend Dame Storks, I must needs break it off here, and conclude it in another chapter.

CHAPTER XXX.

I HEAR THE CONCLUSION OF DAME STORKS'S STORY, AND GAIN FURTHER INSIGHT INTO THE CHARACTER OF MARMADUKE.

ERY little could be done by the honest country couple to lighten the lot of their daughter. She was lawfully married (this they took care to ascertain), and the authority they had once possessed over her as a child had passed into the hands of her husband, now that she was a woman; and it would have been neither right nor lawful for them to have sought to detach her from the new ties and responsibilities she had embraced. All they could do for her was to convey to her, secretly, the sum of money they had abstracted from their hoardings, accompanying the gift with good advice; and then they returned home sorrowing.

The present of money was, as it turned out, the most unfortunate and unwise thing that could have been done for the young wife. Either she was under the necessity of keeping it a secret from her husband, and so commencing a course of concealment and deception; or making it known to him, it opened before him a prospect of obtaining further supplies from the same source, for his own selfish indulgences, in an easier way than by honest industry. As the event proved, William Tindall soon discovered his wife's " good luck," as he called it, and it was not long before this discovery was made the lever for fresh operations. About a month after their return from London, the Storkses received another letter from their daughter, written in much sadness, and part of it evidently under the dictation of her husband. "William tells me to say," so the letter (which was shown to me) went on, "that he has a good opportunity of making use of ten pounds to great advantage, and that he will be obliged if you will send it to him by post. He says he will give you what he calls an I O U for it, and will pay it back again as soon as he has turned it over."

Whether the gamekeeper would have acceded to this request, I cannot say; but all inclination to do so was gone when he read, at the bottom of the letter, a postscript, hurriedly and tremulously written—" Pray don't send the money, father: it will do no good to him or to me." Accordingly a refusal was given; and there came another letter from Tindall himself, insolently demanding a loan, and saying that if it were not sent it would be worse for all parties.

"Have you got that letter, Mrs. Storks?" I asked, interrupting her.

Yes, she had; she had all her daughter's letters, and the hus-

o

band's too, tied up in a bundle, and I should see them. I did see them, and they at once confirmed the secret suspicion which had so long haunted my mind. In short, I had very little doubt remaining that William Tindall and William Bix were one and indivisibly the same; for I could scarcely mistake the bold and fluent handwriting which I had been so accustomed to see daily at St. Judith's. Of course I said nothing about this to Dame Storks, who went on with her story; telling me how this letter so frightened her for her poor daughter's safety, that she prevailed on her husband to yield to the demand. The money was sent, therefore, with an intimation that no more could be furnished; but this intimation did not prevent further applications; and at length, when Storks had been thus fleeced out of nearly fifty pounds, and was determined to draw no further on his almost exhausted hoard, came his daughter's husband in person, to try his skill of persuasion.

"You never knew such a smooth tongue as he had, when he had a mind; at least, I never did," said Dame Storks. "He had got such a beautiful chance of making money, and getting rich fast," he said, if he had only got a friend to help him; that my husband was the best friend he had ever known; and as to the money he had already advanced, it was safe—safe as a bank; and he only wanted a little more to help him to turn one more corner, and set him going straight forward. And if my husband hadn't the money at hand (it was twenty-five pounds he wanted), and would only write his name to a bit of paper he had got with him, it would be all the same; and, long before the money was wanted to be paid back, he should have hundreds of pounds, which were slipping away from him now, for want of that paltry twenty-five. And then our poor girl was to be a lady, and everything was to be so smooth and agreeable. Oh, dear! oh, dear!"

"And so the end of it was that your husband was persuaded to put his name to the bill of exchange?" said I, rather vain, I dare say, that my commercial education at St. Judith's had given me sufficient insight into such matters as to enable me to understand the old lady's story, and to give a name to the " bit of paper " she had mentioned.

"Yes," she said; " that was the name they gave it; and my husband did put his name to it after the man had been two or three days hanging about. And I never blamed Storks for it, though it was a dear signing to him; but the good-for-nothing fellow had so much to say for himself, and made himself so pleasant with us and with all our neighbours, that he made us believe, for the time, that black was white; and the long and short of it is, that my husband signed the bill, as you say."

"And had to pay the money afterwards."

"Ah! you are right there, too, Master George," said Dame Storks, with a heavy sigh. " Pay it he did, six months afterwards, and had to borrow the money to do it with too. But it was little we thought about money then. There was a worse trial than that to come."

This " worse trial " was, as the reader may suppose, the desertion of the poor young wife by her unprincipled, or rather her bad-principled husband, when he found that he had got all that he could get out of her and her friends; and her return home in utter destitution, and the mother of the infant Sophy. Her short married life had been a very sad one, made up, as it was, of ill-treatment, neglect, semi-starvation, constant reproaches and insults: and she soon died broken-hearted.

This—very imperfectly told—is the abstract of Dame Storks's story; and, as I have before said, it left me in scarcely any doubt that, if need were, I could reveal at once the whereabout of the fugitive husband; for, besides the handwriting, which I had seen and identified, and the strong impression made on my mind that every trait of the character of William Tindall exactly tallied with all that I knew of William Bix, *alias* Mr. Smithers—besides these proofs and suspicions, the time when the events I have just recorded happened dovetailed very accurately into a gap in my uncle's history of which Betsy Miller had never given me any account.   But wherefore should I proclaim the discovery I had made, or rather the confirmation of my previous suspicions? What good could have resulted from my saying, "I know where your little Sophy's father is to be found, and I know what his real name is?"   Boy as I was at that time, I had more prudence than to commit an error like that.   It would have pleased me better if I could have felt assured that no future events would ever bring such painful knowledge to the gamekeeper's cottage.   And, though I felt that this could not be calculated on, I made up my mind that no word of mine should betray the additional secret of which I was now possessed.

But one thing perplexed me, and this was, that Dame Storks, with all her bitter experience in the history of her daughter, should have been so oblivious of the possibility of a similar fate hanging over that daughter's child, our little Sophy, and should have permitted her growing intimacy with, and fondness for, Marmaduke.   But then, on the other hand, she had known Marmaduke from a child, and she might have thought that the best way of securing her safety and happiness was to permit matters to take their natural course.   And really she had no reason to anticipate that Marmaduke Tozer would or could turn out to be a second William Tindall.

From these thoughts I was recalled by the return of the boy and girl from their ramble in the park; and Marmaduke and I bent our steps towards his home.

"So you have been hearing all about Sophy's father, have you?" said he, as we walked along.

"What makes you think so?" I asked.

"Oh, nothing particular, only I saw that bundle of old letters on the table." Marmaduke said this with some vexation, I thought.

"You know all about the story, then, do you?" said I, in some surprise.

"I should think so. I heard it ever so long ago."

"Oh! you never told me anything about it."

"What would have been the good of telling you? Don't you see, Hurly, that when we are married—Sophy and I—we shouldn't want—at least, I shouldn't want—everybody to know all about who she was, and where she sprang from, and—and all the rest of it?"

"Well, but I am not everybody," I said.

"No; and, after all, it doesn't signify much; only I wasn't going to tell you. But, now you know it, what do you think about it?"

I told him what I thought about it, omitting my fancied discovery, however, and adding sagely, "But you speak very confidently about marrying Sophy."

"Well?"

"Well, you forgot how many years you will have to wait. And what are you going to do between now and then?"

"What do you mean about 'going to do,' Hurly?" he demanded, turning round on me, sharply.

"I mean what are you going to do for a living?"

"What are *you* going to do, Hurly?" he asked.

"Work," said I—"work at something or other."

"Work away, then," responded Marmaduke, laughing; "but you don't think that I am going to be such a dolt, do you?"

"What will you do, then?" I wished to know.

"Just what I am doing now. Look here, Hurly: I suppose

you know that I shall be coming in for Mr. Falconer's money when he dies?"

"Mr. Falconer isn't dead yet," I remarked.

"There, don't be jealous. I dare say you will get some of it. And if you don't, I expect I shall be able to spare some. But I suppose you are in the right of it to work. All I have got to say is, that it doesn't suit my taste."

I need not repeat any more of this conversation. I should not have put down any of it if it had not left the painful impression on my mind, that the self-willed boy had already begun to be corrupted by the anticipation of his future greatness. I did not then know, as I afterwards knew, how his self-consequence had been inflated, and his self-indulgence encouraged, by the secret influence of the man whom he knew only as Mr. Smithers, who had his own purposes to serve in every word he uttered, and in every act he performed.

I have nothing more to tell of any importance to my story, respecting my visit to Marmaduke and his mother. After the lapse of another day or two, I was on the coach-top travelling towards London. Late in the day I arrived safely at the old house in Silver Square, to the great joy of my dear grandfather and Betsy Miller.

And now that one-half of my story is told, I may stop for one moment or two, to describe, as far as I am able, the true position in which I stood at this time, in relation to God and eternity. And I do this the more earnestly and freely, because I believe I was but the type and exemplar of multitudes of my own age. By God's grace, then, I had been kept from many of the rampant evils, and gross sins, and destructive vanities of youth. As subsidiary means, I doubtless owe this to the training (gentle yet forcible) to which I had been subjected, and to the example which had *always* been set before me by those whom I best loved; partly, too,

BACK TO LONDON.

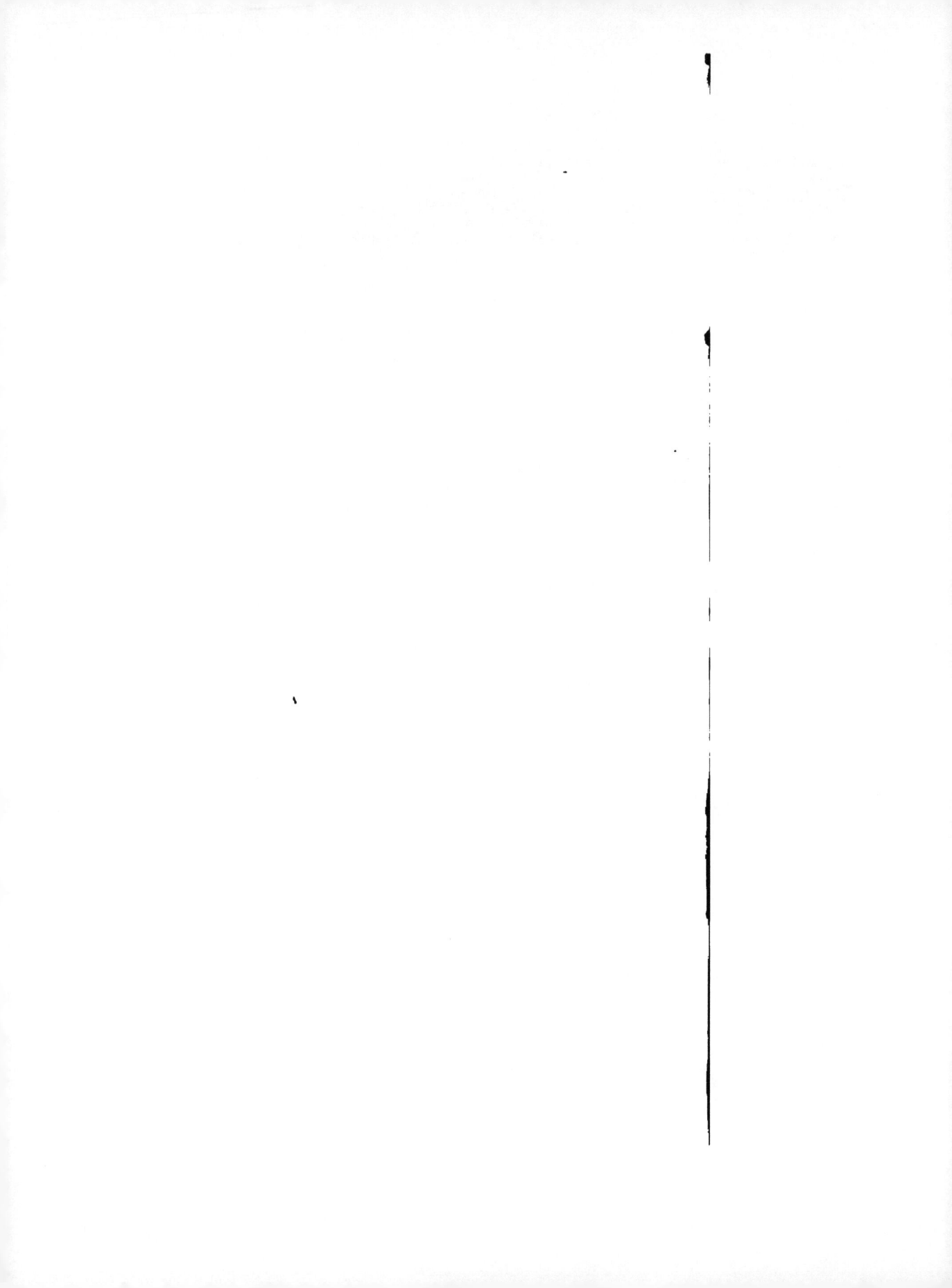

I have no doubt, to the hideous spectacle I had more than once witnessed, of the practice of vice, and its apparent effects on one unhappy votary. Nor can I leave out of this account, the beneficial results which followed my familiar acquaintance with the letter of the Holy Scriptures. Happily, I had never been taught or tempted to despise those divine and holy oracles; but I had learned to treat their sacred truths with reverence and awe. But, for all this, I was, as my readers must have seen, both theoretically and practically deficient in that best of all knowledge, without which, indeed, every one, however high his attainments, and enlarged in mental capability, is essentially ignorant. I knew nothing of the true meaning and intent and extent of the Gospel of Christ; had never been told (so far as I can remember) that I, as a sinner, needed the regulating influences of the Holy Spirit, as well as pardon for manifold transgressions. I had been brought up to think that religion consisted in outward forms, not in any hearty agreement with a loving God and Father, through faith in a blessed Saviour and co-equal Son. If I could be virtuous (and this, after a manner and feebly, I had striven to be), it was all that I supposed would ever be demanded of me: I did not know that God required of me piety and faith,—character founded on religion —usefulness flowing from love to himself. I was not aware that my best doings (whatever they might be) were imperfect; that I needed mercy to pardon sin; the Holy Spirit to implant heavenly strength; grace to renew and sanctify the heart; the atonement of Christ believed, trusted in, and pleaded in prayer, as the source of hope and ground of acceptance. Of all this I was ignorant; these grand and solemn verities had never been set before me; and the whole course of my education, combined with the deceitfulness of the human heart, had gone far in stifling the uneasiness which I recollect sometimes troubled my mind when I read the plain statements of Scripture which seemed strongly to set in against the creed in which I had been brought up.

What more can I say, except that the following description of a mere formal profession of religion is faithfully (so far as it goes) descriptive of my own condition up to the time of which I am now writing :—

> " With all pollutions stained,
>   Thy hallowed courts I trod :
> Thy name and temple I profaned,
>   And dared to call thee God.
>
> " Nigh with my lips I drew ;
>   My lips were all unclean :
> Thee, with my heart, I never knew ;
>   My heart was full of sin.
>
> " Far from the living Lord,
>   As far as hell from heaven,
> Thy purity I still abhorred,
>   Nor looked to be forgiven.
>
> " The worship God approves
>   To him I would not pay :
> My selfish ends, and creature-loves,
>   Had stolen my heart away.
>
> " My sin and nakedness
>   I studied to disguise,
> Spoke to my soul a flattering peace,
>   And put out my own eyes.
>
> " In fig-leaves I appeared,
>   Nor with my form would part ;
> But still retained a conscience seared,
>   A hard, deceitful heart."

Such, then, was my character at this time. That it ought not to have been so I sorrowfully acknowledge, for the Bible, with which I was familiar, condemned me ; and the Gospel told me that the goodness in which I trusted could never save me. But at that time a veil was upon my heart in the reading of the Scriptures. Blessed be God, it was afterwards removed; and that even at the time when I knew him not as he should be known, his restraining grace kept me back from shameful and open transgression.

CHAPTER XXXI.

"WHAT SHALL WE DO WITH HIM?" A CONSULTATION WHICH LEADS TO NOTHING.

"AND now, Hurly, my boy, we must talk a little about what is going to be done with you."

"Yes, grandfather; I am quite ready."

"You will have to work, you know—to work at something or other," said dear old Anthony Bix as he brushed away the refuse dust of a mighty pinch of Prince's Mixture, which had besprinkled his closely-plaited shirt-frill.

We were in my grandfather's office; and it was on the second morning after my return to London, the first day having been considered sacred to mutual rejoicings at our reunion, and to an extraordinarily extravagant dinner prepared by Betsy Miller, to which my venerable relative had added a glass or two of really rare and excellent wine.

"I expect I shall have to work, grandfather," said I, replying to his assertion; "and the thought of it does not afflict me very much."

"No, no: why should it? No reason at all; no reason at all. We all come into the world to work, you know. I have had to work pretty hard in my time, and do now—yes, and I am none the worse for it, Hurly."

My poor dear grandfather! He really believed what he said when he said that he worked hard; but there were those who would have envied him his leisurely occupation. It is curious enough, however, that I have rarely met with a person who has anything to do who does not flatter himself, and try to persuade others, that he works hard. More curious still, perhaps, it is the man who has nothing to do who has the hardest time of all.

"And what would you like to work at, Hurly?" asked my grandfather, continuing the conversation.

I had not thought much about this, and I said so. Perhaps my grandfather had, and would give me his advice.

The old gentleman took another pinch of snuff. Having accomplished this, with another brushing of his shirt-frill, "We had better consult Betsy Miller and Mr. Filby," he said.

I had expected this. Betsy Miller and Mr. Filby were my grandfather's privy counsellors and ministers of state, as I very well knew; and nothing of importance, apart from my grandfather's particular agency duties for Mr. Falconer, was transacted without their advice. And I may add that many a monarch has had worse advisers than they were, in their degree.

"Mr. Filby will be here presently, Hurly," continued my grandfather: "I sent a note to him yesterday. We will wait till he arrives."

I had not long to wait. There soon came a ring at the door, and directly afterwards my old acquaintance Mr. Filby, law-stationer, of Fetter Lane, was introduced by Mrs. Miller.

"Don't go away, Betsy: we shall want you," said my grandfather, as he extended his hand to the visitor. "Come in and sit down."

She came in and sat down. Mr. Filby also sat down; so did my grandfather. I was already seated; and it so happened that they formed a semicircle in front of me, Betsy in the middle.

" I sent you word that I wanted your advice, Mr. Filby," said my kind old relative—" about this poor boy, Hurly."

" What has he been doing, Anthony ? " asked the law-stationer, grimly.

" Growing up to man's estate pretty nearly, while we have been trundling down-hill, my friend," replied Anthony Bix.

" Umph ! is that all ? " demanded the other ; and he seemed rather disappointed, as I then thought, that I had not been guilty of some grand misdemeanour. He had a low opinion of boys in general—an opinion which had not been softened by advancing age.

Betsy Miller turned round and eyed the law-stationer keenly. " And what would you have had of Hurly ? " she demanded. " He has a right to be growing up, hasn't he, Mr. Filby ? "

" No doubt of it, Mrs. Miller," said the cynic ; " but I don't think my friend Anthony fetched me all the way from Fetter Lane to tell me that the boy is grown. If I were his tailor, it might be interesting to me to know it ; but I aren't, you see."

" Pho, pho !" said my grandfather. " Didn't I say I wanted your advice, Filby ? And I want yours too, Betsy. It is my misfortune, perhaps, that I haven't many friends, and I must make the best of those I have. The question is, what's to be done with the boy ? "

" Just so," rejoined the law-stationer, stroking his chin, and looking severely at me.

Betsy held her peace.

" Hurly is come to an age, you see," continued my grandfather, " when he must be looking out to be making a man of himself. He has had a good education. He isn't altogether without expectations ; but that's neither here nor there, and has nothing to do with the present time."

" How old is he ? " demanded Mr. Filby.

"Sixteen, my friend ; and a month or two over."

The law-stationer gave a dissatisfied grunt. "Ought to have been apprenticed two years ago or more. *I* was—had to put on apron and sleeves, and sleep under a counter, when I was just turned thirteen. He is too old to be good for anything now."

"Don't mind my old friend, Hurly," said my grandfather, smiling and reaching forward to pat me on the knee : "he doesn't mean it."

"Doesn't he? He does, though."

"No, no, you don't. Your bark is worse than your bite, Filby."

"Very well ; have your own way, then," retorted the growler. "But you can't deny that two good years have been thrown away."

"Not thrown away, Filby ; no, no," said my grandfather, mildly. "Hurly has been laying in a good stock of knowledge, and you know that's a useful thing."

"'Better than house or land,'" chimed in Betsy Miller ; "for 'when land and money are all spent, then learning is most excellent.' There, then, Mr. Filby."

"That depends on other things, Mrs. Miller," said the stationer, who seemed determined not to be beaten. "I think you and I have known cases to the contrary, Anthony."

My grandfather heaved a heavy sigh.

"Well, I confess I was a blockhead to be saying that, now !" said the penitent. "I deserve to be kicked, that's what I deserve, for touching that old sore. There, never mind, old friend. And don't you mind me either, Hurly. I was only joking, you know ; and I dare say we shall make something of you after all, though you are sixteen, eh? Come now, let us look at your writing—that's the main thing, or one of them. You know the three R's, don't you—reading, 'riting, and 'rithmetic, as somebody says? Ha, ha ! Get through them with credit, and you'll get through the world. As to your Latin, and Greek, and Hebrew, and mathematics, they'll do you no good, if you have got 'em. So now, let us see after your R's."

With no very good grace I rose from my seat, and proceeded in quest of my latest copy-book, which, by the way, my grandfather had not yet seen.

The effect it produced was very extraordinary, and, to me, very unaccountable, till I remembered who my writing-master had been, and that I, by copying his hand, had insensibly acquired a close resemblance to it. My poor grandfather turned pale, and his hand trembled so that he could scarcely hold the book; and when he silently handed it to Mr. Filby, that gentleman uttered a hasty exclamation. I did not know then, as I knew afterwards, how many expensive specimens of a similar penmanship had passed through his hand.

"It runs in the family," said he, in a low tone; "that's plain enough—hope other things don't run along with it." But, in spite of this expression of hope, I could see that his distrust was awakened. He tried to keep it down, however; but I believe it influenced his subsequent advice.

My grandfather was the first to recover his equanimity. "A curious similarity," I heard him whisper to Mr. Filby; "but you see Hurly writes a good hand," he said aloud. "And we will take for granted that he knows how to cast up a column of figures as well. So, now, the question is, What shall we do with him?"

It seemed at that time rather singular that, considering the interest Mr. Falconer had taken in my education, he had not settled this question also out of hand. Instead of having done this, he had not only discharged my last half-year's account with Mr. Thompson without any intimation of any further interest in my future prospects, but had also discontinued my quarterly allowance of pocket-money. Of course, I had nothing to complain of in this reticence, especially as I knew that it had also been exercised with regard to my fellow-*protégé*, Marmaduke Tozer. Still it was rather unaccountable. I did not know till some time afterwards that his silence was the result of a long and sèvere illness, which not only prostrated his body to a condition of infantine weakness, but enfeebled his mind and memory. From the effects of this illness he never entirely recovered, though he lingered on in a state of painful debility. But let me do my kind patron the justice to say that one of the first deeds of his partial convalescence was to transmit to my grandfather an order for five hundred pounds, to be laid out on my business training as might be seen desirable; but this was after my course had been chalked out for me. The same benevolence was at the same time, through another channel, extended to Marmaduke, as I afterwards learned.

From this digression I return to the consultation, which was doomed, however, to a speedy interruption as far as I was concerned in it.

"What shall we do with him?" The words were scarcely out of my grandfather's mouth when a hearty ring at the house-bell caused Betsy Miller to start from her seat, and to rush from the office to the front door, leaving the door of the office so much ajar as to give me, from the position in which I was placed, a perspective view, not only of the hall, but into Silver Square, when the hall door was opened.

The hall door was opened, and, to my relief and delight, I saw, plainly enough, my late schoolfellow and friend Edwin Millman standing on the steps, with a radiant countenance. To spring from my chair almost before he had opened his lips to Betsy Miller, and to rush across the hall before he was half through his message, were matters of course.

Edwin had come to invite me to spend the day with him at his home, which was in Gracechurch Street. He—or his father for him—had planned out a day's holiday. We were to go together to the British Museum, which would occupy some three or four hours; then we were to get to Gracechurch Street in a hackney-coach in time for a late dinner; and then I was to be sent back again to Silver Square at a comfortable time for getting to bed. All this, of course, subject to my grandfather's consent. Only, if Edwin succeeded in his mission, there was no time to be lost; and he couldn't come in, on any account, only to stay in the hall while I changed my attire, if it needed changing.

"Wait a minute, Edwin," was soon said; and, in another second, I was back again in the office.

"Grandfather, you can settle this business without me; can't you, now?" and I repeated the invitation I had received.

"Why, what a hurry you are in!" said Mr. Anthony Bix.

"Pretty cool, too," added Mr. Filby, "to walk off while we are considering your welfare."

"Oh, you can consider that as well without me as with me. I can trust to you for that, grandfather."

"And so you may," my grandfather returned, softly; "so go along if you will; but what are we to make of you, Hurly?"

"Anything you like, sir: I'll promise to agree to it," said I, and went away laughing.

CHAPTER XXXII.

THE MILLMANS AT HOME.

NOW gaily Edwin and I started off, arm-in-arm, from Silver Square, through the busy city, until we reached the quieter retreats of Bloomsbury; how we passed under the old gateway of the Museum, and roamed from room to room amidst stuffed birds, and beasts, and fishes, preserved beetles, and butter-

P

flies, and centipedes, old-world relics from Egyptian tombs, which showed that the men, women, and children of thousands of years ago were vastly like the men, women, and children of our day; how we satiated our sight with the sculptures of ancient Greece and Rome; how we wondered at the fossil remains of extinct existences; how, when the eye was, for that time, tired of seeing, we once more emerged into the busy streets, and hailed a hackney-coach (for cabs were not then), which conveyed us to our destination—need not here to be told at full. It was four o'clock when Edwin's home was reached, and I was introduced, little thinking how many happy hours I should thereafter be permitted to spend beneath that roof.

It was a commonplace house, no doubt, narrow and high; not to be compared with the old mansion of Sir Miles Silver, with which I was so familiar. There were scores of houses like it in Gracechurch Street alone; thousands like it within a mile of its site. Its ground floor was occupied by offices and counting-houses; for Mr. Millman was a merchant. On the floors above were sufficient apartments for the merchant's small family; the day not having yet arrived when almost every citizen, crowded and elbowed out from a city residence, should perforce have to seek a home in the wide and yet widening suburbs of the modern Babylon.

During our rattle over the stones in the hackney-coach, Edwin had found time to tell me that he was soon to take a seat and desk in his father's counting-house—which I expected. He spoke also of his sister Mary and his aunt Rhoda—his father's sister—in terms of boyish enthusiasm. Of course I had heard of these ladies many times before. Trust to schoolboys for exalting sisters, aunts, and mothers, or any other female relations, in the ears of their companions. At any rate, Edwin had done this; and I was prepared to find in aunt Rhoda a paragon of matronly wisdom and kindness, and in Mary Millman a perfect specimen of girlish loveliness. I am sure I wished to do so ; and it is no treason to say that I was disappointed. I dare say I was wanting in good taste and due appreciation ; or, perhaps, my admiration had been forestalled by Betsy Miller and Sophy Tindall. But, whatever the cause of my indifference, I may as well confess that, for a middle-aged lady, I thought aunt Rhoda was stiff and formal, and, for a young lady in her teens, that Edwin's sister was too quiet and retiring by half. This was my first impression on being introduced to them. A rather tall and thin chit of a girl was Mary Millman, with limp brown hair very primly parted over her white forehead, and smoothly combed down behind her ears, without a curl to set off the pallid cheeks, which were tinged with just the slightest shade of a blush when she reluctantly, as I thought, suffered me to take her by the hand, that, for one single moment only, lay in mine, and was then withdrawn without returning the slight pressure by which, with the clumsy but innocent gallantry of sixteen, I attempted to initiate our first meeting. Oh, Mary, dear ! to think what a goose I made of myself then, and what invidious comparisons I drew in my mind between you and the blooming little cousin of mine down in Kent ! And what a strange, forward, familiar boy you must have thought me to be, in spite of all your prepossessions in my favour, gathered from your brother's warm encomiums of the schoolfellow whom he would persist in saying had saved his life. Ah, well, the time was to come when our thoughts of each other underwent a curious change.

As to aunt Rhoda, I acknowledged to myself that she was a comfortable-looking lady—very good-tempered, evidently ; and with a wonderful reverence for her brother, whom I verily believe she considered to be the best fellow in London, let the second best be whoever he might. She was very fond of her niece and nephew also; but I fancied she did not take kindly to me at first. She was one of those persons, not unfrequently to be met with, whose affections and sympathies are so concentrated within a very limited circle, where they have full play and burn very brightly, that they can scarcely extend beyond it. It struck me, too, at the time, that this good lady was unnecessarily jealous of the frank and hearty love borne towards me by her nephew, as though I was robbing others of what was their own peculiar property. But, perhaps, I was mistaken in this.

You are not to suppose, however, that I was made very unhappy by the slight disappointment of my expectations. If aunt Rhoda condescended rather unnecessarily, and Mary shrank within herself, like a sensitive plant, which, indeed, she resembled, I had a hearty reception from Edwin's father, which was worth having. I had a good dinner, too, which was not to be despised; and when, by-and-by, we adjourned into the drawing-room, and ceremony began to thaw under Mr. Millman's genial influence, I gradually forgot that I was a stranger. Before the time fixed for my return to Silver Square, I had been insensibly drawn out to speak of my history, and found myself, almost without my knowing it, and quite without my intending it, giving an account of the grand consultation from which I had that morning been withdrawn, and my present uncertainty as to my future course.

On the other hand, I know I was delighted as well as instructed by the conversation of Edwin's father. It was a style of conversation quite new to me. In his earlier days he had travelled rather extensively, and his reminiscences of former adventures were full of interest. He was evidently a keen observer of men and manners, and he scattered before us the fruits of his experience without bitterness or malice, but rather as one who had been an amused spectator of the vagaries and inconsistencies of his fellow-creatures. In all this Mr. Millman manifested no conscious superiority, evinced no pretensions to wisdom or wit. He wished to please; to do this he knew that he must put his companions at ease with themselves; and he succeeded—succeeded so well that the evening passed quickly and happily, and before it was broken up we were put in such good humour with one another all round that aunt Rhoda unbent herself to tell me that I must come and see Edwin again, and I began to think that Edwin's sister was not, after all, so very plain-featured and uninteresting.

CHAPTER XXXIII.

I ESCAPE BEING SENT TO SEA, DIVULGE ONE OF MY SECRETS, AND RECEIVE STRICT INJUNCTIONS.

"AND how did you get on after I left you this morning, Betsy?"

"Get on!" said Betsy, with a strong gesture of disgust. "Hurly, that Filby is a worriting weasel—that's what he is, my dear."

"Why, Betsy! what has Mr. Filby been doing?" I asked in some surprise. In general I knew that my grandfather's two ministers of state were on good terms with each other, though they occasionally sparred in a good-humoured sort of way.

"Doing! what has that Filby been doing? I am thankful he hasn't been doing anything. But 'tis what he has been saying."

"About me, Betsy?"

"About you, Hurly; yes, nothing less. What do you think he wants to make of you, or wants your grandfather to make of you?" said Betsy Miller, fuming.

"I really have not the slightest idea. Perhaps he has been proposing to take me apprentice to himself," I surmised. "He said something about apron and sleeves, and sleeping under the counter, I remember. Was that it?"

"Worse than that, and that would be bad enough," returned Betsy; "but nothing would do for that man but you must be sent to sea. There, then! what do you think of Mr. Filby for a spiteful old parchment-seller?"

"To sea! Well, I don't think that's a bad idea, Betsy. Why should I not go to sea?"

"Don't talk nonsense, Hurly; don't," said Betsy Miller, sharply. "You might as well say why shouldn't you go and jump off the top of the monument?"

"There's some little difference, I think. But why do you suppose Mr. Filby hit upon that expedient of getting rid of me?" I asked.

"You may well say getting rid of you," replied Mrs. Miller, warmly; "and as to why he hit upon it—what signifies, only that he is a crusty old bachelor? I haven't patience with him."

Let me repeat that Betsy Miller had usually a great deal of patience with Mr. Filby. And, especially during the three years I had been at school, I had reason to believe, partly from observation, and partly from various hints and inuendoes thrown out by Betsy herself, that a pleasant mutual understanding had sprung up between them which might possibly end in matrimony. On the present occasion, however, a breach seemed to have been made in their friendship.

"Well, it doesn't matter why Mr. Filby recommended my being sent to sea," I said. "It signifies more what my grandfather thinks of the plan. I told him I would agree to anything, you know; and, to tell you the truth, Betsy, I have had a thought that I should like to be a sailor."

" And it is a good thing there are wiser heads than yours in the world, Hurly," said Mrs. Miller. " You a sailor, too ! Wait till there isn't a street-crossing to sweep, or a birch-broom to be got for love or money."

" But what did my grandfather say about it ?" I persisted in asking.

" He said that he wouldn't hear of such a thing, Hurly ; and then the old parchment-seller took himself off in a huff ; and if he never comes back again, we can do uncommonly well without him. And that's what I say."

" But not what you think, Betsy. You know better than that. And there's more sense in Mr. Filby than you think. I could tell you a secret : shall I ?"

And so, by a strong effort, I got myself at length to speak of my uncle William. I did not divulge all I knew, or fancied I had discovered ; but I told of his being a teacher, under a false name, at the school I had just left ; and of my having learnt writing of him till I supposed I had copied his style of penmanship ; that I was convinced both my grandfather and Mr. Filby had noticed this similarity, and that, consequently, Mr. Filby (who, by the way, from the nature of his business, was a connoisseur in handwriting, and professed to be able to discover hidden traits of character in down-strokes and up-strokes) augured all kinds of evil to me and of me ; the only escape from which was to put me out of the way of doing the mischief which he verily believed was ready within me to burst out in bud, blossom, and fruit. All this because my writing resembled that of my unprincipled uncle !

Betsy Miller was at first dumb-stricken by my revelations ; and when she recovered breath to speak, her words came out at first in a succession of abrupt exclamations, in manner like the pops of a bottle of ginger-beer when first opened, and in matter as follows:—"That bad, base man! That wicked wretch! To go to practise deception like that! He a writing-master! And a Latin-master! Oh, be thankful, Hurly! Dear me, if he had corrupted you! To think of his impudence, and his daring ever to show himself again among gentlemen! My poor Hurly, what an escape you have had! That bad, wicked William Bix!"

"I could tell you something more about him," I said when I could edge in a few words, and feeling half disposed to bestow my full confidence upon her relative to my meeting with him as a quack-doctor, and the discovery I had made, or believed I had made, of a certain chapter in his history. But Betsy cut me short.

"Don't tell me any more, Hurly. You can tell me nothing good; and I know too much that's bad already. I won't hear any more ; and, Hurly, whatever you do, don't breathe a syllable of what you have told me to your grandfather."

"But, Betsy, don't you think he will be glad to hear that my uncle——"

"Don't call him your uncle, Hurly. He isn't worthy of the name," Betsy interjected.

"Well, William Bix, then; don't you think that grandfather will be glad to hear that he is more respectable than he was, and wishes to keep so ?"

"Didn't he get into his situation by deception, Hurly ? You have just told me so, I think. And hasn't he some deep, wicked scheme in his bad heart ? Oh, that man ! No, don't speak about him to my poor old master, Hurly, I beg of you."

"I will not, then, if you think I had better not; and I must not say any more about him to you. But I may ask you one or two questions. Was William Bix ever married ?

"He married ? He ?" almost shrieked Betsy, with such marks

of genuine astonishment at the inquiry that I was satisfied she knew nothing of it, if it were so.

"Don't say any more, Betsy," I rejoined; "and I agree with you that his wife, if he ever had one, was to be pitied. But can you tell me if, when he was hanging loose about London, twelve or fourteen years ago, he went by any other name?"

"I can't think why you ask such questions, Hurly," said Mrs. Miller; "and, if I were you, I wouldn't be over-curious to know anything more than you can help about that bad man. The best thing I can wish for you, where he is concerned, is that you may never meet him again."

"Yes; but, Betsy, was he known by any other name?" I persisted in asking.

"Well, if you must know," said Betsy, reluctantly, "I believe that he had the grace to go by some other name. But, bless you, Hurly, talk about names, William Bix has had a many different names; but what signifies names when the thing itself is bad as bad can be?"

I thought of the quotation, "What's in a name? A rose would smell as sweet if called by any other name." I merely said, however, "So William Bix *has* gone by other names besides that of Smithers, then?"

"You may trust him for that," said Betsy. "A villain is not at a loss for a name."

"And one of those names began with a T—Tin something—Tintax, or Tinfoil, or——"

"Tindall," said Betsy, testily.

I was right, then; and Sophy Tindall *was* my cousin.

CHAPTER XXXIV.

A LECTURE—"WHAT TO DO WITH HIM?" THE PROBLEM SOLVED
—FIVE HUNDRED POUNDS! WHAT TO DO WITH THAT? ANOTHER
QUESTION.

THE question "What to do with him?" having been
abruptly adjourned in consequence of Mr. Filby's
obnoxious proposal to send me to sea, I was for some time
permitted to take my own course, and employ myself as I saw fit.
To be frank, notwithstanding my expressed willingness to work in
any way my grandfather might choose, I am afraid I was willing
to be idle. At any rate, I had no objection to putting off the time
for actual exertion in the race of life. And reason good, as I then
thought. Had I not worked hard at school? And did I not need
a little breathing-time? Was it not true—as Betsy Miller took
care to tell me, for my encouragement, I suppose—that "all wo·k
and no play makes Jack a dull boy"? Besides, I need not be
idle: there were "lots of things" I could do, even in Silver
Square; if nothing else, I could go on with my old studies, and
commence new ones; while, by way of change, I could spend
many an odd day—and did, too—in exploring the nooks and
corners of the great city, which, cockney-bred as I was, was an
unknown region to me, save and except the immediate surround-
ings of my home, and a few of the principal streets branching out
of the City proper.

I think, also, that my grandfather was very well content with
my remaining in this state of semi-indolence and freedom. It kept
me near him, and it saved him trouble sometimes, because I could
transact for him many little affairs which otherwise would have

devolved upon himself. Of course, Mr. Filby looked rather sourly upon me, as one devoted to destruction; but this was as much due to my unfortunate handwriting as to my easily-acquired desultory habits.   And I cared very little for what Mr. Filby thought— that crusty old bachelor, as Betsy called him.

I say now—writing after so long a lapse of time—that it was an evil thing for me to have it in my power to waste so many precious hours and days and weeks. It would have been yet worse for me if my idleness had been confirmed. Happily, however, a day of deliverance from its bondage was at hand.

As may be supposed, my visit to Edwin Millman at his home led to his coming, a few days afterwards, to see me at mine. Then, when I found I had more time at my disposal than I had calculated on, I made my way again and again to Gracechurch Street, without formal invitation, and was kindly received. On one of these occasions, however, Mr. Millman gave me a good-natured lecture on my present want of purpose.

"You remind me, Hurly," said he—and, by the way, I may as well remark here that, somehow or other, among friends, Hurly had become fixed upon me as my proper name—"you remind me, Hurly, of the fable of the boy who had so much time upon his hands, and was so tired of his own solitariness, that he made a round, one fine morning, in search of a companion. He went to the bee, if I remember aright, and said, 'Come and play with me.' But Mistress Bee said, 'I am too busy; I have got to gather honey; so I cannot go with you.' Then he went to the dog, and said, 'Come and play with me.' But the dog said, 'I have my master's business to attend to; so I cannot go with you.' Then he went to the bird; but the bird had got her young to feed; and, in short, the child found that all the world besides himself had some duty to perform, and that he alone seemed to be living to no purpose."

"I am sorry you think so meanly of me, sir," I said, blushing scarlet.

"My dear Hurly," replied my kind friend, "I do not think meanly of you at all. I am only anxious to see you well employed. I have seen so many young men, of good natural abilities and excellent dispositions, make shipwreck of their future hopes, and sink down into mere idlers or something worse, by being placed, as they thought, above the necessity for exertion, that I fear for you."

"I do not want to be an idler," I said, with rather a mortified heart, "and I do not think myself above the necessity for exertion; but——" I could not proceed with my self-vindication, and my kind adviser took up my words.

"You do not want to be an idler; and yet you are one, you know, and have been any day and every day these last three months. You do not think yourself above the necessity for exertion, and yet you make no exertion. What are we to make of that?" he asked, with a benevolent smile.

"I would have gone to sea—I should have been glad to go— but my grandfather would not hear of it," I said, bitterly.

"There are as good fish out of the sea, perhaps, as there are in it," he replied, reversing the proverb. "You are not obliged to be unemployed on land because you cannot work on the sea, are you?"

"No, sir," I replied, in a subdued tone.

"I knew a young fellow, about your own age, some twenty years ago," continued my mentor, "who found himself in much the same position as yours. He had kind, but rather mistaken friends, who were willing enough that the lad should be free from the restraints, and what they perhaps considered to be the curse of labour. He had ·moderate expectations, which would have warranted the idea that he might pass through life comfortably enough without troubling himself with work; and so, in effect, he was told. Happily, however, the youth had good sense and activity; added to these, and what gave them their true value, he had religious principle. He saw clearly enough, therefore, that it would not do; that a few more months or a year or two of indolence would fix him for life as a cumberer of the ground; that idleness was already eating into his heart like rust. So he made a wise resolution: he would get work; if he had to work for nothing, he would do it; if he had to pay for doing it, he would still do it. The very day on which he made up his mind to this course he set out on it. How many rebuffs he met with, and how many disappointments he had to bear, I cannot say; but he persevered, and he succeeded. That is to say, he obtained what he was determined to have—an employer and work. He worked hard, and was happy. Whether he obtained wealth or not is nothing to the purpose—of very little consequence; but he was both happy and useful, instead of being, in after-life, as there was great danger of his becoming, a miserable burden to himself and others. "Now, Hurly," added my friend, "what is to prevent you from doing likewise?"

This was Mr. Millman's lecture, as far as I can remember it. My kind and fatherly friend did not wantonly wound me without a balm ready at hand. Before we parted he had offered to take me into his own offices, and on terms so favourable that it would have been madness in me had I refused, a thing which I certainly had no desire to do.

"It is the very best I can do for the preserver of my son's life," he said, when I attempted to thank him; "and, setting that altogether aside, I am pleased to secure, in this way, a companion and friend for my son. The obligation is quite on my part, believe me."

So, the next day, with my grandfather's consent, I took my seat at a desk in Gracechurch Street, and, after a month's trial, I signed articles of apprenticeship to Mr. Millman.

Friend Filby shook his head, sagely, when he was told I was going to be a clerk. "The very worst thing you could have done with the boy—better have made him a blacksmith," he was reported to me, by Betsy Miller, to have said; and I have no doubt he quite expected I should soon have to make my appearance at the Old Bailey for forgery, seeing what a hang-dog handwriting mine was. I cared little for Mr. Filby's opinion, however, and set to work as earnestly as I might.

I must say here that in becoming my employer, Mr. Millman did not in the least cease to be my friend. In fact, I was given to understand that I was not only at liberty, but was expected to spend as many evenings in the week, after office-hours, as I pleased, in his family, on the former familiar terms. I availed myself occasionally of this permission, or invitation; and so, without any further change or incidents worth recording, some two or three months passed rapidly away.

It was after I had been about that space of time in my employment that my grandfather received the letter from Mr. Falconer, with the five-hundred-pound order, of which I have already spoken.

"This is uncommonly kind, and just exactly like himself, Hurly," said Anthony Bix; "but it is rather awkward."

"Awkward, grandfather?"

"Why, yes, Hurly. It has come too late, you see, unless you could give up your engagement with Mr. Millman."

"And why should I do that, if I could do it, my dear grandfather?" I asked.

"Why, then we might article you to the law, and make an attorney of you, or a conveyancer, or a barrister, and you might come to a silk gown by-and-by, or to a judge's coif and ermine.

Dear, dear, who can tell how much might be done for five hundred pounds? Or we might send you to college, Hurly, and put you into orders, and who shall say that you would stop short of a silk apron and lawn sleeves?"

Dear old man! I am sure he believed in his own sudden and momentary visions of my future hypothetical dignity—all lost to me because I had been in such a hurry to get married (I am using his own words), to get married to a mercantile employment.

"If we hadn't been in such a hurry to get you married to a merchant's office, there is no telling what this five hundred pounds might have done for you, Hurly," said my kind old guardian, with a deep-drawn sigh.

"Pray don't make a trouble of that, grandfather," I said: "I am very well content to remain as I am. I am sure I have no vocation for the Church," I added; "and, as to the law, it isn't every lawyer's clerk that comes to be a judge, you know."

My grandfather agreed with this, and, after another regretful sigh, decided that the five hundred pounds would not be wanted—immediately, at any rate.

"I'll lock the order up in my cash-box, Hurly," said he; "for we must not run the risk of offending Mr. Falconer by saying that we can do without his money. Besides, there's no telling what may happen, and it may be very useful to you in pushing you on by-and-by."

"Hadn't you better secure the money at once, grandfather?" I said, half jokingly; "because, as you say, there's no telling what may happen."

"No, no, Hurly. That would be something like obtaining money under false pretences. Mr. Falconer expressly says in his letter, you see, that it is to be put to a certain use—your business training; *training*, you see, expressly. Now it cannot be put to that use: it isn't wanted, is it?"

"Then why not write to Mr. Falconer, and tell him so, grand-father; and ask him what you are to do with it?"

"Perhaps it will be best, Hurly; and—yes, I'll think about it, my boy. In the meantime, I'll put the order under lock and key." And he did so.

This is a simple incident to write about, but the sequel is yet to come. Moreover, I learned from it three things :—*First* (which I had suspected before), that my grandfather had no great wealth of his own in store, otherwise he would freely have bestowed it on my advancement in life in some such way as he had spoken of. I was sure of this. *Second*, that, though strictly honest and con-scientious in his transactions with his patron and the whole world besides, he had the natural desire not to let a good thing escape from his grasp, if he could anyhow retain it without doing violence to good worldly principles of integrity. And, *third*, that a habit of procrastination was growing upon him, indicative of the infirmity of purpose which generally (as I have seen) accompanies old age. For it is a fact, account for it as we may, that the nearer our years bring us towards the grave, the more indisposed are we to do, with all our remaining mental might, that which our hands find to do.

CHAPTER XXXV.

A VISIT FROM MARMADUKE TOZER—TROUBLE LOOMING IN THE DISTANT HORIZON.

ONE evening—I think it must have been two or three months after the conference I have just recorded, and it was winter-time I know—on returning from my day's work to Silver Square, I was informed by Betsy Miller that a visitor had that afternoon called to see me, and would call again at eight o'clock.

"A visitor! what name, Betsy?"

"He wouldn't leave his name. It was of no consequence, he said."

"What sort of person is he?" I asked.

"A handsome young gentleman (not so good-looking as you, though, Hurly)," said Betsy, who, in her blind partiality for me, would not admit any inferiority on my part, "with a red shawl handkerchief round his neck, and a great-coat on, for all the world as if it was made out of a blanket, and covered with great white bone buttons, bigger than a crown-piece. He looked all buttons."

I knew no young gentleman to whom this description would apply, for my circle of acquaintances was very limited; nor could any cross-questioning elicit from Betsy any further information than that I had better wait and see.

I had not long to wait. At the appointed time a sounding knock at the door announced my visitor—

Marmaduke Tozer.

"Surprised to see me, aren't you, Hurly?" was his first greeting.

I confessed to the surprise, but said that I was glad—I *was* pleased —to see him. "You are come to stay here, of course?" I added.

No; he didn't know about that. It mightn't be convenient, perhaps; in short, he was staying at a hotel, and had been in London two or three days—had been paying a visit to the Browns, at Blackheath (I remembered Quercus and Philander Brown at old Thompson's, didn't I?), and had run up to London "for a spree," but couldn't go away without looking me up. All this and more Marmaduke said in a drawling sort of way, with an assumption of ease for which I was not altogether prepared, while he stood in the hall, fidgeting with the big buttons of

Q

his drab Witney, as though he were not altogether accustomed to them.

"My dear fellow, how could you think of being at an inn when you know here's a house big enough for a dozen such as you, and a hearty welcome besides? You must not think of going away from Silver Square to-night, nor all the while you are in London. Grandfather will be quite vexed if you do."

"I don't know about that, Hurly," said he, with an absent stare. "This is a queer old place—haunted, too, isn't it? And the old gentleman (your grand-dad I mean) mightn't be best pleased to have me hanging about for a week or so."

"He shall answer for himself," I said, and, disappearing, presently returned with my grandfather, whom I found in his office.

There was no need for much persuasion, after all; for Marmaduke (as became a young man who had expectations) had grown increasingly careful of money, and told me presently, in confidence, that living at a hotel was "preciously dear." So we started to the "Belle Sauvage" to bring away his portmanteau, and in less than an hour had returned with it to Silver Square. Meanwhile Betsy Miller had prepared a room for our unexpected visitor, and a rather superior supper.

Divested of his rough coat and shawl, which made him look like a substantial grazier, Marmaduke did not seem much altered in the short space of time since we had last parted with each other, except that he was grown stouter, and that an air of languid indolence had stolen over him—such an air as I might have had if Mr. Millman had not prevented it in time. He got on very well with my grandfather, however; and presently, when we had finished supper and Marmaduke and I were left together, we glided into confidential conversation.

"You are surprised to see me in London, Hurly," said he.

There was no particular reason why I should be surprised, seeing that some thousands of country people enter London and depart from it every day. I told him, however, that I certainly had not expected to see him—which was true; and asked him if any especial business had caused the journey—which, perhaps, was impertinent.

"Business! Oh no. I thought you knew me better than that, Hurly," said he, laughing. "Bother business! It was only a whim. I promised the Browns that I would go and see them some day; and they wrote for me to come, and I have been a week at Blackheath, as I told you—and a nice place they have there, too, I can tell you; their father is a rich fellow, you know; and so, being there, I thought I might as well come on to this little village and see what it is like, and" (yawning) "here I am, heigho!"

"A pleasant change for you, at any rate," I remarked. "You must be tired, I should think, of always being at home, with nothing to do."

"Oh, you are there, are you, Hurly? I dare say you think much of yourself because you are a merchant's clerk"—I should explain that I had, some time before, written to Marmaduke, informing him of my engagements—"but you must know I am going to set to work too. So I shall be even with you." He said this good-humouredly, of course, but with a degree of affected nonchalance, as I thought, which provoked me to reply that I was glad to hear he had come to his senses, and had made the discovery that work was a desirable condition of human life.

Marmaduke laughed. "I don't say that I think so," he replied; "but circumstances alter cases, as we used to say at St. Judith's. By the way, I have something to tell you about St. Judith's presently that will surprise you; but that will keep. Circumstances alter cases, as I said; and my case is altered."

" Ah ?"

" Five hundred pounds, for instance," continued Marmaduke.

" Oh ! you had five hundred pounds from Mr. Falconer for your business training, had you, Marmaduke?" This was the first time I heard of it. " So had I. Well?"

I noticed that Marmaduke seemed rather surprised, not to say startled and annoyed, when I told him of my having shared in our common patron's bounty. He made no remark about this, however, but said—

" Well, you see, I wasn't in training for business, and the lawyer who corresponded with my mother (what's his name? Fawley, of Hatton Garden) said it was necessary I should have a business, in order that the money might be legitimately—that was the word—legitimately applied; and that it couldn't be touched without."

" Just so; I see."

" It was a great bore, of course," he went on; " but I wasn't going to lose the five hundred pounds, so I went to a farmer a few miles off, who was looking out, as I knew, for a pupil. I soon settled the matter with him, and agreed to be articled to him for four years—all a farce, you know, because I am not going to turn clodhopper, don't you think it. But it made it all right for the money. Wilkins (that's the farmer's name) will get half of it, though, for my board and lodging, and the rest goes for my personal expenses; so I have set up a horse and joined the East Kent Hunt. 'Tisn't bad, is it? And it suits me well enough, for I began to get tired of living at home, with nobody but my mother to speak to."

" And Sophy," I added.

" Oh, yes, Sophy, of course. But, you see, I am near enough now to see her as often as I like; and, if we should be married——"

"IF!" I could not help this exclamation of surprise. I knew, of course, that "there's many a slip between the cup and the lip." But I was not prepared for the cool recognition of this proverbial saying by the boy-lover who, six or eight months before, would have been ready to fly into high heroics if I had ventured to hint at any serious impediments in the course of his love, or any change in his own mind.

"Why not 'if'?" he asked, sharply. "There's no telling what may happen, is there? But I'll say *when*, then—when we are married I may take it into my head to have a farm, and it will be as well to pretend to know something about farming, eh?"

"Better really to know something about it," I thought; but I did not utter the words: I was too anxious about Sophy to hold an argument on any other score.

"And how is Sophy?" I asked; "and old Dame Storks and her gamekeeping husband—are they well?"

"Oh, all right. Sophy is a sweet little thing, isn't she, Hurly?"

I said yes, she was; and that I should be deeply grieved if any trouble were to happen to her.

Marmaduke did not reply to this, but shifted the subject of conversation.

"I was going to tell you about St. Judith's," he said; "and a queer thing that has happened there."

"True. What is it?"

"Why, you see, I rode over there a month or six weeks ago, to have a look at the old place."

"And to exhibit yourself on horseback, in your new capacity as a gentleman-farmer," thought I to myself. But I only said, "Yes, very natural."

"You remember old Smithers?" said Marmaduke.

" Yes, of course, very well. What of him ?"

" He had been found out to be a regular impostor. What do you think of that ?"

I might have said that I was not surprised at it; but I only asked, " How ? In what way ?"

It was in this way :—By some curious concatenation of events, Mr. Thompson and the principal of the boarding-school near London, whence Mr. Smithers professed to have his testimonials, fell in with each other, and it then came to light that a gross deception had been practised on the former gentleman. The result was that Mr. Smithers had been summarily and ignominiously dismissed.

This, in other words, was Marmaduke's story. I gathered from it, however, that my wretched uncle had so far kept good faith with me as not to betray my innocent complicity in his deception. And for this I was grateful to his memory. But I was sorry to find that Marmaduke thought very lightly of the grave offence committed by Mr. Smithers—looked upon it, indeed, as a good joke, and a justifiable expedient.

" I like the fellow for his cleverness," he said, " and shall tell him so if ever I fall in with him."

" Which you may do sooner than you fancy," I thought; for it occurred to me then, not for the first time, that William Bix, or Tindall, or Smithers, had found out, in his underhand way, how matters stood between Marmaduke and Sophy, and would step forward, in due time, to reap his own harvest in that fertile ground.

Our night conference ended here, and I may briefly add that Marmaduke spent a week or more at Silver Square; that is to say, he made my grandfather's house a convenient lodging-house, while following his own will in the disposal of his idle time, and in enjoying his " spree."

It came as a matter of course that I should invite Edwin Millman to meet his and my old schoolfellow; and, one day during the visit, we both obtained leave of absence, and accompanied Marmaduke to Blackheath, to see the Browns. We were cordially enough received by the parents of Quercus and Philander, and spent a pleasant day with our former companions; but we received no great encouragement to repeat our visit. I believe the reason of this was that we (that is, Edwin and I) were only City clerks, and the Browns were people of some independent property. Marmaduke had not erroneously said that they lived in a fine mansion, surrounded by pretty pleasure-grounds, and appeared to live in what was then considered excellent style. I must not omit to say that Quercus and Philander (sonorous names!) had two sisters—fine, rattling girls they seemed to be—and that much polite attention was paid to them by Marmaduke Tozer.

CHAPTER XXXVI.

AT FAIRMOUTH, IN DEVONSHIRE, WHERE I MET WITH AN OLD ACQUAINTANCE IN A NEW CHARACTER.

NOW take my readers onward to a time between two and three years after my first introduction to business life. In consequence of some slight symptoms of pulmonary disease, young Millman was recommended by the doctors to pass a few weeks in Devonshire; and, at his earnest request, I was permitted to accompany him. It was early in spring, and it was the first lengthened holiday either Edwin or myself had taken since we left school. We were in the heyday of youth; and, as my companion's indisposition was not of such a nature or degree as to interfere with his full enjoyment of the charms of nature, and, moreover, as we were sufficiently supplied with funds, and had no urgent cares of life pressing upon us, we made the best we could of our short-lived liberty—especially when, after a few days' sojourn at a small town on the coast, Edwin's threatening symptoms seemed entirely to have disappeared.

Oh, how many delicious rambles we took over the hills! How many reckless, galloping rides on our spirited Exmoor ponies through the wonderful Devonshire lanes of which so many stories tell, on which so much poetic enthusiasm has been expended! How many gentle lulling sails we had on the rippled water of the broad bay, which reminded us of St. Judith's, and brought up reminiscences of our old school-days! I sometimes think of that Devonshire holiday with strange feelings of delight, mingled with remembrances of great and grave sorrow. For with that holiday ended my romance of youth, and my first bitter experience of the vicissitudes of life. I will not anticipate, however.

We had been three or four weeks in—let me give the place a name, and call it Fairmouth. A stream, or a concatenation of streams, from the neighbouring hills, widening into a pretty little river when the valley was reached, ran into the bay. The town was tolerably full of visitors, principally from the surrounding provinces; but we had made no acquaintance with any of them— partly from diffidence, I suppose, and partly because we were each satisfied with the other's society. There was no great abundance of amusement for idlers in Fairmouth. Through the winter I believe there had been balls and concerts for those who patronised such gaieties; and for the more sober-minded portion of the community there had been lectures, public meetings of benevolent societies, and exhibitions of waxworks and wild beasts. But there had come a lull in these modest dissipations; and the Fair-

A HOLIDAY RAMBLE IN DEVONSHIRE.

mouthians were supposed to be agog and gaping for some new excitement when, one fine morning, handbills were circulated from house to house, and posting-bills stuck upon the walls, announcing that Washington Rexworthy, Esq., would favour the nobility, gentry, and inhabitants generally of Fairmouth with a series of entertainments, extending through an entire working-day week, at the assembly-room of the Star and Garter, in the High Street. The entertainments were to consist of recitations from Milton, Shakespeare, Burns, and other poets; ventriloquism; imitations of various celebrated orators and actors; and feats of legerdemain; interspersed and varied by performances on musical glasses. All these difficult and diverse accomplishments, being combined in Washington Rexworthy, were to be exercised for the amusement of his audience, and his own benefit, between the hours of seven and ten. Front seats, 2s.; back seats, 1s.; gallery, 6d.; and children half-price.

Ridiculous as this bill of intellectual fare seems to me as I now write it down from memory, it was tempting enough then to two young men whose opportunities for recreation had been comparatively few, and who, just then, had more time on their hands than they well knew what to do with. Accordingly we purchased tickets and presented ourselves at the door of the assembly-room on the first evening of the entertainment.

It did not appear as though Fairmouth had been taken much by surprise by Washington Rexworthy. Either his name did not please, or his promises were not ample enough, or the pleasure-seekers were not yet recovered from the effects of the recent plethora of amusements, or they had not much money to spend; for, whatever the cause, the room was nearly empty when we entered, and, after a quarter of an hour and more had passed away, and the hands of the dial in front of the gallery pointed at that much after seven o'clock, only about a score of people were scattered over the back seats—the front or dress seats being quite empty.

Everybody knows—that is, everybody who is accustomed to public entertainments of this nature—what a keen appreciation audiences seem to have of the value of time, and how impatient they are of delay. Being very much like the rest of the world, therefore, the small company in the Fairmouth assembly-room began to show rather strong symptoms that they considered themselves to be ill-used. First, there was a comparison of watches with the visible timepiece ; next, there were subdued murmurings, which gradually swelled into very audible grumblings ; then followed shouts of " Time, time !" accompanied by coughing and stamping of the feet. Then a parcel of schoolboys (from the Fairmouth Day and Boarding Academy), who had been admitted into the gallery at half-price, I suppose thought it good fun to produce theretofore-concealed penny whistles and cat-calls, with which they raised a perfectly hideous din. Eventually, however, the tumult was stilled by the appearance, on the platform or stage, of a well-known character in Fairmouth—a little, shabby, eccentric, and dissipated genius, who picked up a scanty livelihood by teaching music and drawing, and who, it appeared, had been engaged to accompany some of the performances on a jingling harpsichord, or, by the same means, to fill up gaps in the entertainment. Shuffling towards the instrument, which was a piece of stock furniture belonging to the assembly-room, this professional gentleman sat down, ran over the keys in ordinary music-master style, and commenced an overture, which so far pacified the audience as that it gave promise of the speedy commencement of the lagging performance.

Ten minutes were thus consumed, and then a curtain at the back of the platform was drawn aside, and the hitherto concealed Washington Rexworthy advanced.

"What a singular-looking fellow!" whispered Edwin to me, as the performer silently bowed, laid his hand theatrically on his breast, and then looked around him, as I thought, in some dismay at the paucity of his patrons.

He was a strange-looking man, certainly; of middle age, or rather past; so, at least, his face would have said, though its evidence would have been partly contradicted by the remarkably fresh, and luxuriant, and glossy curling locks of deepest jet which surmounted his brow, almost covered his forehead, and rose pyramidically to a kind of blunt ridge on the top of his head, as was some time the fashion among fops when George IV. was Prince Regent. He was rather neatly dressed, in evening costume, and the hand laid upon his heart was neatly gloved in white kid.

"Ladies and gentlemen," said the orator, looking around him again with a forlorn smile, "I have the pleasure of appearing before you this evening——"

The voice, tone, manner, were enough. Before he opened his lips I had felt strangely perplexed. He was, and he wasn't, like William Bix; but I was sure now, without the shadow of a doubt, that my mercurial and unprincipled uncle was before me—in a new character.

"Don't you know him, Edwin?" I whispered to my companion.

"Seems as if I had met him, or seen him, or heard him somewhere before; but I cannot think where," he returned, with a puzzled look.

"At St. Judith's, for instance?" I said.

"At St. Judith's! Yes, to be sure. Why, 'tis Smithers, our old writing-master!"

CHAPTER XXXVII.

AN ENTERTAINMENT, A CONVERSATION, AND A SUMMONS.

NOW Washington Rexworthy's entertainment went on and "went off" that evening, I have but a very faint remembrance. I know that in one of his recitations from Milton he personated Satan in his address to the sun, telling that luminary how he hated his beams; that presently, with Macbeth, he asked an invisible something at which he appeared to be staring, three feet from his nose, if it were a dagger, and why shouldn't he clutch it. I recollect, too, though very imperfectly, a number of glass vessels, ranging in size from that of an egg-cup to a punch-bowl, each half-filled with water, being put in due order on a long table or board, behind which he stood; and his drawing out from them some sounds resembling shrieks and groans, by means of a moistened finger rubbed upon their edges. Some remembrance I have, also, of his attempts at ventriloquism, which proved to be so much of a failure as to provoke derisive cheers and laughter from the boys in the gallery overhead, and a few vigorous hisses from an ill-mannered tailor on one of the back benches, which, however, brought down upon the malcontent the unfortunate (for him) but tempting cry of " Goose, goose!" from others of the audience, and so diverted attention and indignation from the poor ventriloquist. Finally, I believe, the evening's entertainment closed with the National Anthem, after an apparently impromptu address from the performer, in which he thanked his intelligent patrons for their patronage, and announced his intention of repeating his performances on the following evening, when he hoped to meet a more numerous assembly, composed of the wit, fashion, mind, and taste of the romantic town of Fairmouth; "united with the youthful, ardent intelligence of our friends from the metropolis," he added, glancing with such a meaning smile towards the bench on which Edwin and I were seated, that my hope that we had not been recognised was lost.

It is one of the disadvantages of secrets, even when they are right and proper, and honestly kept, that they sometimes place the custodier in a false position towards his immediate friends and familiar acquaintances. Here was I, for instance, on brotherly terms with Edwin Millman, and under deep obligations to his family; desirous, also, of exercising towards him the same entire confidence which I knew he reposed in me; and yet conscious of acting with duplicity towards him, not of my own free will, but because others, whether I would or not, had chosen to repose confidence in me.

Painfully feeling this, as we returned to our lodgings in Fairmouth, I would have avoided speaking of the evening's entertainment, and of the performer; while Edwin, ignorant of what was passing in my thoughts, seemed perversely bent on easing his mind of the natural surprise and curiosity which filled it.

"What an extraordinary thing that we should have been brought into contact in this way with poor old Smithers!" he said.

"M-m—ah, yes; it is rather singular. Look, look, Edwin; there's a beautiful shooting-star. What a train it leaves behind it!"

"A meteor! Ah, a very fine one—very commonly seen on fine nights at this time of year," he rejoined, following the direction of my hand with his eyes till the evanescent streak of pale light had vanished.

"I wonder what meteors really are?" said I.

"There are a good many kinds of meteors," replied Edwin,

repeating, without thinking at the moment that he derived his information from an old school-book of natural philosophy, or something of that sort, with which we had both been familiar enough at St. Judith's: "there are luminous and fiery meteors, for instance; and these include the Halo, the Parhelion, or mock sun, the Rainbow, the Fata Morgana, the Ignis Fatuus, the Aurora Borealis, Lightning, and the Stella Cadens, or falling star, such as that we have just witnessed."

"True; I remember all that; but what is a falling star—Stella Cadens?" I asked, glad to get away from Washington Rexworthy on any pretence.

"Ignis Fatuus, Aurora Borealis, the large Fire Balls, and the smaller ones, called falling stars, are said to be produced by certain——" said Edwin, dreamily; and then, rousing himself suddenly, he added, laughing, "But you know all this as well as I do, Hurly. I was thinking of poor Smithers. He seems a sort of Ignis Fatuus. I hope he won't turn out to be Stella Cadens. Hurly, I should like to see him."

"See him! We have seen enough of him this evening, have we not, Edwin?"

"Ah, but I mean see him in private. I wonder where he lodges? Suppose we were to call on him to-morrow?"

"Oh, that isn't worth while, is it? You know why he left St. Judith's. And he has changed his name, too; and your father said the other day he had no faith in any man who needed two names."

I should say here that Edwin had heard the story of Smithers's disgrace at St. Judith's from Marmaduke.

"But the poor fellow may be wanting a little help," said compassionating Edwin. "I thought he looked very woe-begone, though he did put a good countenance on just now; and I am sure, if he does not get a fuller room all the rest of the week than he has done this evening, it will be a losing speculation for him."

"For all that, I think it will be wiser for us to avoid him, if we can; at least, I would not search him out. I am afraid he is a worthless fellow."

"I am afraid he is; indeed, he must be, to have got into the situation at St. Judith's as he did. But, oh, Hurly," added Edwin, "if we all had our deserts, who would escape whipping? The poor fellow may be needy, if he isn't faultless; he must eat and drink, to live, you know. And, besides, he really was a good-natured fellow at school, for an usher, wasn't he?"

"You don't know so much about him as I do," I groaned.

"Why, I always thought that you and he were rather thick together at St. Judith's. What can make you so shy of him now?" Edwin asked. "Not, of course, that it would be right to keep company with him, being what we know he must be; but we might pass a word or two with him; and if he should want a little help, and could be got to say so—don't you see?"

What could I do? I could see that, in the kindness of his heart, and to avoid wounding the feelings of our old teacher, as well as in the hope of doing him some little service, Edwin was determined to find him out in his lodgings, wherever they might be; and that, if I did not accompany him, he would go alone. I knew, also, or could very easily imagine, that this renewal of acquaintance would be fraught with danger to my friend, as well as possible annoyance to myself. I made another attempt, therefore, to turn Edwin from his purpose.

"How uncommonly earnest you are, Hurly!" said he, with much surprise. "You seem as though you thought some dreadful thing would happen from my passing a few friendly words with the poor fellow. Why, it was you and he between you—you principally, Hurly, but he helped afterwards, you know—who saved my life when I was all but drowned; and it would be very ungrateful——"

R

"Your father made him a handsome present, Edwin," said I, hastily; for I knew (though not till long after the event) that Mr. Millman put a twenty-pound note into Mr. Smithers's hand, as an acknowledgment of the service he had rendered.

"And you think that I ought to cry 'Quits,' then?" said Edwin, laughing; "but that was my father's gift, not mine, you know; and I think I owe the poor fellow something—at any rate, I mean to show him that I am not too proud to acknowledge him."

"You don't know so much of him as I do, or perhaps you would think differently," I repeated.

"You have seen him before to-night, since we left school then?"

"No; but I saw him two or three times, and knew a great deal too much about him, before I went to school. I knew him first more than ten years ago; and his name is not Smithers any more than it is Rexworthy. His name is Bix; and he is my own uncle—my mother's brother." I whispered this in my friend's ear, though there was no one near us. It might have seemed as though I were afraid that the very stones of the pavement on which we were then walking would hear me.

"Hurly!"

"It is all true, Edwin; and I will tell you all when we get to our lodgings. Don't let us talk about it in the street."

We soon reached our lodgings, and I poured into Edwin's ear the tale of my uncle's boyhood and youth, as I had heard it from Betsy Miller—told how and when I first met with him, and had been enjoined to secrecy; how I next fell in with him in Wingham, in Kent, under the disguise of a quack doctor; how I was led to suspect, and afterwards had my suspicions confirmed, that he was paternally related to the little Sophy Tindall whose praises I had often sounded in Edwin's ears. Then I went on to tell of my surprise and terror when, three years afterwards, he made his appearance at St. Judith's, under another name; and how, under the compulsion of his dark threats, I had promised to keep secret my previous knowledge of him. All this, and more, I told Edwin Millman, who sat with eyes wide open and a listening countenance till I had finished.

"What a strange story!" he then ejaculated.

"Isn't it? But you don't blame me for not speaking of it, do you, Edwin?"

"No, Hurly. You couldn't help yourself, that I can see."

"I can assure you," I continued, "that I have suffered a great deal from knowing all these things, without being able to speak of them to any one."

"I don't wonder at it, Hurly; it is a great nuisance to have anybody's secrets to keep whether one likes it or not. But what puzzles me is why your uncle should have gone to St. Judith's at all."

"Don't you see," I replied, "that he had got his eye upon Marmaduke, and has still; and that he means to get a share in Mr. Falconer's fortune by-and-by; and that, when he found that I was at St. Judith's, he thought it necessary to stop my mouth as soon as he could by pretending to take me into his confidence?"

"I suppose that must be it," said my companion. "He is a clever fellow, though, for all he is a knave. I must call him that, in spite of his being your uncle. It is curious that we should meet with him here, isn't it?"

I agreed that it was.

"Does it enter your thoughts that he planned it?" Edwin asked.

"Planned?"

"Yes; planned to pounce upon you, knowing you to be here."

"I do not see how he could get that knowledge, nor what

advantage he can promise himself by following me to Fairmouth," I answered.

"Do you remember my father saying a little while ago that great rogues often take the most circuitous routes to accomplish their ends, when it would seem to others that a straight cut would be not only the shortest, but the easiest way ?"

I remembered this very well, but did not see the bearing of the remark.

" I think I do, though I do not pretend to be very wise either," said Edwin. " Wait a moment : let me see. You say that your uncle has never been to Silver Square since that first time of your having any knowledge of him ?"

" Never, I am sure."

" Can you guess why he has not ?"

"Oh yes ; very easily. He is a coward, and is afraid of Betsy Miller ; he knows, too, that he is still in Mr. Falconer's power, and he has been told that if he annoys my poor grandfather, that power will be used against him."

" All that is plain enough. But, though he does not go to Silver Square, there is nothing to prevent his going near it, is there ? And, from some source or other, he may pick up a pretty accurate knowledge of all that is going on there."

I acknowledged this, and readily thought of the shopkeeper close by, with whom Betsy Miller dealt, and with whose wife she was in the habit of occasionally interchanging friendly words.

" Just so," observed Edwin, with a magisterial gravity which amused me, though I was in no very amusable humour ; " and from that personage your uncle—I am sorry to give him that designation, but he has so many aliases, you know—your uncle may easily have obtained a knowledge of your present journey."

I remembered that my uncle had once spoken of the rumours

in and around Silver Square that I was to be Mr. Falconer's heir, and I thought Edwin's conjèctures to be probable. "But," added I, "what possible good can he think to do himself by fastening upon me? Or, if he wished to do it, why not in London, without being at the trouble of coming to Fairmouth?"

"I think I can answer those questions, too," continued Edwin. "Supposing, for instance, that he wishes to have two strings to his bow, and so retain a hold upon you? He may think that, after all, it is not absolutely certain that you may not turn out to be Mr. Falconer's principal legatee; at any rate, he may believe that you will be remembered in that gentleman's will; and you may be sure that your uncle would like to have some claim upon you, of friendship, or gratitude, or, perhaps, of terror."

"I can understand that," I said.

"And then," he went on, "there is your grandfather's property, which he may think worth looking after, in case of its not being left to him."

I shook my head. "I believe that, at one time or other, Uncle William has had pretty nearly the whole of my grandfather's savings, and that there is very little for him to leave to any one," I said.

"Your uncle may not know this," rejoined Edwin.

"But supposing all that, why should he follow me down here?"

"For a good reason why. He knows that in London you have friends—my father, for instance; that is to say, he may probably know it, and judges it more prudent on his part to catch you at a disadvantage here, where you have no one besides a young fellow like me to stand between you and harm."

I thought then that many an older friend would have shown less judgment and acute perception than Edwin, and I said something to this effect.

My friend laughed. "Don't trust to that," he said. "I know I have not half your determination, at any rate, and should be more easily taken in. The only thing is that, in this case, not being so personally interested in this Rexworthy (to give him his present name) as you are, I may naturally see into his designs a little more clearly. And this is only a perhaps."

"But this entertainment of his—it must have taken some time to get up, and—and, in short, I don't see why he should fancy it worth his trouble. He might have followed us here without such a complicated scheme."

"Yes, but suppose the scheme not to be so complicated as it seems at first sight. Think, Hurly: it is three years since your uncle, as Mr. Smithers, left St. Judith's. And since then he must have picked up a living, somehow. What more likely than that he should have returned to his vagabond habits, and taken up this new trade as more profitable than that of selling either spectacles or physic? A very little outlay would have been sufficient for his musical glasses, conjuring apparatus, and other stage properties; or they might even have been hired. Then, if you noticed, he was not particularly adroit in his performances: sufficiently so, perhaps, to amuse the frequenters of the low, sixpenny, half-theatrical places in London where such men as he manage to keep just within statute law; but it did not seem to me this evening as though he were accustomed to entertain a very select audience, and I fancy this made him feel more awkward than he need have been."

"It may be so," said I; "but I fancy, if the poor fellow has really taken up that line of life, he has not made much out of it."

"Hurly, my father said something to me once that I have never forgotten. He was talking about an unfortunate man who, though he was very clever, had never succeeded in anything. I was wondering how it was. 'Oh,' said my father, 'there's no occasion for much wonder. There are a great many clever people in the world who take extraordinary pains to starve, when they might fatten, if they would, without difficulty.' "

"Well," said I, "here my wretched uncle is; and the question is, what shall we do?"

"Let us plan for that to-morrow," said Edwin. "He won't break in upon us to-night, at any rate; and to-morrow will be a new day."

To-morrow *was* a new day, and gave me something to think about of more moment than my vagabond uncle. It brought a letter to me from Betsy Miller, entreating me to return home as soon as I could. My grandfather had received intelligence of the death of Mr. Falconer, and the shock was so great that he himself was incapable of writing to me; but she—Betsy Miller—desired earnestly to see me forthwith.

"I will go back with you, Hurly," said Edwin.

"No, don't do that: stay out your holiday," said I. "You have a fortnight's longer leave, you know."

"Oh, but I am all right now; and I want to get home. Besides, it will be no holiday for me here when you are gone."

So we hastily packed up our portmanteaus, and that day bade good-bye to Fairmouth. And whether Washington Rexworthy's entertainment succeeded during the remainder of the week we never knew. We learned, however, from our landlady, who had occasion to write to Edwin Millman, that that gentleman called at our lodgings about an hour after we left them, and seemed "put out" when he learned that we had left Fairmouth, and should not return.

CHAPTER XXXVIII.

DARKNESS.

EACHING London on the evening of the day after our leaving Fairmouth, Edwin and I took a hackney-coach, which, having set me down at my grandfather's door in Silver Square, conveyed my companion to his home in Gracechurch Street.

"I am so glad you are come, Hurly," was Betsy Miller's first salutation, when, after wiping her eyes with the corner of her apron, she seized me by the hand, and hurried me into our common sitting-room.

"Where and how is my grandfather?" I asked, seeing that he was not present.

"He is in his office, Hurly, and is much as he was when I wrote to you. But the first thing is to get you something to eat and drink. You have been travelling a terrible long way, you know."

This was true; and true also that I was hungry. I was yet more anxious, however, and said that I would go and see my grandfather while Betsy was preparing the meal.

"I wouldn't if I were you, Hurly," the faithful creature exclaimed, hastily; "and yet," she added, "why not now? The shock must come."

More alarmed by this intimation than I can very well express, I hastened across the hall, and tapped at the door of the office. Receiving no audible summons to "come in," I cautiously opened the door.

My poor grandfather was seated on the floor, nursing a doll. He was fearfully altered in appearance; but I will not attempt to

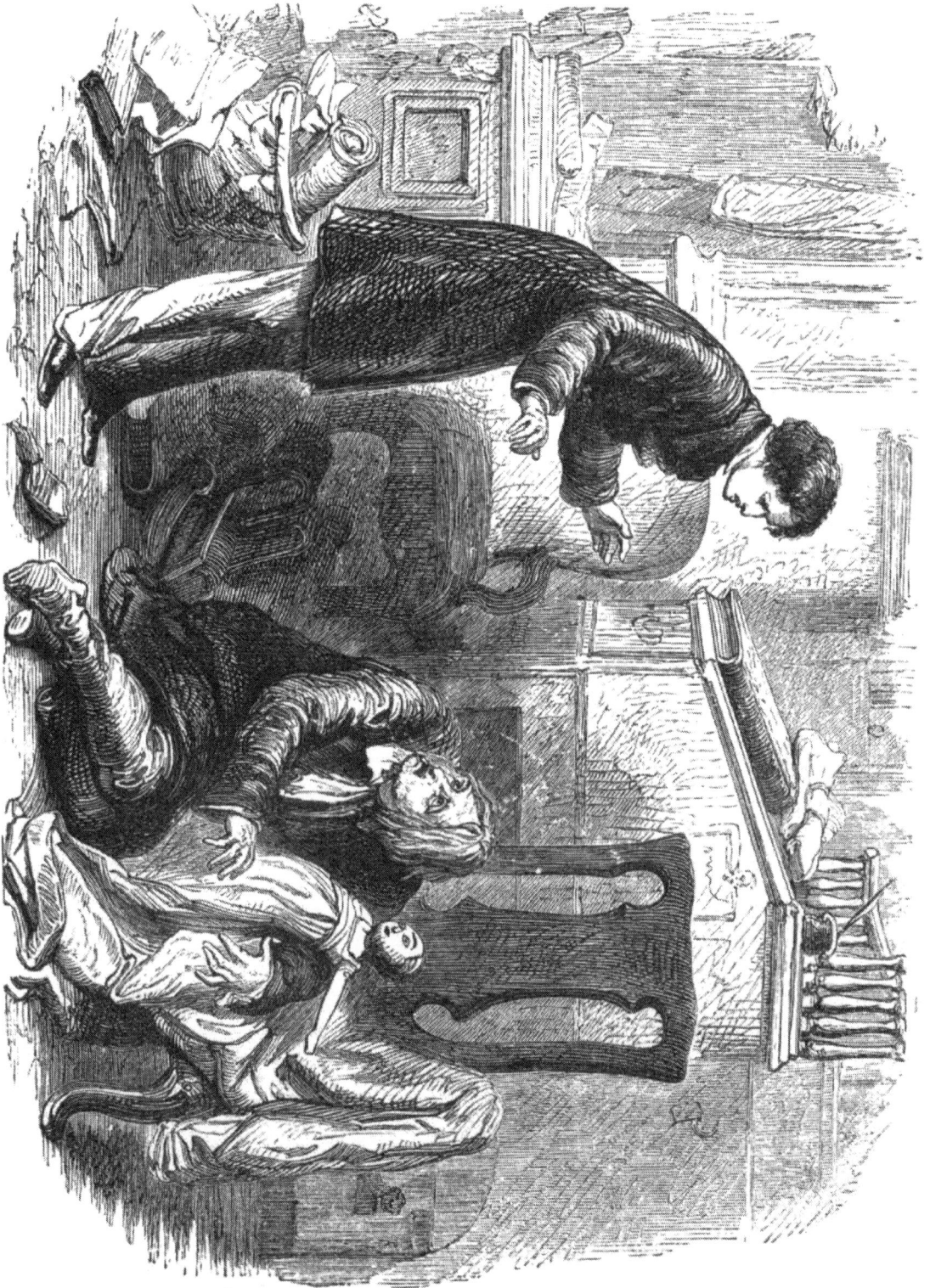

OLD MR. BIX'S HALLUCINATION.

describe the plain marks and indications of, at least, temporary insanity.

"Grandfather! dear grandfather!"

"Hush, hush!" he whispered, rocking the puppet resemblance of babyhood gently to and fro. "Hush, hush!"

"Grandfather! Do you not know me?"

He looked up into my face with a ghastly smile, then down upon the thing in his arms with maudlin admiration. "William," he said, in a low tone of fondness: "his name is William;" and, raising it to his bending face, he pressed his lips to the wooden forehead.

I could bear no more. Shrinking back, I closed the door reverently on the humiliating spectacle, and returned to Betsy Miller.

"This is terrible!" I said.

"You may well say so, Hurly. I couldn't bear to tell you of it in my letter."

"How long has my poor grandfather been in this state?" I asked.

"Ever since the letter came from abroad, and that's a week ago yesterday. He sat in a maze, like, after he had read it, for a matter of three or four hours, it may be; and when I went into the office I couldn't make any sense of him at all. His poor wits were all gone wool-gathering, Hurly."

"And then, Betsy?"

"I tried to coax him and bring him round, Hurly, and asked him what the letter was about; for I didn't know then, of course. But I could make nothing of my poor master, only he told me to go away and not worry him. So I went, hoping he would come to if I left him alone—but, Hurly, I won't tell you any more till you have put something into your mouth: it isn't of any use for you to starve yourself. If you do, I shall have two patients upon my hands instead of one; and there's no use in that."

Good Betsy! She attempted to speak gaily; but her heart was heavy, and tears stood in her eyes, though she smiled. She had busied herself in hastily spreading a cloth, and loading the table with substantial viands; and now she stood with her arms folded in an old-fashioned manner of hers which I full well knew denoted determination. It may be supposed that I had no appetite left—my hunger was gone; but I compelled myself to go through the ceremony of eating, though every morsel I swallowed seemed as though it would choke me. At length I pushed away my plate, and Betsy, seeing that I could do no more, condescended to relax.

It would be both painful and tedious to follow Betsy Miller's narrative of my grandfather's sudden affliction. It is sufficient to say that through the remainder of the day of his seizure, and far into the next, he remained in a state of stupor from which it was exceedingly difficult to rouse him for food or rest. Then, on the evening of the second day, a sudden change came over him, manifesting itself in violent and abusive language (my poor grandfather! to think that *he* should ever be violent and abusive!) and in loud lamentations that his child—his little Willy—had been taken from him. Roaming over the desolate, empty house in this state, and turning over the contents of closets, drawers, boxes, and cupboards, which had not been explored for many a year, he happened to light on a little hoard of my dear mother's and my uncle's playthings, which had been stored away when they ceased to be children——oh, so long, long ago!—and which I had been occasionally permitted to look at as something very sacred, in the days of my childhood.

With a wild cry of delight the poor maniac seized upon these hidden treasures. It seemed as though they recalled some long-forgotten incidents of the past, and reproduced in his disturbed mind images or shadows of the little ones who had played about him in their infancy. With a yet more maniacal shout, he disentombed and disentangled from the heap of worthless relics the great wooden doll which I had seen him dangling, and rushed away with it to his office.

"He doesn't part with it, night or day," continued Betsy; "only the first night I stole it when he was asleep, and dressed it decent-like, as you saw it, and put it back again in his arms without his waking. And there he sits all day long, hushabying, for fear the baby should wake; and at night he takes it to bed with him, and lays it down by his side, with his arm underneath. He thinks 'tis his William. He has no thought for anything else; your grandmother is clean gone out of his mind, and so is your mother, Hurly. As for me, he knows no more of me than if I was a complete stranger."

"He did not seem to know me," I rejoined, and asked, "Does he take any food?"

"Very little, Hurly; scarcely enough to keep life in him; and he sleeps but little, either. Times and times I slip into his room o' nights, and only that second night, when I dressed the doll, have I found him with his eyes shut. He dozes a little in the daytime, and that is about all the sleep he gets, I think."

"I am afraid you have had little sleep yourself, my good old nurse," said I, looking more attentively than I had before done at her red and swollen eyelids and her careworn face. It seemed to me then that since we parted, not much more than a month before, she had aged at least five years.

"My dear, don't think about me," she replied; "it matters very little whether I look old or young; and, as to not getting any sleep, that will cure itself some of these days. I'll take it out all in a lump. The thing to think about now is what is to be done."

"We must get advice as soon as we can."

"If you mean doctor's advice, that has been took already," said Betsy. "Our old doctor—Dr. Squills, you know—has been to see your poor dear grandfather, and comes in every day; and all he says is, 'We must wait, Betsy; we must wait. The symptoms will change by-and-by.'"

"We must get further advice."

"Not to send my good old master to the mad-house, Hurly! That's what Dr. Squills said at first; and, if I didn't give him a setting down, don't you ever believe me again."

I had no doubt that Betsy did give the gentleman "a setting down." And, not wishing the same or a similar operation to be performed on me, I hastened to appease her jealous suspicion. "I did not think of such a thing as sending my grandfather to a lunatic asylum," I said.

"Because," continued Betsy, "sooner than send the dear old gentleman to one of them malignancy places, I'd have my hand chopped off. Yes, I'd chop 'em both off myself at the wristeses. There!"

What Betsy meant by "malignancy" may be explained, I suppose, by malignant, or evilly disposed. How she could have performed the deed she threatened, she never attempted to explain. I only know that it was a favourite maledictory phrase of hers, when excited. And even this admitted of variations or degrees. In a moderate heat she would threaten her *wrists;* when warmer, she spoke of her *wristes;* it was only when in a boiling, effervescing state of passion that her eloquence rose to *wristeses.* I knew then what was to be expected by the party to whom or by whom she was opposed. I was too wise, therefore, and also too sympathetic with her, to cross her strong prejudices at this time; and I assured her again that a lunatic asylum was the last place in which I should wish to see my poor grandfather, even if I had the power of sending him to one, which of course I had not. "But I am not satisfied with Dr. Squills's skill and judgment in this case," I added ; "and we must call in a second physician to-morrow."

Betsy was very agreeable to this, and then, turning to another matter, she informed me that, on the day after the receipt of the foreign letter, Mr. Fawley, the lawyer, called at Silver Square, and was shocked to find my grandfather in such a state of mental affliction ; that it was from Mr. Fawley that she had learned the purport of the letter, and it was he who had advised her to write to me, and recall me home. She added that Mr. Fawley had repeated his visit daily, and had had consultations with Dr. Squills, saying that it was of the utmost importance that my grandfather should, if possible, be speedily restored to a state in which business could be transacted with him. " An easy thing for a lawyer to say," added Betsy ; " but twenty lawyers, and twenty to that, can't do it."

I need not repeat what further transpired that evening. It was too late to see Mr. Fawley then, and Dr. Squills's diurnal visit had been paid. There was nothing better to be done, therefore, but to wait patiently till the morrow ; only that, after once more contemplating with bitter anguish the melancholy wreck of mind, and persuading Betsy to call in additional help in her household affairs—which she had no difficulty in doing—I hurried to Gracechurch Street, and reported the sorrow into which I was plunged. This did me good, for I received abundant and sincere sympathy, with a peremptory request from Mr. Millman not to think of returning to business until matters at home were in a more satisfactory state.

CHAPTER XXXIX.

A DIGRESSION AND A RETROSPECT.

ND now I may be permitted to break off my narrative of consecutive events, to give one short chapter on matters of more importance than the common, every-day experiences of life.

I have previously spoken of myself as exceedingly ignorant of spiritual truths. It is true, as I have already stated, that in my childhood and boyhood the Bible was very frequently in my hands; but as far as my heart was concerned it was, to a great extent as to its higher teachings, a sealed book. Still, I liked reading its histories; and, as it never entered my head that the time would ever come when professed teachers of Christianity, and grave dignitaries of any section of the Christian Church, would openly declare those histories to be myths and fables—contrary to human science, and impossible when tested by the Rule of Three—I believed them.

I am glad of this now; glad that the reverence which had been instilled into me, first of all, by Betsy Miller, for the Scriptures, was never rudely shaken, in those early days of my life, by the assaults of infidelity, scepticism, rationalism, worldly wisdom, or ignorant prejudice; glad to remember that I, as a boy, received the Bible, and read it, and thought of it, as it is in truth, as the Word of God, and not as the word of man; glad that the profound awe with which I then regarded the very book itself, as being something directly appertaining to the great God who made me, so that I would rather have received a personal hurt than that the Bible in my school-desk should be rudely and irreverently treated, has never forsaken me to this hour. Yes, I am glad of this; glad that I never doubted, never scorned; glad that I can say now—

> " Should all the forms that men devise
> Assault my faith with treach'rous art,
> I'd call them vanity and lies,
> And bind the Gospel to my heart;"

glad to remember how in those early days of my youth, when, in a new romance I was reading, I lighted on these lines—

> " Within this sacred volume lies
> The mystery of mysteries.
> Happiest they of human race
> To whom God has granted grace
> To read, to fear, to hope, to pray,
> To lift the latch and force the way;
> And better had they ne'er been born
> Who read to doubt or read to scorn."

—I say I am glad to remember that, when I came to these lines in the romance, my eyes were made moist and my heart joyful by the discovery that a novelist could speak or write so truly and boldly of God's Bible. I thought it was a noble thing of the then unknown author of those marvellous stories, which in their first freshness so captivated the world, to stand up like a man and a Christian for the blessed Bible. I thought so then, and I think so now.

Well, these being my boyish feelings of reverence and respect for the Bible, I used to read it with interest. I liked its true, yet strange and wonderful histories. In my imagination, I lived before the Flood, and dwelt in Eden's bowers; witnessed, horror-stricken, the first murder; looked on while Noah and his workmen were building the ark, and then saw it floating on the waters. In the same rapt spirit of dreamy forgetfulness of the present I traversed the plains of Mamre, accompanied the old

S

patriarch Abraham, with his youthful Isaac, to the mount of sacrifice, saw the glittering knife for one moment lifted above the bare breast of the submissive victim, and heard the angel's voice calling upon the sacrificing father to forbear. With Isaac I walked abroad in the cool of the evening, and lifting my eyes, saw afar off the train of camels, with Rebekah, the betrothed bride, hasting to meet her future husband. With Jacob—whom I did not like so well as his rougher brother Esau—I laid my head on a stone for a pillow, and dreamed of angels ascending and descending, by their wonderful ladder, to and from heaven. But why do I dwell on these old remembrances now? There is no necessity, at any rate, to go on tearing them up to shreds and tatters: it is enough to say that, before I left school, I suppose there were none of the narrative portions of the Bible, including the Gospels of the New Testament and the Acts of the Apostles, with the leading events of which I was not as intimately acquainted as with the history of my own short life.

And yet—I have said it and repeat it—as far as my spiritual life was concerned, the Bible was to me a sealed book. A veil was on my heart, and I did not apprehend the truths which lay within my grasp. My readers may remember—or shall I repeat?—that, after the narrow escape I had from drowning, I was very much surprised at its being questioned whether, at that time, I were "fit to die." Fitness for death, and judgment hereafter, I had never much thought about. It may be remembered, too, that a few words spoken by Mr. Millman, in his very short sermon—as he pleasantly called it—stirred up in my mind certain doubts as to whether all was safe and right with me ; and, though these doubts did not much disturb me at that time, I trace back to the impression then made the first dawnings of a better life in my soul.

Well, I left school, as I have already recorded, and after a short time became intimate with the Millmans—with Mr. Millman, next to Edwin, especially, not only as my employer, but as my personal friend (if I may presume so to boast) and my adviser. Now this was, undoubtedly, a critical era in my life. I was not indisposed to think well of religion, and to acknowledge that it demanded personal attention; at any rate I was not prejudiced against it, and I was very far from being determined to neglect it; and I was easily impressible—more impressible for evil than for good, doubtless; but I was alive to the beauty of true goodness. I was also observant. I may say this without making any boast of being sharp and clever, because I have known many great simpletons who have possessed this quality.

This, then, was my mental or intellectual position, with regard to vital godliness and evangelical truth, when I first entered Mr. Millman's house. I was ignorant, you see—more ignorant than I ought to have been, all things considered; but I was not unwilling to be taught. As to my moral character, it was outwardly correct. No one could have charged me with any flagrant violation of the duties due to my immediate neighbours. The less I say of the state of my heart, and affections, and desires, however, the better for the purity of these pages. I did not know then—ah, I do not know now entirely and fully—how desperately criminal in the sight of God and all holy beings were the imaginations of my heart, how utterly short I came of the requirements of God's holy and perfect law.

Mr. Millman was a "professor"—that is to say, a professor of religion. I know I am laying myself open to a sneer by using a word, in this connexion, which was more common at the time of which I am writing than it is now. Then it was not unusual to call any member of a Christian church, of whatever denomination, or any regular communicant, and sometimes any constant attendant on an evangelical ministry, by the name of a professor. If the title has entirely dropped, it is of no great consequence. Men and women were none the better for being called professors ; but, at the same time, let me say they were none the worse for it. May be, if self-adopted, it savoured a little of the "Stand by : I am holier than thou;" or of "The temple of the Lord—the temple of the Lord are we," of the ancient Pharisees. But, on the other hand, a consciousness of being looked upon by the surrounding world as "a professor" might have a tendency to promote that circumspection and carefulness in daily walk and conversation which are incumbent on every Christian, and so might induce the true child of God to pray more earnestly, "Hold thou me up in my going, that my feet slip not. Lead me, O Lord, in Thy righteousness, because of those who observe me."

These reflections have led me away from Mr. Millman: let me return. I soon learned, what, indeed, was no secret, that my employer was an active and leading man in the religious society and congregation with which he was connected, and that his name stood prominent and high in what was called "the religious world." My observation of him was, therefore, proportionably keen. I do not say that it was ill-natured ; I do not think it was ; and I am sure it was not suspicious; but it was on the alert. Now, if I had seen, in my employer's daily intercourse with the world, or in any particular business transactions, or in his behaviour in his domestic circle, anything inconsistent with his "profession," I should have been sorry for him, but I might also have been prejudiced against religion itself, or might, at any rate, have been confirmed in my wavering, procrastinating thoughts regarding a personal striving to enter in at the strait gate and narrow way which lead to eternal life.

But I could detect nothing of the sort, for Mr. Millman's practice exactly agreed with his profession. And to this conclusion I was compelled to come, not only in consequence of my own observations, but because of the united and uniform testimony of others. I heard occasionally, from fellow-clerks who were not "professors," covert sneers at Mr. Millman's Methodism; but I never heard a word—no, not a syllable—breathed against his integrity, or his kindness, or his benevolence, or his considerateness; on the contrary, the same gently-scorning tongues would candidly trace home the noblest traits in his character to his religion. "Oh, he will do it, I dare say" (this in reference, perhaps, to some loving attempt at the alleviation of distress and sorrow)—"he will do it: it is just like his Methodism, you know;" or, "Mr. Millman won't be hard upon the poor wretch" (this in reference to an unfortunate debtor): "he is too much of a Methodist for that;" or, "Only prove that you are trying to do your best in his service, and, from principle, Mr. Millman will be your fast friend for life." All this, and much more to the same effect, I heard again and again from the lips of men who would have found fault with the religion of their employer if they could have done so. The apostle James challenges those to whom he writes to show their faith *without* works (if they can), and tells them that he will show his faith *by* his works. I never read this without thinking of Mr. Millman. He, certainly, showed his faith by his works.

It was in his family, however, that Mr. Millman's Christianity stood out in its most affectionate aspect. He had experienced a sad and life-long trial in the death of his wife; but it had evidently wrought in him more fully the peaceable fruits of righteousness. He had, at times, a good deal of care and necessary anxiety in connexion with his extensive business; but care and anxiety never made him morose: so far as I ever witnessed, and I had abundant opportunities for witnessing, he had always a cheerful countenance at home; and, if his heart was not always light, it was always ready to sympathise with his children and friends in their pleasures.   And I must say a word for "aunt Rhoda" here.   She also was a "professor," and it is wonderful the amount of genial kindness and good temper there was wrapped up, so to speak, in her prim formality and old-maidishness.   Aunt Rhoda had had her personal sorrows.   In the days of her youth she was engaged to be married, and, I believe, the wedding-day was fixed, when her affianced husband—a young clergyman—in visiting a fever and poverty-stricken abode in his parish, took the fever and died.   A small locket, containing a minute portion of braided hair, and always worn suspended around her neck by a delicate gold chain, attested to the fidelity with which aunt Rhoda, after the lapse of a quarter of a century or more, clung to the memory of her first and last lover.   Nor was this her only sorrow.   Years later she lost almost all her property by the dishonesty of an agent, in whose power it had been placed; and she had scarcely any other means of support than those derived from teaching, until she became her bereaved brother's housekeeper.   To some minds these troubles would have been a perpetual source of morbid melancholy, and a standing excuse for irritability of temper; but, with aunt Rhoda, they seemed to produce an opposite effect; and I never recall her to mind without thinking of the words of the prophet, " The work of righteousness shall be peace ; and the effect of righteousness, quietness, and assurance for ever.   And my people shall dwell in a peaceable habitation, and in sure dwellings, and in quiet resting-places ; when it shall hail, coming down on the forest ; and the city shall be low in a low place."

Without further enlargement on this subject, I shall only say that the constant observation of such beneficent and morally healthy traits in the characters of two foremost "professors" (scorn the term if you like, reader, but not the thing) wrought a beneficial effect on my mind which no amount of mere talk would have produced. In their case I saw that evangelical religion was a reality; that while faith was the foundation, deeds were the edifice; if faith was the root, deeds were the branches, and the fruit; "faith, working by love."

And I verily believe that, by these means, God was graciously pleased to bring home conviction to my soul—a conviction that these, my kind and faithful friends, had something that I needed, and that that something was a cordial reception of Christ Jesus as my Saviour, and following him as my example. And I do sincerely feel assured that the Divine Spirit of God so effectually, though gradually, enlightened my mind and opened my eyes, at this time, to apprehend the foulness of my nature, and the need of soul-cleansing as well as pardon for past sins, and to behold wondrous things out of God's law, as to lead me, in the hope of heavenly strength being imparted, to resolve to give myself first to the Lord, and then to his people, according to the will of God.

If it be asked of me what all this has to do with the story I have undertaken to tell, I have only to say that, to my mind, it forms an integral part of it. At all events, I have this to say, that I do not know how I could so well have borne the present trial of my grandfather's terrible affliction, and the future vexations which I have yet to record, if I had not experienced the truthfulness, and fidelity, and certainty of the Divine promises— "Call upon me in the day of trouble: I will deliver thee, and thou shalt glorify me." "Cast thy burden upon the Lord, and he shall sustain thee." "When thou passest through the waters, I will be with thee; and through the rivers, they shall not overflow thee: when thou walkest through the fire, thou shalt not be burned; neither shall the flame kindle upon thee."

For I was in the greater trouble seeing that, added to the sorrowful stroke which had fallen on my grandfather, I had suddenly a weight of responsibility laid upon me which I was ill able to bear. Besides myself, poor demented Anthony Bix had no legal representative at hand, and I was not much over nineteen years old. It made matters the worse for me that, do what I might, I should usurp the power of my wretched uncle William; and it added to my perplexity that, at that moment, I knew in what direction he was to be sought for. But could I recall him? would it be right for me to communicate with him, knowing what I knew of him?

I could not decide.

CHAPTER XL.

A CONSULTATION OF DOCTORS, ASSISTED BY A LAWYER.

PASSING an anxious night, I arose on the morning after my return from Fairmouth still perplexed and undecided with regard to my course of duty. My poor grandfather was in the same bewildered state of mind, rejecting, fretfully, all persuasions and attempts to rouse him, and quiet only when the wooden doll was in his arms. To my relief Dr. Squills came early to visit his patient, and readily agreed with my proposal to call in an eminent physician—the consulting physician, I believe, of one of the public lunatic asylums of London, the mad-houses, as they were then generally called; while, by a kind of figure of speech, the physician referred to was spoken of as the mad-doctor.

An hour or two later in the day, then, the two doctors made their appearance, and shut themselves in with the patient, while Betsy Miller and I waited without. Presently, after a long consultation apart, they returned to us.

"Can you make anything of my poor grandfather?" I timidly asked the great man.

"Oh yes," said the mad-doctor. "It is one of those very common cases which we meet with every day in our profession—a very painful profession, Mr. Burley, but one that brings its rewards with it, in enabling us to mitigate the sufferings of poor human nature. A very common case, as I was saying, produced by a sudden shock, doubtless, which has thrown a mind, not originally very strong (if I may be allowed to say so), off its balance."

"Can you hold out any hope of my grandfather's recovery, doctor?" was my next question.

"We may hope, sir; but we must not be too sanguine," he replied. "If our respected friend were younger, there would be no ground for despairing of the resources of art, and the effects of gentle treatment; but at his age we must be allowed to pronounce it a serious and critical case."

"Thank you, doctor, for your candour," I said, sorrowfully.

"I have not kept back from my friend Dr. Squills," continued the physician, "my decided opinion, in which he agrees with me, that the wiser course would be to place our respected patient under the judicious care of our admirable institution, the Bethlehem——."

I saw an angry storm rising in Betsy Miller's countenance, and, fearing another explosion of wrath similar to that which Dr. Squills had already experienced, and from which, I could see, he nervously shrank, I hastened to assure the doctor that, unless as a very last resort in case of urgent, threatening danger, the idea of my poor grandfather's confinement in a lunatic asylum could not be entertained.

"Just so," replied he, with much suavity. "I have understood from my friend that there are strong objections, founded on prejudice, no doubt; but even prejudices are to be respected where they do not endanger life, and health, and safety; and we are happy to perceive, in the case of our patient, that the present phase of his mental disease is rather that of harmless delusion than of active mischievousness. Besides, the patient is feeble—very feeble."

My poor grandfather!

"I have been suggesting to Dr. Squills," continued the mad-doctor, "the propriety of a male attendant accustomed to cases of this kind—to give his time entirely to the patient, and furnish him with amusement."

There was no objection to this. Indeed, I had thought of it myself, and was happy to see that Betsy Miller fell in with the idea. It was agreed, therefore, that Dr. J—— should, in the course of the day, send to Silver Square an experienced keeper to take the principal charge of my grandfather. This arrangement removed a load of anxiety from my mind. There was another matter, however, on which I resolved to be, at least partly, guided by the advice of the two physicians. It was evident that my grandfather's disturbed mind had concentrated itself, so to speak, on the memory of his child. Then, William Bix, let him be what he might, and what I well knew him to be, was doubtless the legal representative of his father; and, as I knew where and under what circumstances, and in what name, the prodigal son was likely to be found, I desired to know whether I should be justified in withholding from him the knowledge of his father's present condition.

Fortunately, as I was about to enter on this subject, Mr. Fawley the solicitor arrived with his daily inquiry after my grandfather's health, and he joined in our conference.

The doctors' decision was plain and decided. They had, in fact, arrived at it before I spoke; for Dr. Squills (these family doctors, of course, as a rule, know most of their patients' family secrets) had, in their previous consultation, revealed to his friend some part at least of what he knew of my grandfather's circumstances and of my uncle's character.

"The son must not come near the house; at any rate he must be kept away from the patient," said Dr. J——; "that is a matter on which my friend Dr. Squills and myself have made up our minds. It might do no harm, for possibly the patient would not recognise him; but the probability is that he would, and in that case we could not answer for consequences. The shock to the nervous system would be too great, and from a harmless maniac the patient might become a furious madman, or, quite as probably, almost immediate death would ensue."

"Do I understand you, doctor, that there is a chance of my friend Bix recovering his senses if kept perfectly quiet?" demanded the lawyer.

"It is the only chance we have," replied Dr. J—— oracularly.

"Very well, then; fortified by this opinion, I advise our young friend" (this to me) "not to trouble himself about his uncle," said Mr. Fawley. "We all know enough about William Bix—at least I do—to be assured that the less we have to do with him the better; and as he chooses to run about the country under an assumed name and in disguise, let him keep to them both. We are not bound to know Washington Rexworthy as William Bix. If we want him, we will advertise for him under his proper name."

And so the matter was settled for that time, and the doctors soon afterwards took their leave. But the lawyer remained, and drew me aside into another room.

"This is an awkward affair, Mr. Burley," said he.

"It is very painful, sir."

"Painful, yes; painful to you especially. Painful to me, to see my old friend in such a state; but, speaking professionally, it is especially awkward also; coming at this time, too, when your grandfather's wits are all required to be in due order."

"About Mr. Falconer's affairs, I suppose."

"Just so. Mr. Falconer was—there's no harm in saying it—a singular man. There are those who don't hesitate to think that he had always a bee in his bonnet, as folks say ; at any rate, he has made a singular will, and your grandfather is his sole executor—a very foolish proceeding, considering your grandfather's age, and the large property there is to manage. I told Mr. Falconer so when I drew up the will. But he pooh-poohed me ; and now you see the consequences."

I did not see the consequences so plainly as the lawyer did ; but I did not say this, and Mr. Fawley further informed me that the will being in his possession, and he having some power under it (he did not then explain what) to act professionally as my grandfather's legal adviser, he had taken such steps as were immediately necessary, hoping soon to be rid of the responsibility.

"There's one thing more," he added. "Your grandfather was always rather close and secret, you know—in his money matters, I mean ; and I doubt now whether he has five pounds in the house ; or, if he has, whether you or Betsy know where to lay your hands upon it."

This was true, and I said so.

"Well, what are you going to do ? You can't keep house for nothing ; and these doctors, and the man that's coming, must be paid, you know."

Betsy Miller and I had thought of this. It had been my grandfather's practice to place a certain sum weekly in her hands for current expenses, to be duly accounted for ; and the last payment she had received was exhausted. It happened, however, that Betsy had a hoard of her own, and also that I had a few pounds ; and we had agreed to make use of these joint resources.

"No, no," said the lawyer, when I told him this ; "you'll

never get it back again, perhaps; who can tell? You must let me be your treasurer. I am safe to get paid." He put ten pounds into my hand as he said this. "Make it go as far as you can, but don't spare for anything," he added; "and when you want more, come to me. Don't spend your own money—not a sixpence of it."

Saying this, he departed.

CHAPTER XLI.

UNEXPECTED VISITORS AT SILVER SQUARE. MR. FALCONER'S SINGULAR WILL.

WHATEVER mystery (if any) might be wrapped up in Mr. Fawley's allusion to Mr. Falconer's "singular will," I thought but little about it. It was more to me that my poor grandfather should be properly cared for, and, if possible, restored to his right mind. It was a great relief, therefore, when, later in the day, a person arrived with proper credentials from Dr. J——, and entered at once upon his prescribed duties.

I cannot tell how he managed it, for he was a quiet little man, with no appearance of either moral or physical force about him; but he had not been an hour in attendance on my grandfather before he had gained an ascendancy over the patient which neither Betsy Miller nor myself, with all our previous knowledge of his character, and all our affectionate concern, had been able to exercise. Coming prepared to act as valet, he produced my grandfather, at the expiration of that time, newly shaven and shorn, with his hair nicely arranged and repowdered, and his clothing trimly brushed and adjusted; and, in the gentle manner of an affectionate, confidential friend, he was walking arm-in-arm with the afflicted man across and across the marble-paved hall, addressing him in pleasant soothing words; having, as I afterwards learned, persuaded the monomaniac that it would be better for the child (that is to say, the wooden doll) to be laid gently to sleep in an extemporized cot in the office.

In the same unassuming, but potential manner, this man (Jonathan, he was called) suggested and won over my grandfather to agree with him that the old office was an unwholesome place for a delicate infant, and that one of the rooms in the upper part of the house would be vastly preferable as a nursery; explaining afterwards to Betsy Miller and myself that it was desirable to remove the patient from his ordinary place of business. Accordingly, a room was prepared, and before the day closed in, my poor grandfather and his attendant were duly installed there.

After a like manner, Jonathan prevailed on the patient to take necessary sustenance; in short, such a favourable change had outwardly passed over my grandfather that our hopes were raised as to his ultimate recovery.

That is to say, Betsy Miller's hopes and mine; for Jonathan did not share them. On the contrary, he gave it as his opinion that "the poor old gentleman's mind" was "almost entirely gone."

There were, however, in connexion with what I have already stated, some good results arising from the presence of the placid keeper. In the first place, responsibility was shifted on to more capable shoulders than either Betsy Miller's or mine. And next, I was relieved from the necessity of constant attendance, and was enabled, after the lapse of a day or two, to resume my duties in Gracechurch Street. I need scarcely add, that I received from Mr. Millman and his family continued proofs of their sympathy.

Two or three weeks passed away without much alteration in my grandfather, only that the cloud which rested on his mind assumed sometimes a darker and sometimes a lighter complexion; but it never once was withdrawn—never once. Meanwhile, of course, the physicians were regular in their visits; and so was Mr. Fawley, fidgety, but kind, not confidential, however. I thought, sometimes, that he might have enlightened me as to the nature of Mr. Falconer's will, or to what extent, if any, I was beneficially interested in it. But he did not. He told me once that he had taken measures, or must soon take measures—I don't remember which—for the proving of it; and this was all I heard.

It was two or three weeks, then, after my return from Fairmouth, that, on going home from business one evening, and letting myself in by means of a latch-key (which I had some time used, to save Betsy the trouble of opening the door to me), I fancied I heard footsteps in the dining-room; and, on pushing open the door, I found it occupied by Mrs. Tozer and her son. Astonished at this unexpected apparition, I had at first scarcely presence of mind to bid them welcome, especially as the lady seemed to have taken in a double amount of her natural acerbity, while Marmaduke was pacing to and fro over the half-carpeted floor with manifest impatience.

"I thought you were never coming, Hurly," he said, coldly giving me his hand. "Here's my mother, you see."

I muttered some complimentary words, and blundered out two or three incoherent questions and apologies.

"Oh, there's no occasion for that, Hurly," said Marmaduke. "Of course, you didn't know we were coming, so you couldn't have expected us. Have we been long in London? No; only two hours. Have we dined? Yes; we dined on the road, coming up. Will we have tea, or what not? No; we have ordered tea where we ordered beds." All this was spoken in an indescribably sulky air and tone; and all this time Mrs. Tozer had said not a word, but sat immovable as a statue, only that she had once extended her arm to put two cold, and bony, and stiff fingers into my palm when I offered to shake hands with her. She opened her lips now, however.

"You are not more surprised to see me here, sir," she said, in a sepulchral voice, "than I am surprised to find myself beneath this roof—this roof, of all others in London," she added.

"There, that will do," interposed Marmaduke, whose behaviour towards his mother had evidently not improved since my last visit to their house. "What's the use of going over old stories? If you had married Jack Falconer instead of Frank Tozer, you would have had this house for your own. I suppose we all know that; but what's the good of saying it. Here you are now, at all events. You *would* come, you know." Saying this, he turned to me.

"The long and short of it is, Hurly, I don't think we have been well used; at any rate, I haven't. There, I don't want to quarrel; but now you know my mind."

"Not well used, Marmaduke?"

"No, not well used. You know as well as I do that I am Mr. Falconer's nearest of kin, and have had expectations held out to me, and all that sort of thing."

"Well, and what then?" I demanded, rather sternly, if I spoke as I intended.

"What then? Why, I want to know why the news of his death has been kept from me. It is a month ago—ay, six weeks ago, pretty near—since he died; and I never heard of it till two days ago."

"Really," I said, "I am not answerable for that."

"No; but somebody is, if you are not," said he, working himself up into a passion.

"From whom did you receive the intelligence of Mr. Falconer's death?" I asked.

"From whom? Fawley, the lawyer, if you must know."

"And did he not mention why he had not written to you before?"

"Oh, he tells a cock-and-bull story about Mr. Anthony Bix being indisposed and unable to attend to business. As if I could not see as far into a mill-stone as here and there one," said Marmaduke, so insolently that I could not forbear replying—

"You seem to have kept company with clodhopping clowns so long, Marmaduke, that you have learned their manners; and I have only to say that you may see as far into a mill-stone as you please; but you must also please to remember that you are in my grandfather's house, and that——"

Here Marmaduke interrupted me.

"That's the very thing that has got to be proved—whose house it is. If your grandfather isn't well, I am sorry for it," he added; "but that's no reason I should be kept out of anything belonging to me."

"I really do not understand you," I said. "I am not aware that any one wishes to keep you out of anything. You are labouring under some strange mistake, I am sure: but I have no disposition to quarrel, and I cannot explain what I do not know. Had you not better see Mr. Fawley?"

"Yes, and meant to; and I called at his office with mother, but he wasn't in. So I told his clerk I was coming on here, and he might do as he liked about coming after. Here's mother; she can tell you that was what I said, if she will."

Hitherto, after uttering the one sentence I have recorded, Mrs.

T

Tozer had sat stiffly upright, with her eyes (as far as could be seen through her green spectacles) fixed on me, in an old way of hers which I very well remembered. Now she spoke again.

"It is no pleasure of mine that I am here," she said, in a calm, monotonous tone; "I want nothing, and I expect nothing from Mr. Falconer's will. It is quite true, as Marmaduke says, that, if things had been otherwise ordered, I might have been here now in my own right. But it is as well as it is, and I have no desire for worldly pomps and vanities and wealth. But I will see my son righted, you may depend on it; that is why I am here; and no interlopers shall stand in his way, if there's law to be had." The lady raised her voice a little—not much—as she said this; and then she subsided into silence.

"There, now you know what we mean, Hurly," added Marmaduke; "and you see we don't want to have words with you, but we don't mean to be played with. There's your grandfather, he is old Falconer's executor, we are told, and if he and the lawyer have gone putting their heads together, you understand, it will be the worse for them. It is he—Mr. Anthony Bix—*I* want to see. That idiotic Betsy Miller of yours told us that he wasn't to be seen by anybody; but you had better call him, I think, to save a row, Hurly, or I'll go to him if you like. There's only a plain question or two I want to ask him, without any nonsense, and that won't be much trouble, anyhow, if he is an honest man."

"And 'an honest man's the noblest work of God,' so somebody says, Mr. Marmaduke Tozer. My service to you, young gentleman, to you also, madam; and, as to plain questions, I am here to answer them."

The voice was that of Mr. Fawley; and on turning my head I saw him standing behind me, having just entered the room unseen and unheard. How he came into the house without my knowing it, I could not understand; but it was made clear to me afterwards by Betsy Miller, who, foreboding some awkward complications from the visit, had no sooner safely shut the visitors in the disused dining-room, than she slipped out by a back way and hurried to Mr. Fawley's offices. Fortunately she met him half way as he was coming towards Silver Square, and introduced him into the house by the way in which she had made her exit.

"You see, Hurly," said she, when she was giving this explanation, "I knew Master Marmaduke from his having been here before, and I knew Madam Tozer by the green spectacles you have told me about so often; and I knew what they were likely to have come about by their looking so fierce, and telling me they wanted to see your poor grandfather; and so, thinks I, Hurly shan't have to battle it out by himself if I can help it; and thankful I am I brought up the lawyer in time."

To return. It was not in Mrs. Tozer's way to manifest much surprise at any time. She simply bowed to the addition made to our party, and said quietly, "Mr. Fawley, I presume?" Marmaduke was rather more disconcerted, and muttered something about not expecting, which Mr. Fawley cut short.

"Nay, young gentleman, you left word with my clerk that you were coming here, and that I might follow. I have followed, you see; and, as my time is precious, it will be as well to proceed at once to business. You wish—I think I so understood you—to see Mr. Anthony Bix. You cannot see him. If you demand to know why you cannot see him, I may as well tell you at once that it is forbidden by his medical attendants. I am here, however, as his legal friend and adviser, to answer any questions you may have to put to him. Or perhaps I can save you the trouble. You wish to know, first of all, I presume, why you received intelligence only so recently of the death of your late patron?"

Marmaduke bit his under lip and nodded.

"Simply because my old friend was unable to write, and I waited, in hopes of his recovery. If there has been improper delay, it is my fault, and I am willing to answer for it."

"Oh, it doesn't matter, I suppose; only one doesn't like to be treated with neglect," Marmaduke muttered.

"No one likes to be treated with neglect," said the lawyer. "And now your next question."

"You told me, in your letter, that I was interested with Mr. Falconer's will, as, of course, I expected to be."

"And you wish to know to what extent and in what manner. Nothing can be more reasonable; and it is quite reasonable also that you, madam "—a bow to Mrs. Tozer, stiffly returned—"as your son's natural and legal guardian, should take an interest in the matter. I felt so satisfied of this, when I heard that you called at my office, that "—the lawyer drew from his breast-pocket as he spoke a flat packet tied up with red tape, which he began at once to undo—"that I put a certified copy of Mr. Falconer's will in my pocket. The will itself is in safe keeping, and can be inspected at your pleasure another day." Saying this, Mr. Fawley unfolded the foolscap.

"I will just remark," continued the lawyer, as he took a seat and adjusted his eye-glasses, "that our friend Falconer had a way of his own of doing things, and did not choose to be dictated to. He did not consult me when he made his will, I assure you." With this preface Mr. Fawley began to read.

Now there is this peculiarity about legal documents, as far as I am concerned, that they naturally bewilder me; so, after vainly endeavouring to follow the lawyer through all the verbosity of the document he held in his hand, I gave up the attempt in despair. Not so did Mrs. Tozer, however. I remember now how eagerly she listened; and the questions she afterwards sharply put to the lawyer proved that she was keenly alive to her son's interest, however indifferent she might be to her own, while, at the same time, they enlightened me as to the nature of the will.

"If I understand the will aright," said the lady, while Mr. Fawley was re-folding the paper, "the whole of the estate is left to be enjoyed by Anthony Bix, without any deductions, as long as he lives?"

"The whole estate, real and personal, without any deductions, except the payment of certain small legacies to Mr. Falconer's former dependants abroad, and the payment also of the legacy duty; yes, madam."

"And also that Anthony Bix is appointed sole executor?" continued Mrs. Tozer.

"Sole executor," repeated the lawyer, "giving power, however, to me, as the legal friend and adviser both of the testator and the legatee, to act for the latter in case of illness, age, or other incapacity.

"Rather a strange bequest," said the lady.

"In what way strange, madam?" demanded the lawyer.

"What is Anthony Bix that he should be favoured in this way?" she asked. "Only a paid servant," she added, answering her own question.

"And an attached and faithful friend. I may say that for Mr. Bix. As to the strangeness of the bequest, I have said that the will is a singular will; but it is indisputably the testator's last will and testament, and we must take it as it is. However, madam, you have noted, I dare say, that the bequest is not absolute: it is left in trust, conditionally."

"I was coming to that, sir. At the death of Anthony Bix, the whole of the personal property devolves to my son Marmaduke Tozer?"

"The whole of it, madam. All the funded property here set down, and of which only the interest is enjoyable by the present holder, and also all other moveable goods and chattels : the furniture of this house, for instance.   Also all moneys lent out at interest, according to the accounts forwarded from time to time by Mr. Bix, as Mr. Falconer's agent."

" I understand that.   Then the real property——"

" Consisting of certain houses in Silver Square, duly catalogued."

" Consisting of certain houses in Silver Square, duly catalogued," the lady repeated, " is to be divided ?"

" To be divided, madam, in tolerably equal portions, according to their assumed value—each portion being particularly scheduled, so as to prevent unpleasant disputes or misunderstandings hereafter.   Mr. Falconer was anxious, you see, that these should be avoided."

" And one of those portions will eventually come to my son Marmaduke ?   I am anxious to understand this."

" Absolutely to your son, madam, without further deductions; and I may congratulate him on the prospect—I may say the certainty—of a very pretty property."

" Yes, but when ? I should like to know," interposed Marmaduke, sullenly.   " These old fellows sometimes live to no end of time, especially when there's anything to be got by their dying."

Shall I ever forget the look of indignant contempt which passed over the honest lawyer's countenance at that moment? Marmaduke felt it, and writhed under it.

" I beg your grandfather's pardon, and yours too, Hurly," he muttered.   " Didn't mean any harm ; only it is a bore, you see, waiting to step into a dead man's shoes."

" You will not have to wait long, I am afraid, Marmaduke," I said, with tears in my eyes.

CHAPTER XLII.

SORROW AND ITS ANTIDOTE.

I BROKE off my last chapter rather abruptly; but indeed there was little more to tell respecting Mr. Falconer's will. The only thing of importance was that a moiety of the Silver estate (as it was called) was left to my grandfather's entire and absolute disposal after his death—no mention being made of me.

I could readily understand now why Mr. Fawley had been so silent towards me with regard to the will.

"I was loth to damp your expectations," he said, when Mrs. Tozer and Marmaduke had taken their departure (which they did rather abruptly); "but it is as well for you to know what you have to rest upon."

"I had no right to expect anything from Mr. Falconer," I said, with some bitterness I fear. "He was very good to me when I was a child, and gave me a good education afterwards; but he never held out any promise to me that I should inherit any part of his property."

"No; but don't you see that, in leaving this half of his real estate at your grandfather's disposal, Mr. Falconer thought he was benefiting you? And don't be discouraged. My friend Bix was a thoughtful and shrewd man in matters of business, and the probability is that he has made a will embracing all possible contingencies like this. I shouldn't wonder, indeed, if he knew what Mr. Falconer was going to do, and has taken measures for you accordingly. Or, if he should not have done so, perhaps even now he may recover his wits, and make things all right in the end."

This was all the encouragement Mr. Fawley could give me; and it was easy to see that he did not half believe in it himself. Presently he too took his departure.

I have many sad, grevious faults, and always have had; but I don't think I was ever mercenary—not *very* mercenary. Nevertheless, I could not, when I was alone that evening, look upon my half-blighted prospects without a pang. I had no reproaches to cast on Mr. Falconer's memory. I could understand why he preferred to leave it with my grandfather to provide for me—having given him the means to do so—rather than that I should look upon himself as my chief benefactor. It was like his disinterestedness. The error he had committed was in taking for granted that his old friend, Anthony Bix, would outlive him, and have energy to carry out what he probably knew to be his patron's wishes. The elder did indeed survive the younger; but it was as though he had died. I am afraid I murmured in my heart rebelliously at the stroke which, in all probability, would so seriously affect my interests.

No; I don't think I was mercenary. I had never wished to be enriched at my uncle William's expense—never desired to deprive him of his just patrimony. If my grandfather had any property of his own to leave behind him, which, for reasons already stated, I very much doubted; but if he had, my uncle's natural claim to that inheritance was greater and stronger than mine, and I had never wished him to be disinherited. But this bequest of Mr. Falconer was not my uncle's just patrimony—was never intended to be his; I felt sure of this. And yet it did not need a lawyer to tell me that, except on the unlikely supposition that my grandfather had made provision for the very contingency which had happened, I should eventually be deprived of all benefit from Mr. Falconer's good intentions towards me.

And there was a reason why I felt this disappointment keenly.

I had not been so long on brotherly terms with Edwin Millman—
on intimate terms with the family in Gracechurch Street—without
having gradually admitted into my day-dreams how happy I might
be if those ties could be rendered permanent and yet more close.
I have previously described my first impressions respecting Mary
Millman; but the three years which had elapsed had wrought its
changes in us both. Mary had bloomed into lovely gracefulness,
and had become a charming young woman. I use these hackneyed
terms now with a smile, but not of contempt, for they are right
and proper. Cold and austere and platonic old age may sneer at
the enthusiastic admiration of green youth, and may say that it is
all vanity and vexation of spirit. But I am pleased to think that
I am neither cold nor austere, nor very platonic. At any rate, I
hope I can not only rejoice with those who rejoice, but also
admire with those who admire. Let the words stand, then, in my
story, as the memory remains in my heart—Mary Millman *was*
personally lovely, graceful, and charming. But the attractions
of her person were surpassed by those of her mind. I had seen
her gentleness, and watched her maturing piety, and noted how
she was the source of happiness to all around her. Was it possible
that, without too great presumption, I might some day ask her to
be my wife?

Well, I had come gradually to think it possible; that is to say,
I was almost certain she liked me, and I was almost equally
certain that Mr. Millman and his maiden sister had witnessed our
growing intimacy (I had almost written attachment) without
displeasure. Why, then, should I not some day ask Mary to
become my wife?

There was only one reason—so I had accustomed myself to
argue—why I should not. Mary's father was undoubtedly
wealthy, and I and my grandfather were poor. I remembered
Mr. Millman once, while speaking of a certain marriage which

had then recently been contracted in the circle of his acquaintance, mentioning this very circumstance as an objection to the match, and saying that a disparity in outward circumstances was often an impediment to future happiness. I believed him to be right: he always was, or seemed to be right, in his judgment of mankind; but I had pleased myself with fancying that some day, as far as Mary and I were concerned, this disparity in circumstances would be removed. I was wrong in building thus upon uncertain expectations; but having began to open my heart to my readers, I shall not, in this particular, conceal its weakness and folly.

And now these hopes of mine were apparently overthrown. I was poor, and in all probability should remain so, unless by my own exertions, and God's blessing on them, I could eventually raise my position. This might be; but how long and unsuccessfully others, as persevering and self-denying as I could ever hope to be, had laboured for wealth, I very well knew. And why should I expect to succeed where they had failed?

All these, and other thoughts—very sad and gloomy, believe me—passed through my mind as I lay tossing on my pillow that night, after Mr. Fawley had left me. I knew where it is said, "Cast thy burden upon the Lord, and he shall sustain thee."—"Casting all your care upon him, for he careth for you;" and I trust I knew the value of these declarations. But they did not alter the fact that I had been living in a fool's paradise, and that I was now being roughly wakened up to the stern realities of disappointment. I felt, too, that to have any claim to the heavenly help therein promised, I must vigorously brace up my mind to the performance of stern duty; and that it is while thus girding on the armour that divine strength is oftenest imparted.

On one thing, at least, I was resolved. I would root out from my heart, if I could—and if I could not do this, I would cut down to the roots—all those luxurious weeds of idle romance which had sprung up there. I would thenceforth, as far as I could, without giving offence, avoid further intimacy with my employer's family. Mr. Millman should, at any rate, see that I had not made his disinterested kindness a stepping-stone to my selfish ends and aims. My grandfather's continued affliction would give me a good reason, at present, for the course on which I had determined; and beyond this, I must patiently wait.

I am glad now that I was thus determined—more glad that I did not trust to my own heart, nor rely on my own strength for carrying it out : glad that I then remembered where it is written —"If any of you lack wisdom, let him ask of God that giveth to all men liberally, and upbraideth not; and it shall be given him." I did lack wisdom; and I did ask of God; and I humbly trust I asked without wavering, and in faith, knowing that He is faithful, who has promised. And let me record, in no vain-glorying, but in fervent gratitude, that what I asked for was given, and something more, for strength equal to the trial was given.

It was hard to part with the anticipations which had grown up in my heart; but I did part with them; and the sacrifice (for it was a sacrifice) did not make me absolutely wretched. Perhaps it is true that no man can be absolutely miserable whose conscience does not accuse him of foul and flagrant misdoing. And, whether this be so or not, I soon found, to my surprise, that I could almost as calmly bend my attention to the necessary transactions of business, and almost as steadily go along "life's dullest, dreariest walk," as though my fairest visions of hope were certain and soon to be realised. I bless God for this.

I was a young Christian then. I had not very long known the true meaning and extent of that Gospel which, in its facts, had so long been familiar to my mind; and I had yet much to learn, as indeed, I have now ; but I had learned this,—that the things which are seen, and temporal, are not worthy to be put into competition or comparison with the things that are unseen and eternal ; and in proportion as my worldly prospects and expectations seemed to fade away, my realisation of the joys of hope and faith and spiritual love, became more and more vivid. I bless God for this too.

And, before I proceed with my story, let me quote what one has written respecting the peculiar resources of a believer for meeting worldly calamity, or inevitable sorrow. " Whatever may be thought of his faith by others, the object it looks at, and the influence it exerts, are realities to *him*. He confides in a benignant Providence ; he believes that all things are regulated by Wisdom and Love ; and that nothing can happen to him except by the will of his Father in heaven. When prostrated by some sudden stroke, or called to endure what is incident to humanity, what all one time or other must sustain, he has not to submit to it as the unintelligent result of the working of a mere machine ;—he has not to regard himself either as a victim beneath the iron foot of material laws, or as the sport of capricious accident or chance. To *him* 'there is a God that judgeth in the earth ;'—a presiding and regal personality, with thought and love, purposes and ends ;—who directs all things 'according to the counsel of His own will,' but whose will is, that 'all things shall work together for good to them that love Him.' He refers every event to the Supreme reason, the Infinite intelligence, believing that He, whom he thus regards, is alike just, benevolent, and merciful. He expects from his trials moral advantages, believing them to be intelligently administered. He finds support in prayer to God in heaven, solace in resignation to His will on earth. He is conscious of Divine strength springing from hope and faith,—from the belief that 'the sufferings of this present time' are exactly what he needs to fit him for his anticipated higher life; and that 'they are not worthy to be compared with the glory that is to be hereafter revealed.' He is 'persuaded' that nothing 'can separate him from the love of God that is in Christ Jesus;'—that nothing can occur beyond the strength of faith to sustain, or transcending the resources of religion to relieve. He cannot be overwhelmed by a sudden surprise, nor crushed, though he may be stunned, by a blow. He will not be 'swallowed up with overmuch sorrow,' nor be left without inheritance, even should his worldly all be destroyed;—for 'he has in himself, and in heaven, a better, even an enduring substance.' The Christian man, because his faith is a reality to himself, can come forth, uncrushed and uncomplaining, from severe sorrow; can reappear, in his sphere of duty, with calm countenance and unabated vigour, feeling that he possesses internal resources of repose and strength. Work can be done again though some may be withdrawn whose presence and companionship made labour light; and earth can be enjoyed though its scenes may have lost to him some of their attractions. To *him* the darkest cloud has a silver lining; sorrow may continue for a night, but light is sown in the darkness, and joy returns with the day."*

I do not say that all these effects were produced in me, in all their fulness; for, as I have said, I was young in the Christian life, and my faith was weak; but I bless God that enough of them was known and felt by me to make life not only endurable, but pleasant, even under the anticipated loss of a fortune and——Mary Millman.

I return now to my story.

* The Rev. T. Binney in " Is it Possible to Make the Best of Both Worlds ?"

CHAPTER XLIII.

DRAWING TOWARDS AN END—ANOTHER VISITOR AT SILVER SQUARE.

MY grandfather's malady continued unabated; but the symptoms underwent a change. The wooden doll was discarded, and the name of Willy was never more mentioned by him. No name was mentioned by him; his memory was gone.

Yet, in this new phase of the mysterious disease, there was less than before that was absolutely painful. Quiet and docile, the aged man sat, day after day, gazing with childlike curiosity on a book of pictures which Jonathan had introduced for his amusement. It was evident that they conveyed no ideas to his mind, and that they were ever new to him; but the bright gaudy colours pleased him, and that was enough.

My poor grandfather regained his former courtesy of manner also, and his extreme nicety in dress. He was pleased to be under his attendant's hands, and would have submitted to be shaved and brushed and combed every hour in the day, with much personal gratification, I have no doubt. He put me in mind of Marmaduke, who once spoke very enthusiastically of the delightful sensation he experienced in having his hair brushed by a celebrated perruquier; and I suppose there was something in the operation which soothed my grandfather's disturbed mind. My mention of Marmaduke reminds me that, about a week after his and his mother's unexpected and unpleasant visit to Silver Square, I received a letter from him, apologising for the ill-temper and rudeness he manifested towards me on that visit. I was glad of this, but should have been better pleased if he had not attempted to lay the blame of his conduct on his mother. "She would come with me, and I did not want her to be meddling in my affairs, so I was put out. And then, instead of going home at once and leaving me in London, she would stick to me like a leech; so I could not even go to Blackheath—to the Browns, you know—without having her hanging on. And, as I wasn't going to stand that, I had to give them the go-by. Provoking, wasn't it?" Now, I did not like this, nor did I like his reiterating the assertion that it was a bore to have to wait till my grandfather died before he could "come into his property." I thought it cold-hearted. Nevertheless, I was glad I had not had a downright quarrel with Marmaduke.

To return to my grandfather—I have said that in the second stage of his malady he regained his former courtesy of manner. He was pleased when called upon to receive visitors—bowing to them with courtly formality, desiring his attendant to hand seats to them, and pressing them to take refreshment. And as every person who entered his apartment—his doctors, Betsy Miller, and myself included—was to him a visitor and a stranger, both my grandfather and Jonathan were kept pretty well employed through the day. The real visitors were not numerous, certainly; but some were admitted: Mr. Fawley, for instance, who frequently called, in the vain hope of perceiving some gleams of returning intelligence; and Mr. Millman and Edwin, who, because I rarely spent an evening with them now, sometimes came to Silver Square; and Mr. Filby, who made it his business to call occasionally upon his old friend, and speak a few comforting and confidential words to Mrs. Betsy. And I may as well remark here, that Mr. Filby's prejudice in my disfavour did not last long, though it did last as long as I retained in my caligraphy any manifest traces of the teaching of Mr. Smithers. But, this being

swallowed up, or superseded by the standard business-hand cultivated in Gracechurch Street, Mr. Filby's hopes of me returned.

And so some months passed with little variation; and if I sometimes felt my heart heavy and sorrowful, I was not without some
gleams of comfort. I had striven—imperfectly and feebly, no doubt,
but not quite unsuccessfully—against the fond fancy in which I
had once indulged; and, as I had done this at what I believed to
be the stern call of duty, I had at least the satisfaction of knowing that I *had* striven and was still striving.

One thing that puzzled and rather hurt me was that Mr. Millman seemed silently to approve of my keeping away from the
home society at Gracechurch Street. And once, when Edwin said
to me in his presence, "You never come to see us now, Hurly;
and Mary is quite vexed: she is sure she must have offended you.
Of course we cannot expect you, because of your poor grandfather,
to spend so much time with us as you used to do; but you might
run up-stairs now and then, if it were only for five minutes at a
time"—I say, when Edwin said this, Mr. Millman said, sharply
and coldly I thought—

"Hurly is quite right, Edwin. He knows that under present
circumstances, he has one paramount duty. I am glad that he so
well knows how to perform it."

I felt sure by this, that Mr. Millman guessed what was passing
and had passed in my mind, and that he was glad I had relieved
him from the painful necessity of telling me that my particular
attentions to his daughter could not be permitted.

"It is best so—best so," I sighed, in the bitterness of my heart.

Full employment is the best remedy for gloomy, morbid
thoughts; and, happily, I had at this time work enough to
keep me pretty constantly employed. Of course I had my
duties at Gracechurch Street—principally correspondence and
book-keeping—to engage my entire attention there. And on

my return in the evening to Silver Square I was busied in my
grandfather's office, assisting an accountant's clerk in the adjust-
ment of his—or rather, of his late patron's—affairs, under the
direction of Mr. Fawley.

Now, almost everybody knows, or can conjecture, that however
methodical and correct a person may be in the transaction of his
business and the general management of his concerns, and the
arrangement of his papers, if by reason of death or absence, or
sickness, these duties are suddenly thrown upon a stranger,
numberless perplexities arise, which, if the principal were present
to explain, would be made perfectly clear. My grandfather had
always prided himself in the perspicuity of his business habits, and
the transparency of all his transactions during the long term of
his agency: and not without reason. Yet, when we first entered
on the examination of his books and papers, we found ourselves
plunged into a chaos of figures, and statements, and balances,
which puzzled us exceedingly. No doubt the clear head of
Anthony Bix would have set us right in a few minutes; but we
had not his clear head to help us, and on some occasions many
hours, and even many evenings, were occupied before, with
regard to some particular item, we could arrive at a satisfactory
result. Then there were packets of letters embracing the whole
term of my grandfather's agency, and old books relating to long
bygone money transactions, to be carefully examined: so that the
work went slowly on.

At length, however, our labours drew to a close; and I had the
satisfaction of witnessing that my grandfather's integrity and
fidelity towards his employer stood out very plainly manifested.

It was as plainly manifested that he himself—apart from the
princely bequest of Mr. Falconer—was a poor man. This, however, as I have before intimated, was no new discovery to me. I
had pretty well known that the constant demands made upon him

U

by his profligate son, for many years, and the obligations he had taken upon himself on that son's behoof, had swallowed up the entire savings of his life. And now that, at length, riches had been suddenly heaped upon him, he was incapable of enjoying them.

Very gradually, and yet perceptibly, my grandfather's bodily health began and continued to fail, and his strength to diminish, until at length he was unable to rise from his bed, and it was evident that he was drawing near to the end of his mortal course. It was on a gloomy November day that, as I sat by his bedside, watching the labouring breath and almost corpse-like features of the dying old man, I thought I noticed a sudden brightening of his eyes, and a look of intelligence flitting across his countenance. It was as though a ray of mental light had darted into his soul, just as sometimes I have seen the close of a dark stormy day cheered by the gleams of the setting sun.

"Hurly!" The voice was very feeble; but it was the old familiar voice in the old affectionate tones I had so long missed. He moved his hand towards me, and I bent down and pressed my lips upon it.

"You know me, grandfather?"

He smiled very kindly, yet there was a look of perplexed trouble on his face. He raised his hand, and laid it on his forehead, as men do sometimes when trying to remember.

"I have been ill, I think, Hurly. Was it yesterday—yesterday?"

"Dear grandfather! you have been ill many months."

"Months! Many months!" Oh, how he started with astonishment and almost unbelief! "Many months, Hurly?" He endeavoured to rise as he repeated these words, and then fell back helplessly on his pillow. Then he with difficulty raised his attenuated hand and held it before him. "Many months!" he said again: "and with so much to do, so much to do, Hurly."

" Do not think of that now, dear grandfather ; time enough to think of that when you get well again." Was it wrong of me to say this, fearing as I did that he would never get well again— that the sudden requickening of his intellect for a brief space was the sure sign of his speedy departure ?

I do not know ; but I know that he was more faithful to himself than I was to him.

"I begin to understand it, Hurly," he whispered, mournfully ; "I shall never get well again." Then he laid his hand tremulously on mine. "Pray for me, my dear ; pray, pray for the poor miserable sinner, who has done the things he ought not to have done, and left undone what he ought to have done. Pray, my dear, pray !" And I knelt by his side.

"Thank you, Hurly," he said in broken tones, when I presently rose from my knees. "I see more clearly now—more clearly. ' God be merciful to me a sinner.' " He closed his eyes, and his lips moved ; but no sound escaped them. Presently his eyelids again rose. "Hurly, have I been dreaming, or has some one told me that my dear friend John Falconer is—is gone from this world ?"

"It is true, grandfather."

He sobbed sorrowfully. "And my son—my poor boy William ?"

I had not time to frame an answer. For some few minutes I had heard a sound of voices down-stairs, and recognised those of Betsy Miller and Jonathan, as in tones of remonstrance and rebuke. Now the voices were louder, and there was a shuffling on the stairs ; and I heard another voice, louder and more harsh than theirs. I knew the voice, and hastened to the chamber door.

"A pretty thing, indeed, to keep me away from my own father ! Stand back, I tell you," said the approaching visitor.

I closed the door behind me gently, and hastened to meet him.

"Hush, uncle William, hush ! My poor grandfather is dying ;"

and, as I said this, I laid my hand on the intruder's arm, and by persuasive force drew him into another room—an unused chamber. For a moment returning to Betsy and Jonathan, I told them of the change in the dying man; then I went back to William Bix.

He was in woeful plight—more shabby, I think, than on my first acquaintance with him ten years before. He was almost barefoot; his coat—an old drab surtout, dirty and weather-stained, hung loosely upon him in rags; his own natural hair, shaggy and untrimmed, fell down over his forehead; and his cheeks were hollow and haggard.

"Yes," he said, observing my horrified look, I suppose: "a nice reputable fellow I am to look at. A regular prodigal son, eh, Hurly?"

"You look as though you had been ill," I said.

"I have been ill—laid up three months in a parish poor-house with fever, and turned out to starve, or to beg, or to steal, as soon as the fever left me: but here I am, you see; and I want to know what all this is about the old man—they tell me he is very bad."

"Your father is dying," I said. "You will be glad to know he was speaking affectionately of you not ten minutes ago."

"Was he, Hurly? Was he—was he—was he? I must see him. I *will* see him."

I could not understand then, I do not care to decide now, whether this sudden passionate outburst was assumed or real. There is no doubt that William Bix had been very much weakened by the fever, which, as I afterwards learned, had laid hold upon him two or three months after I saw him at Fairmouth, and while he was wandering in the West of England, picking up a scanty living, if even that, by his so-called entertainment. Un-friended and unknown, he got into debt—so far as a close-fisted landlady would let him—at his temporary lodgings; and then, after disposing of his musical glasses, and the very clothes he had worn, he was summarily ejected, wrapped in a blanket, and consigned to the tender mercies of a workhouse; whence, when he was scarcely able to crawl, he was afterwards reclothed, after a fashion, and discharged, and had begged his way to London, utterly prostrated in bodily strength, and broken down in spirit by the bitter reflection that his hundred tricks had not saved him; and that, after all, perhaps honesty would have been the best policy. It may be, therefore, that his apparent remorse was genuine. But let it be understood that remorse is not penitence. It springs from a different source; it leads to a different result. There is a "godly sorrow" which "worketh repentance to salvation, not to be repented of:" and there is a sorrow—"the sorrow of the world," which "worketh death."

"You shall see him," I said, as soothingly as I could; "but not as you are." And so, without entering into further particulars, I presently procured him food, which he ate ravenously; and provided him with a suit of my own clothing, which he thankfully put on.

Meanwhile, I learned with satisfaction that my grandfather had subsided into a quiet sleep; and that Dr. Squills, who called while I was with William, had said that, though death was evidently near at hand, the patient might last through another day, perhaps two days.

"And so you are going to harbour that bad man under this roof, are you, Hurly?" said Betsy Miller, after I had fed and clothed the unwelcome guest, and was asking her to prepare a bedroom for him.

"What would you have me do?" I returned.

"You have read the story, Hurly—I did when I was a schoolgirl, and 'tis in the old spelling-book now—about the woodcutter and the frozen adder?"

"I remember it, Betsy."

"Why not profit by it, then, Hurly?"

"I cannot turn my uncle away from his father's house on my own responsibility," I said; "for, if my heart would let me do it, I have no power."

CHAPTER XLIV.

THE CLOSING SCENE OF LIFE, AND ANOTHER SCENE.

DR. SQUILLS'S prediction came to pass. My dear grand-father lived on to the second day, and then peacefully expired. During those two days my uncle William's conduct was decorous enough, though his presence was embarrassing. It is scarcely necessary to say that, after due preparation, he was introduced to the dying patient; but the little flickering of intelligence which I have described was fast departing, and it seemed doubtful whether the father recognised his son. At any rate, the interview was a silent one on both sides; and William did not enter the chamber a second time while breath was in the body of the dying man, but sat moodily silent, hour after hour, smoking tobacco and drinking much water, when he was not eating. By the way, this tobacco-smoking was an old habit of my uncle's, revived and indulged in, at this time, to an enormous excess, though he determinately abstained from strong drink. He had not broken his vow—so he told me on one of the rare occasions on which he opened his lips when we were together; and this was a good thing, surely.

It was on the second day, as foretold by Dr. Squills, and late in the afternoon, that Betsy Miller, who, with Jonathan, was then in attendance in the sick chamber, came hastily to me as I sat in the old office, and whispered, hoarsely—

REAPPEARANCE OF WILLIAM BIX.

"He is going—going fast, Hurly."

I rose and hastened up the broad stairs, calling in on William Bix as I went, and repeating the warning words, adding, "You will be with him at the last, will you not, uncle?"

The wretched man turned very pale, and seemed agitated. "I can't, Hurly; I can't. Don't ask me! I never saw anybody die. You go, and let me know when it is over."

I passed on. Had there been room in my mind then for anything beyond deep affliction and solemn awe, I should assuredly have thought William Bix to be a pitiful, conscience-smitten coward. But this came to me afterwards.

My poor grandfather! He lay quietly on his side, his eyes half closed, and breathing very, very feebly. A great change was even then passing over his countenance, which told too surely that, to use the expressive figures of Scripture, "the silver cord was loosed, the golden bowl broken, the pitcher broken at the fountain, the wheel broken at the cistern;" that "the spirit" was about to take its flight "to God, who gave it." Betsy Miller was standing by his head, and gently wiping the death-dew from her old master's forehead, her own cheeks bathed in tears; while Jonathan, with a grave countenance, held his finger lightly on the wrist of the dying man.

"The pulse has left off beating," he whispered.

"But there's a little breath yet," said Betsy, fondly. She would not give up all hope, even at the very last.

I knelt down, and placed my lips near my grandfather's ear, and asked could he hear me? Did he know me? Alas! there was no response. No sound less piercing than the archangel's last trumpet would ever again rouse that slumbering dust. One convulsive sob, one last expiring breath, and Anthony Bix was dead.

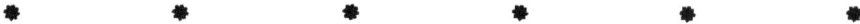

* * * * * *

thought it necessary, Mr. Fawley followed us out of the office, and locked the door behind him, putting the key in his pocket.

There was not a room in the house which did not undergo a similar severe scrutiny; and I was surprised at the knack, or professional instinct, of the lawyer while prosecuting this search, which seemed to direct him to the most apparently unlikely (and yet, perhaps, really the most likely) places in which the document we wanted might have been hidden. It added to the anxiety both of Mr. Fawley and myself, while conducting these proceedings, that we felt in some measure condemned to a wise and prudent silence, because my uncle kept closely by us, at first with a kind of stolid indifference, as though he had no personal interest in what was going on, but after a while with a kind of half-awakened suspicion. It added, also, to the natural pain I felt in being obliged to invade the secrecy of the late owner of the matters we brought to light, that he—my poor grandfather—lay unburied, and that, while we were thus busy, the undertaker's men arrived with the coffin, which was so soon to shut him out from our sight.

Presently we retired—Mr. Fawley and I—to the disused dining-room, while my uncle sat down moodily with his pipe in the kitchen.

"What do you think, sir?" I asked the lawyer.

"That there is no will in the house, Mr. Burley. I am almost certain of this."

"I have very little hope of finding one," I rejoined.

"It was impossible to say; it is yet impossible to be certain. Can you think of any one with whom your grandfather would have been likely to deposit such a document?"

"No one but Mr. Filby, sir."

"*I* have thought of Filby; but he hasn't got it. I saw him

this morning before I came here; and, more than this, he declares his belief that your grandfather had not made a will."

"What makes him think so, sir?"

"He had some conversation with your grandfather on this subject not a year ago, he says; and urged on him the duty of making some certain arrangement of his affairs—for your grandfather confessed to him then that he had never made a will—and the answer he got was to this effect: that he had nothing to bequeath, that he was scarcely solvent, and that therefore he must leave the matter, and you especially, Mr. Burley, in the hands of Providence. It is Filby's impression that your grandfather was so certain that Mr. Falconer, as being the younger man, would outlive him, and that he, Falconer, would take care of your interests, that he did not concern himself about the matter so much as a wise man ought to have done."

"We must give it up, then, Mr. Fawley?"

"I am afraid we must; but——"

What else he might have said I cannot tell. At that moment my uncle entered, pipe in hand; and I could see a curious alteration in his countenance. There was an eager glare about his eyes, and a latent sneer on his lips—latent, I mean, to any one who had not seen so much of William Bix as I had seen of Mr. Smithers at St. Judith's—which convinced me that his suspicion had ripened. Possibly the pipe had aided his reflections on what he had that day observed.

"I wish to ask a question or two," said he, addressing himself to neither of us two in particular, but glancing his dark eyes from one to the other.

"Yes, Bix—do you?" said the lawyer, coolly.

"I do. I want to know what you have been looking for."

"Papers. You saw what I did: I sealed up, as the late Mr. Falconer's representative, all papers connected with his estate."

"The—the what? the *late* Mr. Falconer! What! do you mean to say that that fellow is dead?" shouted my uncle, in excitement.

"Be respectful, if you please, Mr. Bix," said the lawyer. "It can do you no good, and it will do the dead man no harm, to call him a fellow; but I don't like it. In reply to your question—Mr. Falconer *is* dead."

"How is it you haven't told me of this, Hurly?" said William Bix, turning sharply upon me.

"I will answer for your nephew," interposed Mr. Fawley, preventing my reply. "I presume that he thought it could be no possible concern of yours whether Mr. Falconer were dead or living, except that, if he had been living, it was rather dangerous for you to make your appearance here. But that's past and gone; and it is enough for you to be told that Mr. Falconer has been some time dead."

"I don't know that it is enough, though," said my uncle; "and I don't understand this keeping things so uncommonly sly. I don't understand your prying about my father's house, either, in the way you have been doing to-day. Papers—were they? Are you sure it wasn't a *will* you were looking after, and haven't found?"

"You will know in good time whether or not there is a will, and to what extent you are interested in it. But there are other parties besides yourself who probably are thirsting for the same information; so I must recommend you patience."

"Patience, too!" he would have added more, I fancy; but William Bix was not at all sure of his ground, and he contented himself with a silent sneer.

"Yes, patience. We will not exercise it long. So long as your father remains unburied, I intend to exercise authority here. On the day of his funeral I will give account of my stewardship to those whom it may concern; but not until then."

This was said so calmly and quietly, and yet so firmly, that my uncle seemed afraid to reply. At any rate, he went away silently.

From that day, however, to the day of my grandfather's funeral, my uncle was evidently "on his watchtower," as Betsy Miller remarked; and nothing that passed in the house escaped his inquisitive eyes. His manner, too, became changed, from sullen submission to a kind of easy insolence, as one who felt that he had obtained unexpected power over those who were round about him. Meanwhile he did not neglect to avail himself of Mr. Fawley's warrant for a new suit of mourning, and all things conforming, which, in his case, included a complete refit, from top to toe. Obedient to his peremptory orders, these necessaries were all brought home on the third day after my grandfather's death, and two or three days prior to that of the funeral; and the first use to which he put them, or rather to which he put himself when encased in them, was to sally forth into the City, to call on a friend, as he said.

CHAPTER XLV.

THE DAY OF THE FUNERAL.

"MAN that is born of a woman is of few days, and full of trouble. He cometh forth like a flower, and is cut down: he fleeth also as a shadow, and continueth not."

There are few of my readers, perhaps, who have not, at some period of their lives, heard this solemn declaration pronounced over an open grave, and felt themselves, for a moment or two at least, subdued in heart and mind, not only by natural grief for the loss sustained, but by a conviction of the shortness of life and the certainty of their own approaching end—so subdued as to respond to the touching prayers that precede and follow : "O teach us to number our days, that we may apply our hearts unto wisdom." "O holy and most merciful Saviour, deliver us not into the bitter pains of eternal death."

My dear grandfather was buried in the City graveyard close by the old house in Silver Square ; and six mourners, more or less affected by the event, stood silently by while the mournful ceremony proceeded. My uncle William and I, Mr. Filby and Betsy Miller, Mr. Fawley and Mr. Millman—the last-named gentleman at my request, Mr. Filby as an old friend of the deceased, and Mr. Fawley as his and my professional adviser.

The funeral over, we returned to Silver Square.

There were others there waiting our return. Marmaduke Tozer was there ; so was his mother. They had been summoned to London by Mr. Fawley, and invited to attend the funeral. They obeyed the summons, but declined the invitation. They were in deep mourning, however, having put this on some months before for Mr. Falconer ; and they were attended by a satellite in the form of a solicitor, to see, I suppose, that all was fair and above-board, probably suspecting (but it was a needless suspicion) that Mr. Fawley was too deep in the secrets of his two late clients, and too favourably disposed towards myself, to be altogether trusted by them. Another person was present also, not altogether un-expected by Mr. Fawley, I think ; namely, a sharp practitioner, who arrived during our absence, and whom I afterwards dis-covered to be the "friend" whom my uncle had stepped out, in the full bloom of his new suit, to engage in his own interests. Of course the three lawyers behaved with extreme politeness to each other.

We all assembled in the large dining-room of which I have

several times spoken ; and never before had it seemed so gloomy and dismal as on this day. A large fire was lighted in the grate ; but a dozen fires would have brought no warmth to my chilled and desolate heart. One comfort, however, remained to me : my friend and employer, Mr. Millman, sat by my side and encouraged me.

I must briefly speak of the events of that afternoon as I remember them now : the particular details, except here and there, have escaped my memory. I think they were never distinctly impressed on it.

I believe that Mr. Fawley opened the conference by laying before us a statement he had prepared respecting my grandfather's circumstances prior to the death, and irrespective of the will, of Mr. Falconer. Thanks to the industry of the accountant who had so long been employed in the investigation of these affairs, Mr. Fawley had no difficulty in producing evidence sufficient to convince all present that Anthony Bix, down to the time mentioned, was an impoverished man. I do not think that this information surprised those who were not before in the secret. My uncle changed colour a little, but I am willing to attribute this to some remains of natural shame that he himself was the cause of his father's poverty. Apart from this, no symptoms of emotion were shown.

Next, as far as I recollect, Mr. Fawley unfolded the nature of Mr. Falconer's will. As I have already laid this before my readers, there is no need to repeat it. In Marmaduke and his mother, who very well knew its provisions, the re-explication of this will wrought no perceptible effect : they knew it all by heart, no doubt. With William Bix, however, the case was very different. The climax was approaching, and on the turn of the next revelation to be made depended whether he should be doomed to a life of miserable dependence or of shifty scheming, such as he

x

had so long led ; or whether, by a sudden and unexpected trick of fortune (as he would have said), he should be raised to wealth, which must have appeared to him then almost incalculable. He trembled exceedingly ; his countenance underwent continued mutations, now pallid as a corpse, then overspread with a feverish flush ; he could not retain his seat, but rose and paced the room once or twice, and drank a large tumbler full of water. But, notwithstanding all this agitation, I could detect that he followed Mr. Fawley with the keen eye of a gaze-hound ; that he understood and noted all that he heard. I saw him thrust his hand into his bosom, as though he would have stilled, if possible, the rapid beating of his heart ; and once or twice he nervously whispered something in the ear of his solicitor, which met with a responsive nod. Otherwise not a word was spoken until Mr. Fawley ceased ; and even then a deep silence followed, lasting a full minute—a short space of time, truly ; but to some of us there present it seemed long.

Presently my uncle's solicitor spoke. "All this," he said, "only indirectly or hypothetically concerns my client. The next and principal thing is the production of Anthony Bix's will."

"I have no such will to produce. I regret to say," continued Mr. Fawley, "that the will of Anthony Bix has not yet been found."

"You are probably certain, nevertheless," said the other lawyer—laying his hand on my uncle's arm, as though to impose silence—"that such a will is in existence ?"

"A very unnecessary question that, Mr.—Mr.—I beg your pardon ; your name has escaped me, but that is of no consequence —a very unnecessary question to put. How can I be certain that it is in existence when I cannot produce it ? Or, if I were——" He stopped short here.

"If you were, it would make no difference, you would say. Certainly not. And we are to assume, therefore, that there is no will?"

"You must assume what you please," said my lawyer.

"We do assume it, then, and are prepared to act on the assumption."

I shall not pursue the discussion, which was continued for some time, and in which Marmaduke's (or Mrs. Tozer's) lawyer took part. It is sufficient to say that, though Mr. Fawley zealously and generously supported my faded and obsolete interests, he could not resist the argument that, at present at least, my supposed claims could not be sustained. Then my uncle spoke.

"This house is mine, then, it seems, Hurly" (it was in my uncle's schedule); "and all that it contains belongs to Mr. Marmaduke Tozer, who probably does not remember in me his old friend Smithers, of St. Judith's."

Marmaduke started in wild amazement. For my own part I did not wonder at Marmaduke's lapse of memory or recognition; for, besides that my uncle's almost farcical disguise at St. Judith's was very complete, his recent illness had wrought a considerable change in him, and his full suit of fashionable mourning added to the metamorphosis.

"Well! and if it isn't, too!" exclaimed Marmaduke, for a moment forgetting the present momentous business. Meanwhile Mrs. Tozer had taken off her green spectacles—to see more clearly, I suppose—and her keen eyes rested on the countenance of William Bix. Despite the anxious care under which my depressed spirits were suffering, I had some curiosity as to whether the lady would recognise in the former teacher of her son the optician who had sold her the spectacles, or the Monsieur le Grand of whom she had purchased drugs. And she did at length remember him, but in neither of these characters. Hitherto she had scarcely spoken throughout the conference; but now she uttered sharply the question, "Is not your name Tindall?"

"Not at this present time, madam," returned my uncle, coolly; adding, "There was a time when I might have answered to that name."

"I thought so," rejoined Mrs. Tozer, almost as coolly, and replacing her spectacles.

"Setting aside this by-play," continued William Bix, turning to me, "as this house is mine, and the furniture Marmaduke Tozer's, you probably do not intend to remain long in possession. I need scarcely say to my old acquaintance, Mrs. Miller, that the sooner she can make it convenient——"

Both mouths were opened now, and prevented his continuing the sentence. Betsy spoke first. She would not demean herself by remaining another night beneath the roof of a house which owned *him* as its master. I said something to the same effect.

"Nay," he said, blandly, "I am in no such hurry as that. Take your own time, Hurly. I can wait; and I dare say Marmaduke will not take your bed from under you."

"We will save my client the possibility of such a danger, and your clients," turning to Mrs. Tozer's lawyer, "from the temptation to commit such an outrage," said Mr. Fawley. "Mr. Burley, you will consider yourself, for the present, as my guest."

"I must put in a prior claim," rejoined Mr. Millman.

And when we had retired from the room in which the above scene had transpired, Mr. Millman, said, "Come home with me, Hurly; and you too, Mrs. Betsy."

But here Mr. Filby interposed. "Mrs. Betsy Miller and I," he said, "have come to a pretty clear understanding that she is to be Betsy Filby as soon as she likes; and the sooner the better;

so, with many thanks for your generous kindness, sir, I have to propose——"

What Mr. Filby had to propose may be guessed by the result; but he did not complete his sentence, for Betsy struck in.

Striding up to me, and taking both my hands between her own, and with tears streaming down her kindly face, she said, "I'll never leave you, Hurly, till you tell me to go. I brought you up from a child, and never but once laid hands on you in anger; and we have always been like mother and son—you know we have; and I'll never leave you; I'll go where you go, and be your faithful servant, as I was your grandfather's."

"If you hadn't stopped me, Betsy," said the *old parchment-seller* (oh, Betsy, Betsy; they were your words, once upon a time!)—"if you hadn't stopped me, you would have heard that I had no thought of separating you from Hurly. There's room enough in my house for you both."

My readers can guess why I thankfully embraced this offer in preference to that of Mr. Millman. And so, presently, our meeting broke up.

CHAPTER XLVI.

A WEDDING—A NEW HOME—WILLIAM BIX IN A NEW ASPECT.

HAVE a vivid recollection of the marriage of my faithful friend Betsy Miller with her patiently-waiting admirer Mr. Filby. This event took place about a month after our departure from Silver Square. In the intervening time Betsy and I had taken up our abode in temporary lodgings near Somers Town, and not far from the green fields (made yellow by buttercups) in which some of the pleasantest out-of-door hours of my childhood had been spent, with Betsy as my "guide, philosopher, and friend." Alas for the mutability of all earthly things, however! the green fields had, by this time, become brick-fields—such of them as had not already been overspread with an intricate labyrinth of streets, and mimic squares, and blocks of houses, some already finished, others in course of erection. Fortunately it was winter-time during our short sojourn there, or pretty near it; so the changes did not seem so great and depressing.

From these semi, or demi-semi-country lodgings, we took flight one morning in a vehicle then called a "glass coach," which conveyed us to a neighbouring church, where I enacted (much to the merriment of an old wizen-faced pew-opener) the part of *father* to the mature bride.

We never returned to our lodgings. The wedding-day was spent very quietly in Mr. Filby's house in Fetter Lane (some pleasant allusion being made, in the course of the day, to newly-forged fetters); and that house was thenceforward, for six years, my home.

There never was a more comfortable elderly couple, I think, than Mr. and Mrs. Filby. They had no pressing cares; for he had well feathered his nest, and she did not marry altogether portionless. It is astonishing how savings may accumulate when there is no inclination to spend. I believe that Betsy's wages as my grandfather's housekeeper were but moderate in yearly amount; but in the many years of her servitude, the aggregate accumulation of her savings (which she had put out to safe interest and compound interest) was not much less than two hundred pounds.

Money, however, does not produce domestic happiness, though easy circumstances, which include money, tend to promote it. Apart from this, the "old parchment-seller" and his spouse were well suited to each other. They had kindred tastes, and, though these tastes did not range over a great variety of objects (I may say this without disparaging the memory of these dear friends, who have long since been dead), they were not less contented on this account.

Nor were they the less happy that true Christian piety formed the basis of their real though sober affection for each other. I have heretofore spoken of my old nurse as conscientious in her religious duties, such as she understood them to be ; but, on the other hand, as being much in the dark respecting the true nature and design of the gospel. A change, however, had gradually passed upon her, very pleasing to witness, and this change had been ripened by the sorrows of the past months; for those sorrows drove her to Him who says—" Come unto me, all ye that labour and are heavy laden, and I will give you rest:"—and in thus going to Christ she found even more than she sought, while she lost what was worth the losing—even her self-dependence, and the last remnants of pharisaical pride. As to Mr. Filby, respecting whose religious character I have heretofore been silent, I found, on better acquaintance, reason to believe that, with all his peculiarities, he was a humble and devout Christian.

One thing in which these good friends of mine cordially agreed, was their kindness towards, and their sympathy with me, rendered the more cordial on the part of Mr. Filby by the conviction that he had, for a little while, wronged me in his thoughts; and the more intense on both their parts on account of the disappointment of my hopes, and also because of one particular instance of injustice (as they esteemed it) which I had suffered at the hands of Mrs. Tozer and her son.

It will be remembered that, when my grandfather received an order on Mr. Falconer's London banker for five hundred pounds, to be applied to my business training, he put it away safely in a cash-box, deferring to some future time the consideration of how it should be used. Unfortunately, my grandfather's habit of procrastination continued to grow upon him with increasing age; and, as the money was really never wanted for the specific purpose mentioned, it had lapsed, in some way or other, into Mr. Falconer's personal estate, which was bequeathed to Marmaduke, and the order, from some peculiarity in its wording, I believe, was of no use. So Mr. Fawley told me, after taking counsel's opinion.

"It is a hard case, Hurly," he said: "but, unless we can work upon their sense of justice and moral right, Marmaduke (and his mother as his legal guardian) must have the money." Acting on my behalf, therefore, he made a proposal that the five hundred pounds should be given to me.

I will do Marmaduke the justice to say that he was, at that time, willing enough to accede to the proposal; but Mrs. Tozer was hard as adamant.

"Not five hundred farthings of it—not five farthings of it, with my consent," she said, fiercely. And the end of it was, that I did not obtain five farthings of Mr. Falconer's intended generous bounty.

As may naturally be supposed, very little intercourse thereafter subsisted between the fortunate legatees and myself, while my interest in the old house of my childhood gradually died away. I was aware, however, of a great sale of some part of the Silver property, and heard that, with his share of the proceeds, Marmaduke (when he came of age) purchased an estate in Kent, and set up for a country gentleman. This was the last I heard of him for some time, until other events, of which I shall presently speak, brought us once more into contact.

As to my uncle, or (as I shall henceforth call him) William Bix, I had no temptation nor desire to renew acquaintance with him under his new and improved circumstances; but it was impossible to avoid hearing of him. Just about the time when the sudden change in his fortunes took place, sprang up one of those extraordinary manias for wild speculations in commerce, which have upset for the time the sobriety of the whole nation, and have brought about such strange revolutions in the fortunes and histories of thousands of individuals and families. It is not my intention to enter into the particulars of these speculations, nor to expose the rottenness of the system on which they were based; for mine is but a humble history of private adventures and experiences. It comes within the scope of these memoirs, however, to record that the name of William Bix began, in the course of two or three years, to appear very prominently in connexion with more than one company whose professed object was to bestow immense and previously unheard-of benefits on society at large. In particular, there was one association of which he was announced, in multitudes of florid advertisements, as being the resident director, and the offices of which were in Silver Square.

I do not know whether any person ever thought it worth his while to pry very deeply into the antecedents of the man who thus prominently thrust himself before the eyes of the public. I am inclined to think, however, that no very close inquiries were made. Wealth, or the repute of wealth, like charity, "covereth a multitude of sins"—in great mercantile cities especially—and it was enough to know that William Bix had this reputation. I remember being once in a City coffee-room, taking my five o'clock cup of tea, when something like the following dialogue passed, in the next box to mine, between two gentlemen whom I knew as belonging to the upper class of City men, who were dining (as I had reason to know through more than one of my senses) off a haunch of venison :—

"Who is this William Bix, of whom we hear and see so much?"

asked one of the venison eaters, laying down the morning paper in which, as I suppose, he had caught a glimpse of the name.

"Oh, don't you know? Why, he is *un nouveau riche,* a new man, but warm—warm," was the reply.

"Where does he spring from?"

"Who knows? We don't care so much where a man springs from as where he springs to. But I believe I have heard something about him, too. He is the son of an old fellow who did agency work for the owner of the Silver estate, and who came in for most of the property when the owner died. The son has got it now."

"He *is* the same man of whom I have heard some rather queer stories, then. Not much good in him, I should think."

"Oh, none the worse for having had a little rough experience. All the more likely to get on now that he has the chance. A sharp, clever fellow, I understand; and great confidence is placed in him. Not a better name in all London now for this sort of thing. Shares looking up in all the companies he is connected with. Sure to double his fortune in no time."

And then they went on eating their venison in silence.

You will believe me, reader, that it was through no idle, prying curiosity that I overheard the above dialogue. I could scarcely help hearing it; the speakers spoke so audibly, and I sat so near.

It was a singular coincidence that, on the very next day after William Bix's name had thus been mentioned in my hearing, I was passing near to the Stock Exchange, and suddenly came upon the man himself. The recognition was instant and mutual, though I might have been pardoned if I had not recognised, in the rotund, clean-looking, extravagantly-clad, and bejewelled exquisite, who looked like a foreign count at least, the miserable wretch who, two or three years before, sneaked into Silver Square.

IN A CITY COFFEE-ROOM.

I should have passed him without word or sign—for what had I in common with him?—but he prevented me.

"I am glad to have met you, Hurly," said he, in his old way of condescending familiarity, to which I had been accustomed at St. Judith's. "Why don't you call in upon me sometimes?"

"There is no reason why I should, sir," I said, rather haughtily, perhaps.

"Yes, there is," he rejoined, with an affectation of good-humour. "I am your nearest relative—that's one reason; and another is, I might put something in your way worth having. I have been going to look you up for some months past; but I haven't had time, exactly."

"I am obliged to you," I replied; "but I cannot see that any good can possibly arise from our renewing our old acquaintance; and, as I am in a hurry just now——"

He laid his hand on my shoulder, and looked steadily in my face. There was a dark scowl upon his countenance, but it passed away.

"There are not many men who would speak to William Bix now-a-days in that tone and manner, Hurly," he said, in a low and guarded voice; "but I suppose you have not forgiven me yet for having the good luck to be the son of my father. That's silly, my dear Hurly."

"You cannot forget that there are——"

"That there are other reasons for your giving me the cold shoulder," said he, laughing, and thus filling up in his own way the sentence I had hesitated to complete. "Such as my aliases and the naughty tricks I played when I was under the necessity of fighting my way through the world somehow. Pho! all that is over; and who cares to remember such old stories against a fellow who has money, and can make others as well as himself rich?"

I made no reply; for to what purpose would it have been if I had answered him?

He went on in a more serious fashion. "Look you, Hurly: you say you are in a hurry; so am I. I have wasted too much time already, when every moment is worth gold to me. But I'll tell you why you ought to come and see me. My daughter, your cousin Sophy—ah! I thought I should make you start—is living with me in Silver Square. You had a kindness for her once, and she has still for you—the more so for her being now aware of your relationship. She is in trouble, and—strange as it may seem to you—so am I, on her account. You may perhaps help her out of it; so now do as you please; come and see us this evening, or leave us alone. Good-bye." Saying this, William Bix released me, and pushed his way into the Exchange.

CHAPTER XLVII.

THE OLD HOME—REVELATIONS—COUSIN SOPHY.

WILLIAM BIX had held out to me the only inducement which could have drawn me to his house. He had said truly that I had a kindness for Sophy once; and I might have added that I had a kindly, affectionate, cousinly interest in her still. In the years which had transpired since we last saw each other I had often thought of the gamekeeper's darling little granddaughter, and, especially of late, had wondered how she had been affected by the changes which had taken place. And so she was in London, and in trouble; poor child! Yes, I would do battle with my repugnance towards her father—I would go and see my cousin.

I took my way from Gracechurch Street, by the old familiar route, and found myself in Silver Square for the first time since it ceased to be my home. No perceptible alteration had taken place in the square. I could see, by the brass plates on the doors as I passed, that many of the houses had the same tenants; and the enclosure in the centre looked much as it did in other days, so that I could almost fancy that my remembrances dated back but a day. On arriving at the former mansion of Sir Miles, however, the illusion was dispelled. Renovating builders had been at work; compost and paint, and Corinthian pillars and plate-glass, had transformed the sombre old-fashioned house into a gaudy mansion. But the improvements were no improvements to me; they did not seem to fit nicely. It was like putting an ancient and comfortable-looking matron into the costume of a modern belle.

I knocked at the door, and it was opened to me by a tall porter in brilliant livery; and I was shown into the old office, which was now fitted up as a private study—so I was given to understand it was called—the porter saying, when I gave my name, that Mr. Bix was expecting me, and would see me in his study. In passing through the hall, I perceived that its old appurtenances had disappeared, and that on the door of the former dining-room was inscribed, in gold letters, the words "Board Room." In fact, I discovered afterwards that all the rooms on the ground-floor of the house were used as offices.

William Bix was seated in his richly-furnished study. "I felt sure you would come, Hurly," said he, offering me his hand, which I could not very well refuse to take; "and, as I should like a few words with you before you see Sophy, I told the porter to show you in here. It isn't everybody I admit into this room; but you are privileged. By the way, we meet as friends, I hope?"

"Not as enemies. I have no personal enmity against you, Mr. Bix," I said.

"That's well: we may come to friendship sooner or later."

I hoped not; but I did not say so.

"And we meet on terms of mutual confidence?" he continued.

"In anything relating to my cousin Sophy," I said, quickly. "You told me of her being in trouble, and that perhaps I could help her out of it."

"True; but first of all I must explain. You wonder at her being here at all; don't you, Hurly?"

I told him no, I did not very much wonder. I had heard of the history of Sophy's mother from old Mrs. Storks, and had guessed at his relation to Sophy before he had virtually acknowledged it to me. Also, that I had always given him credit for affection towards the child; and that therefore it was natural that he should come forward and acknowledge her when he became rich. All this and more I said, in other words.

"I am obliged to you for having done me so much justice," said William Bix; "and it is no more than justice. I did love the child, as I do now, more than ever; and I risked discovery again and again to catch only a sight of her pretty face. I went rather too far, though, when I caught her up in my arms that day in the park; and I owe you something, Hurly, that you never betrayed me. But the child always haunted me; and I would have gone through fire and water to keep her from harm; and so I will now." He said this very fiercely, I thought; and I turned off the subject by asking how he managed to gain possession of Sophy.

"Oh," he replied, with a bright laugh, "in the old-fashioned romantic style. You have read stories, I dare say, of fathers disappearing, and being set down as dead, leaving a child or two to the tender mercies of the world; and then suddenly making their appearance in very grand style, in coaches and four, with silver-laced footmen, and all the rest of it. Well, I copied all this nonsense, went down to the gamekeeper's cottage like a lord,

told a good story for myself, scattered money about pretty pro-
fusely, dazzled the old grandmother, became reconciled, and
whisked off the young damsel in a twinkling, before she knew
whether to laugh or to cry."

"And poor Sophy is unhappy now, I suppose, at having exchanged the freedom of her country life for the restrictions of her
new and more splendid home? And she pines for the kindly
old faces which used to smile upon her?"

"You are mistaken, Hurly; I know you are mistaken. If I
thought as you do, I would—but it is not so. Sophy is too wise
and too old not to see the advantages of her present position.
She isn't a mere girl now, as she was when you last saw her. She
is a woman, and has got woman's thoughts in her mind, and
woman's feelings in her heart. You and I little know what
those thoughts and feelings are; but we can guess at them,
Hurly." William Bix spoke in a quick, hurried manner in
saying this; and then he added more deliberately—

"No, Sophy knows that she is well off, and has a true female
instinct for money and money's worth; but she is in trouble
nevertheless. Shall I tell you, in one word, what ails her?"

"In one word?"

"Yes; the word is Marmaduke."

I guessed as much. I remembered those old days of child-
courtship in the park; and I had never forgotten Marmaduke's
later " If."

"Yes," continued William Bix; "Marmaduke is trifling with
her affections, and she is beginning to suspect it."

I was sorry to hear it, I said; but I did not see in what way I
could help my cousin.

"You can do something that I cannot do," he replied. "Look
you, Hurly," he went on: " I never liked Marmaduke, and I knew
more about him as a boy than ever you did. I did not like him;

he came of a bad stock; and, little as you may think it—knowing me to be what I was, or what I am, if you like—I would have put a stop to his baby-courtship if I could. But I couldn't help it. How could I, when I could not show myself openly? I did what I could on that one occasion which you may remember, when I called upon her as Monsieur le Grand, in putting Marmaduke's mother up to the goings on at the gamekeeper's cottage; but that did no good, so I was obliged to let things take their course. Well, they did take their course—their natural course, I suppose—as you know very well. And, by-and-by, when I found out that Marmaduke was likely to be old Falconer's heir, I made up my mind not to interfere. But yet, I tell you honestly, I would rather have had Sophy married to a country carpenter than to Frank Tozer's son."

William Bix said this so earnestly, and with such apparent sincerity, that I could not help believing him; but it was inexplicable to me. I could only imagine that the one bright speck of parental love in his heart redeemed it from the utter darkness of its habitual depravity.

"You have wondered, I dare say," continued William Bix, "how it was I overcame my habit of drunkenness. I told you once that I made the effort from motives of self-interest. This was true, but not the whole truth. I thought of Sophy, and her innocence, and pictured to myself what she would feel and think if it should ever come to her knowledge that her father lived and died a drunkard. It was this reflection that confirmed me in my resolution that, do what else I might, I would not inflict this burning shame and disgrace upon my daughter."

I could not but believe him: he was so earnest.

"You see now, Hurly," he went on, more deliberately, "that, whatever I may be to all the world besides, I am capable of making sacrifices for my child; and when I saw, as I easily did when I brought Sophy home, that matters had gone so far that it would be a heart-breaking affair if Marmaduke were lost to her, I determined that the poor child should have her fancy; for, after all, there was nothing that *I* could positively object to in the young fellow; and—well, to tell the truth, his money *was* no objection. I can read in your face that's what you are thinking of, Hurly.'"

I was thinking so—was thinking, too, that, after all, there was a full pound of the dross of self-interest to the single grain of pure love for which I had just given the incomprehensible man credit. I thought that, if Marmaduke's expected prize in the chances of Mr. Falconer's will had turned up a blank, William Bix probably might not have been so keenly alive to Sophy's disappointed hopes—supposing that they were to be disappointed.

Thinking this, I merely said, " You said that I could help Sophy Tindall out of her trouble, sir."

"Sophy Bix, Hurly. Let the Tindall be forgotten," he said, hastily; adding, " Yes, you can do something which I cannot very well do. You can see Marmaduke. He knows that you know what has passed between himself and your cousin, and you may bring him to an explanation. I cannot do it."

I did not ask him why. There was no need to ask it, for I knew. It is one of the common, ordinary, worldly disadvantages of crooked courses, that the man who adopts them has no title to expect ingenuous straightforwardness from others. People (in general, perhaps) think that honest, open-hearted, sincere, and unsuspecting men are more liable to double-dealing and deception than rogues. I believe this to be a great mistake, and that it is the deceitful man who is the oftenest deceived—the cheat who is the oftenest cheated. On the other hand, the very uprightness and integrity of a good man are his best preservatives.

I did not, therefore, ask William Bix why he thought I could better succeed than himself in obtaining an explanation of Marmaduke's intentions; but I objected that my intercourse with Marmaduke had long ceased, and that I did not wish to renew it; also that I could not, unless the cause was very urgent, leave London at that time, even for a day.

"There is no need for your leaving London," he replied. "Marmaduke is in London—that is to say, he is now visiting at Blackheath. You remember the Browns at St. Judith's, with those ridiculous names? Well, he is there. By the way, Marmaduke's mother is dead—she died three months ago—and he is come to London to shake off the blues, he says; so you won't have to go out of town to see him. In fact, you shall see him here; for of course we keep up our connexion, and are the best friends in the world."

"And yet you cannot trust him?"

"Not a bit of it—no more than he trusts me," said William Bix. "You look horrified; but when you have seen as much of the world as I have, Hurly, you will come round to my way of thinking, that our very best friends are the last people in the world to be trusted."

"That depends upon whom we bestow friendship, I should think," I said.

"Possibly; but that's nothing to the purpose. I can trust you, at all events; and you will oblige me, I know. There will be an evening party here to-morrow night. Come, and you will meet Marmaduke, and you can easily find or make an opportunity of speaking to him alone. And now let us go to your cousin; you will find her, I flatter myself, very much improved since you last saw her, a wild little woodland bird on the Kentish downs." Saying this, my uncle (I will once more give him this title) rose, opened the door, and motioned me up the broad staircase.

Nothing I had hitherto experienced or observed in the world had more surprised me than the apparent ease with which William

Bix had cast off the slough of his former vagabondism, and adapted himself to his wonderfully improved fortunes : or rather had emerged from the chrysalis state in which I had formerly known him, into his present butterfly existence. I had to see more of this on the following day; but in the interview I had just held with him there was an impressiveness of manner and a sort of assumed superiority which would have imposed, I think, on other and wiser men than myself. It was acted, no doubt; but it was such capital acting that it seemed real.

So, when, after conducting me to the habitable part of his house, he gently tapped at a particular door, and waited till a soft voice within gave permission to enter, and when he presently introduced me to my cousin, and said, with a quiet and almost melancholy smile, "You have much to tell one another, and I should only be in your way," I almost forgot, for the time, what William Bix had been, what, in his heart, he still was, and could think of him for a minute or two only as a well-bred gentleman. And yet I knew that he was acting a part he had previously planned.

In a moment or two he was gone ; and after the first greeting with my cousin I looked round me. I was in a room on the second floor of the old mansion which had once been a bed-chamber; and in the early years of my remembrance, like the greater number of rooms in the house, it was unused. I had a very clear remembrance of its former gloomy state—the dark, moth-eaten hangings, the massive bed-pillars and heavy dressing-table, and large wardrobe of solid mahogany, but black with age. All was changed now. The apartment had become a lady's bower. Gay paper covered the walls, a brilliant carpet the floor; delicate silk curtains festooned the window; a dainty couch and pleasant lounging chairs, softly cushioned; a handsome table of some exquisitely beautiful foreign wood, inlaid with mother-ofpearl; a bookcase filled with gorgeously-bound volumes, glittering in purple, crimson, and gold; a small piano, bearing the name of one of the most fashionable London makers; a pretty cabinet, a delicate work-table—all these and similar tokens proved that no expense had been spared to please and dazzle the occupant of that fairy-like retreat; for this was Sophy's own room.

Nor had money been grudged in preparing my cousin to be the queen of this small domain. I learned, presently, from her own lips, that on her first coming to London her father provided her with private teachers; and as a good foundation had already been laid in her education, I have no doubt she would have passed muster in a crowd. Moreover, she had her own maid, and her own carriage also, so she told me; and her own way in everything, she added, with a melancholy smile, as though that was not much to be proud of.

In spite of all this, Sophy was not spoiled. I think she was one of those whom it is very difficult to spoil. She was altered no doubt. When I last had seen her, she was a girl; now she was a woman, or nearly approaching womanhood; but this was the greatest difference I could detect in her, excepting (and it was a great exception) that in her lowlier state of childhood she was without care, joyous and free, and that now she was anxious and troubled. She tried to restrain her tears when we talked of her grandparents, and their pretty cottage, and the park, and the first time we met; but the attempt was vain. I tried to comfort her, by speaking of her present superior position; but she only sighed mournfully. She ought to be very happy, she acknowledged; at any rate, she ought to be grateful; and she hoped she was not ungrateful; for her father, whatever he had been to others (I knew what she meant by others—she was thinking of her mother), was kind and indulgent to her. But—and here she stopped short in her confessions—"let us speak of something else, Hurly," she said.

And so we spoke of something else; she showed me her books, and we talked about her favourite authors; she opened her portfolios of drawings, and I praised them, not flatteringly either; for she had been an apt pupil; she sat down, at my entreaty, to her piano, and she played some simple melodies with taste, and sang very sweetly.

"You will come and see me again, Hurly; will you not?" she said, when I rose to leave. "I don't mean to-morrow night, when there is to be a grand party, and you say you have promised to come; but when we can have a little quiet together, as we have had this evening. And you will think as kindly as you can of my father; for he is very good to me." And so we parted.

———

CHAPTER XLVIII.

AN EVENING PARTY AT SILVER SQUARE.

WITH what mingled feelings of repugnance and awakened interest I bent my steps, on the following evening, to Silver Square, would be so difficult to explain that I shall not attempt an explanation. It was not late when I arrived, but I found the old mansion lit up with great splendour; and, comparatively early as it was, several carriages had already set down their freights of visitors; and, as I drew near to the door, another and another drove up, so that, for a minute or two, I was held back from seeking admittance. At length, however, there was a slight lull in the fierce attacks made upon the heavy door-knocker, and I ventured up the broad stone steps. In a few moments I had achieved an entrance, and was ushered into the suite of rooms on the first floor, which, in the days of my earlier remembrance, were so deserted and desolate.

The rooms were already tolerably crowded with guests; but the host found time presently to approach me and snatch my hand.

"Glad to see you, Hurly. Was sure you would come," he said, hurriedly. "You won't mind my distributing my attentions principally among these people; must do the polite, you know," he whispered in my ear. "There's money to be made by it; you understand?"

I told him I did understand; and I think I did.

"All hollow-hollow-hollow," said he; "but the world itself, they say, is hollow; and why shouldn't the people on it be hollow too? By the way, your cousin is expecting you; let me lead you to her."

And so, through files of people whom I had never before seen, and past groups of others who were eagerly talking together, but none of whom I knew, William Bix led me quickly on from one room to another; but, rapidly as we went, the fortunate owner found time to say, "Cost a deal of money, all this frippery, Hurly. New carpets, new furniture, new everything. That old harridan (you know who I mean) wouldn't let Marmaduke leave a single stick nor straw behind; sold everything she could lay her hands on; and Marmaduke—ah, I haven't forgotten how he served you about that five hundred pounds—a dirty trick that; but we won't say a word more about it. He is my dear friend, you know."

"Is he here yet?" I asked.

"No, I think not. He comes late to these parties; does not want to see too much of me, nor of Sophy either; but he'll be sure to be here presently. I have laid a bait for him; he likes money as well as ever he did, and—but here we are, and there is Sophy. I will leave you with her for the present, Hurly."

If it had not been for Sophy, and the hope of being of some

little use to her, I think I should have turned my back upon the place, and fled at once to my quiet retreat in Fetter Lane. It seemed as though it were accursed. Hollow! yes, William Bix had spoken truth for once when he said that all was hollow. And was not he the most hollow of all?

And of what use could I be to my cousin? She was in trouble, no doubt. She had almost acknowledged, on the previous evening, that she was not happy; and, without acknowledgment, it was easy enough to see this. But was it in my poor feeble power to make her happy? I seriously questioned, indeed, whether her sorrow arose from the source to which her father attributed it. She might have a lingering attachment to her boy-lover; that was natural enough. But I fancied that her dissatisfaction had a deeper spring than the disappointment of her girlish day-dreams; that she distrusted her father, in spite of the gloss he had put upon his former base desertion and neglect; that she half loathed the false glare by which she was surrounded; and that she longed to return (which, alas! she never could do) to the happier days and scenes of her inexperienced childhood. She had increased in knowledge, and she had increased in sorrow. What help, then, could I give her?

These thoughts had passed through my mind again and again during the day as I sat at my desk in Gracechurch Street; and they came into it now with redoubled force. But it was too late to draw back.

"It is very good of you to come and keep me in countenance, Hurly," said Sophy, as she half rose from a silken couch, in the last room of the suite, and beckoned me to her side. "My father likes to have me here at his grand parties; he says I am an attraction," she added, with a quiet little laugh; "but I would rather be alone in my own room up-stairs. It is all so strange to me."

"Not more strange to you than it is to me, Sophy," I said; "nor so strange; for this is the first time in my life that I have ever mingled in such a crowd. And I have no doubt that your father is right. I do not wonder that he likes to see you here."

"You are not to flatter me," replied Sophy, laying her hand on my arm, and looking almost beseechingly in my face. "I have flattery enough paid me by the bold and disagreeable people my father gets together here. He says he is obliged to invite them. I do not understand it; but, if I had so much money as they say he has, and as he must have, for keeping up all these grand appearances, I would have pleasanter company, or none at all."

"Your father has extensive connexions in the City, and among men who are so busy in making money, that they have no time to spare for cultivating the graces of society, I suppose. By the way, I did not see any ladies as I passed through the larger drawing-rooms. They are not excluded from your parties, I hope?"

"Not entirely, Hurly. You will see presently that I have my own special parliament around me. The members are not arrived yet; but the seats are ready for them, you see, and they will soon be here." Sophy said this with assumed gaiety, as she pointed to several couches ranged round the room. "You must know," continued my cousin, "that this room is what my father calls the ladies' cabin, and no gentleman is admitted to it except by special permission, or unless introduced by a lady. That's why it was unoccupied, all but by poor little me, when you came in."

I felt grateful to William Bix for this sign of precaution, and asked my cousin a question or two respecting the quality and position of the female friends who were thus admitted to her confidence.

"They are a very good sort of people," she answered without hesitation. "They are the wives and daughters of some of my father's City friends. One of them is Mrs. L——, the wife of an alderman, and she has three daughters; another of them is the sister of a great stockbroker, as I believe he is called. They are all proper sort of persons, Hurly, but they seem to me to be very ignorant and vulgar; but then, that is because I am so ignorant myself, and so unaccustomed to society, my father tells me. I see," my cousin added, smiling, "that you do not understand, so well as I do even, the nature of these parties. I should have thought my father would have explained them to you better than I can do. You see my father has a great deal of business to transact, in a variety of ways; and he says that the days are not long enough to do half what he wants to do, so he has these parties; and the gentlemen come early, some of them to buy and sell, and bargain and speculate, and, I am afraid, to gamble, only they don't call it gambling," said Sophy, lowering her voice; "and, as my father tells me, thousands, and thousands, and thousands of pounds have changed hands in those outer rooms of an evening, and yet not a single sovereign to be seen," she added, with a perplexed look.

"Yes, I can partly understand that, Sophy," said I. "Your father" (I could not, in all this dialogue, speak of William Bix as my uncle)—"your father has found out, or improved upon a method of combining business with recreation; and the ladies do not make their appearance, I suppose, till all business is over. A very wise precaution on their part, I should think."

At this moment there was a more than usual stir in the outer rooms; and the next moment came sailing into the ladies' retreat a full-faced, smiling, and rather ponderous dame, accompanied by two younger and thinner ladies, in very fine evening costume and superabundant head-dresses. These ladies, after saluting poor Sophy very affectionately, were introduced to me as Mrs. L—— and the two Misses L—— (of course, the alderman's wife and two of his daughters); and I was introduced to them as Sophy's cousin. But, as they were not acquainted with Sophy's cousin, and did not seem disposed to honour the unknown stranger with more than a condescending and rather formal curtsy, I made my escape, and took a slight tour of inspection through the more crowded drawing-rooms.

There seemed to be a good deal of mysterious business still going on: at least there was confusion enough. Many of the guests were congregated in little clusters, with heads very close together, and in earnest confabulation. Others were seated on sofas, in twos and threes, with memorandum-books in hand comparing notes, as it seemed. Others paced the rooms with nervous steps, solitary and, of course, silent, casting sharp glances on their fellow-guests as they passed them. And others were linked arm-in-arm in private and confidential intercourse. Among these, I presently singled out the two City magnates who the day before had discussed the character and antecedents of William Bix in the coffee-room; and presently, just as I passed, ambled up to them William Bix himself, who, taking by the button him who had pronounced on him the eulogium of being "warm, warm," drew him aside and whispered in his ear. Seeing this, I passed on.

There were, as far as I could see, no servants present to assist in or to interrupt the proceedings of the guests, or to serve as spies or eavesdroppers; but there was a novel—or what appeared to me then to be a novel—arrangement, due, as I fancied, to the fertile contrivance of William Bix, for ministering to the appetite of the guests. This was a long semicircular table at one end of the ante-room, very much like the counter of a railroad refreshment-room of the present day, laden with various kinds of light viands, sweetmeats, decanters of various kinds of choice wines—so I judged from the labels with which they were decorated—and a large array of porcelain plates, wine-glasses, and tumblers. No servant was in attendance even here; the guests perfectly understanding that they were expected to help themselves *ad libitum*, both with regard to time and quantity.

Several gentlemen, indeed, were already doing this when I drew near, and among these I saw Marmaduke Tozer and our old schoolfellow Quercus Brown, who had apparently but just entered.

Not caring at that moment to make myself visible to Marmaduke, I was about to retire, when a hand was laid on my arm, and William Bix led me forward, and brought me face to face with the two young men.

"I need not introduce you to each other," he said, as Marmaduke stared at me with unfeigned astonishment; "but I am glad," he added, "to be the means of bringing old friends together again. Mr. Brown, you too remember my young relative. Or has time wrought such changes that you fail to recognise him?"

Quercus gave me his hand, pleasantly enough, remarking, with a hidden meaning, I thought, that time had brought about marvellous changes in some quarters, certainly; but he remembered George Burley, or Hurly-burly, as I was called at school, well enough, and was very glad to see me.

William Bix was quick to understand the sneer with which young Brown accompanied his first words; and he answered, with admirable composure, that time's changes had been very welcome to him, at any rate; and that there was certainly a slight difference between being usher in a boarding-school and the owner of an establishment like that in which Quercus was now a guest. Thus turning the tables upon the sneerer, the host drew Marmaduke aside, and made some communication to him which, as I could see, gave him some internal satisfaction. Thus left a moment or two together,

Quercus turned to me, and, taking my arm, walked a few paces away with me.

"He had me there, eh, Hurly?" he said, laughing.

"How?"

"Why, about time's changes, and his having been an usher. He is a queer fellow, this uncle of yours; he is your uncle, isn't he? Marmaduke says he is."

"Yes, he is."

"You were precious sly about it down at St. Judith's though. You didn't let any of us know it there. I suppose you were ashamed of your relationship, eh? But circumstances alter cases."

I might have told Brown that I was never more ashamed of my relationship to William Bix than at that present moment of speaking; but I restrained myself, and said only that there were sufficient reasons for my silence at St. Judith's.

"I dare say there were," said he; "and it is no business of mine, at all events. But what I admire in Bix is that he doesn't now try to hide from all the world what he has been; in fact, he tells such strange and incredible stories of his former life that nobody believes him."

I afterwards learned that this was the case; and I am inclined to think that the very immunity which seemed to shield William Bix's character from inconvenient and damaging inquiries arose from the apparent frankness and candour with which he spoke of his former low and disreputable condition. If he had set himself up as an immaculate personage, he would have laid himself open to continued risks of awkward discoveries and mortification, and loss of confidence; but what could be said of or to a man who was always ready to say worse things of himself than others could bring against him?

My short conversation with Quercus Brown was interrupted by

the return of our host and Marmaduke—the latter of whom, with a show of cordiality at least, offered me his hand.

" Bix has been telling me how stupid it is that you and I should fight shy of one another, Hurly; and I am sure I don't want to do so. It wasn't my fault, you know, that you didn't get any of old Falconer's money, was it ?"

I told him that I didn't suppose it was; and that, as to my disappointment, I had long since become reconciled to it. Also, that I was pleased—in a certain limited sense—to meet him again on terms of friendship, though it was not likely that, moving as we did in different spheres, we should often come in contact with each other.

I fancied it was a relief to Marmaduke to hear me say this; and probably this candid declaration of mine determined him to give me no ground of complaint for that night at least. At any rate, he made no attempt to part company with me; and, mindful of the unpleasant but not dishonourable task which had been thrust upon me, I gave myself up for the next hour to his society.

He was glad, I believe, to have a new listener to his rather boastful accounts of his estate in Kent, and of his future intentions. It appeared to me as though he were bitten with the prevailing mania for amassing large gains in the smallest possible space of time; for he talked widely of what he intended to do shortly. The house on his estate was old and inconvenient; he intended shortly to have it pulled down, and had already consulted an architect about the plan for a new mansion. There was also a neighbouring farm which lay convenient for making his estate nice and compact, and this farm he intended to buy as soon as he could afford it. It was to be had for five thousand pounds, more or less, and he expected soon to have that balance in his bank, at all events. Then he intended to lay down some two or three hundred acres in a park, and stock it with deer, and plant it with ornamental trees ; but this was for after-consideration, when his new house was built.

"It will cost a good deal of money, Marmaduke ; I mean, all this which you have been planning."

"Oh, nothing, nothing," he said, with a contemptuous wave of his hand. "Money makes money, you know ; and only just now I had good news of an investment I made only a month ago. A capital fellow Bix is for managing such things. I say, Hurly, I shouldn't wonder if he were to be the making of you at last, if you only manage to work the oracle with him properly. He has lots of shares in lots of things at his disposal. Why shouldn't he put you down for a few hundreds of them ?"

I told my fervent adviser that I did not know why he should, and ventured to remind Marmaduke that a higher authority than any he could quote in favour of rapid gains had laid it down as a certain axiom that "they who will be rich fall into temptation and a snare, and into many foolish and hurtful lusts, which drown men in destruction and perdition."

"Oh, oh !" said Marmaduke, with an unpleasant laugh ; "the grapes are sour, are they ? Well, every one to his taste. If you don't want more than you have got, I do ; and I can run the risk of temptations and snares and all the rest of it."

"I am sorry for that," I replied ; "but you mistake me. I did not say that I do not want more than I have got. For instance, I should be glad of the five hundred pounds to which you know I once had a rightful claim, though not a legal one."

Marmaduke was rather confused ; but he turned off his confusion with another laugh. "You have me fair enough, Hurly," he said ; "but you know I couldn't help it. My mother said you shouldn't have it ; and what could I do ? But I tell you what, Hurly, I'll owe it you. As soon as I have turned two or three corners I shall be all right, and you shall have it, old fellow. I can't give it to you now."

"I didn't expect you to do it; and I don't particularly wish for it now. But perhaps some day I may remind you of your promise."

"All right," said he, glad, I had no doubt, to be quit of the disagreeable subject; "and now, suppose we go and say 'How d'ye do?' to Sophy."

"By all means; but you mentioned your mother. I heard only yesterday of her death. I see you are in mourning for her."

"Oh, it can't be helped, you know," said Marmaduke, heartlessly. "Old folks can't be expected to last for ever."

"Your mother was not so very aged," I observed.

"Nor yet so very young. She was no chicken. But I believe she fretted herself to death. She wanted to have the handling of all my money, after I came of age; and I wasn't going to stand that, you see."

There was no use in pursuing the subject, which evidently was an unpleasant one to Marmaduke, while it was equally painful to me to hear him speak thus of his mother. We passed on, therefore.

By this time the guests in the rooms had been joined by others—ladies as well as gentlemen—and some of them had settled down to cards. Others still remained grouped together in conversation, above the hum of which, however, rose sounds of sweet music from the inner room of all. Hastening thither, we found it pretty well crowded with a mixed company, who were listening, or professing to listen, to the soft strains of a very sentimental song, accompanied by the twanging of a harp. The performer appeared to be professional; and, for my part, I was glad that my cousin had neither hand nor voice in the performance. She was seated where I had left her earlier in the evening, and was surrounded by worshippers,

z

either of her beauty or her father's wealth: it would have been hard to say distinctly which. She coloured slightly when she saw by whom I was accompanied; but she rose to meet us, and gave her hand to Marmaduke.

CHAPTER XLIX.

A FEW MORE WORDS WITH MARMADUKE TOZER.

"ONE word or two before I go, Marmaduke." It was an hour or two past midnight; the rooms were still crowded, and I had bidden good-bye to Sophy, who, poor dear, seemed wearied and languid, as no doubt she was. I had seen nothing of Sophy's father for some time. The last time in the evening that I had passed a word with him, he said, "Remember your engagement, Hurly; get an explanation from Marmaduke, if possible. Go into my study with him; you will find lights there, and you will be more private and quiet. Mind, I depend on you." And, as I had inwardly resolved that as this was the first, so it should be the last night of my being seen in such society, especially at such a time, and as, moreover, I had no disposition to carry on a renewal of acquaintance with Marmaduke, I determined if possible to get through that explanation at once. I was the more moved to this, I think, by having observed the air of constraint with which Marmaduke had addressed a few words to Sophy, and the evident pain which, I fancied, this coolness on his part had occasioned.

And I have to observe here that I have very grave doubts now as to the propriety of my course at that particular time. That

William Bix was making a tool of me, I knew then perhaps as
well as I know it now; but I was willing to submit to this
degradation for the sake of my cousin. Nevertheless, I was
clearly out of the right way when I consented to join in such a
company even for a single night; or, having been innocently
drawn into it, not knowing the materials of which it was composed, I was undoubtedly wrong in not leaving it when I made
the discovery. It was of God's mercy that I did not imbibe
contamination from the immoral atmosphere by which I was
surrounded; and I have no reason to suppose that this mercy
would have been extended to me if I had wilfully and deliberately
ventured a second time within the evil influences of such a godless
company. My doubts, therefore, as to the propriety of my
course have no reference to that which I now know to have been
decidedly wrong, but to my interference at all in so delicate a
matter as that for which my services were engaged. I do not
think I had much right to call Marmaduke to account for his
fickleness, if he were fickle and unfaithful; and if I had, it was
not at all likely that my arguments would turn him from any
line of conduct he might see fit to pursue. My only plea is, or
rather would then have been, that I was sincerely interested in
my cousin's welfare, and, like a warm-tempered, impetuous, and
inexperienced youth, was very ignorant and wide of the mark,
in the way I endeavoured to set about promoting it. These
reflections have led me further than I intended; let me return
to my story.

I had sought Marmaduke, who soon left the ladies' drawing-
room, and I found him, after some time, at the refreshment-table
where I had first met him. There was a noisy company around
him, and I plainly perceived that he, as well as others, had been
too freely availing himself of the privileges of a guest. And this,
again, should have induced me to pause; but, as I have said, I

determined to have the explanation over that night, or rather morning.

"A word or two before I go," I said, touching Marmaduke's elbow.

"Oh! what is it?" he demanded.

"I will tell you where we can be a little more quiet. Let us descend; we can go into my uncle's study, I believe."

"Very good. Just one glass more first," said he, filling up his wine-glass and throwing it off. "Now, then, I am at your service."

We found lights in the study, as William Bix had said, and no one there.

"Marmaduke," I said, opening the conversation, "you remember, when we were boys together, your telling me that it was your intention to marry Sophy Tindall at some future time."

"Did I say so? Ah, well, possibly I may remember it; and what then, Hurly?" said Marmaduke, carelessly.

"I have rather wondered at your delay in the accomplishment of that design," I replied.

"Have you, though? But how can I or any other man marry a nonentity? Answer me that, Hurly."

I did answer, that I held my cousin to be an entity.

"Your cousin, yes; but Sophy Tindall, no. There is no Sophy Tindall: she is the nonentity."

"The name is changed, certainly," said I, "but the person remains."

"The same, but not the same, my dear fellow. Now, look you, Hurly. You have been set on by Bix to badger me about Sophy: I can see it in your serious phiz. And I might ask you what business you have to interfere in my private affairs?"

"The sincere interest I feel in Sophy's happiness must be my excuse, Marmaduke."

" Pho ! And how do you know that Sophy would be any the happier for having me for a husband ?" he asked ; and then he added, " but come now, I'll be frank, because, after all, you are a good sort of fellow, and I don't want to quarrel with you. You want to know if I mean to marry your cousin. Suppose I say no, I don't mean to marry her. Then you ask me why I don't mean to marry her ; and I might say, in the first place, because I mean to marry somebody else ; and a man cannot very well have two wives, in England at least, without rather awkward consequences. Next, you will tell me that I am acting dishonourably towards your cousin. I deny it—altogether deny it, Hurly. Because I played at love-making when I was a silly boy, is that a reason why I should turn the play into earnest now I am a wiser man ?"

" You told me once, Marmaduke, that you had never played at love-making. You were earnest then," said I.

" You interrupt me, Hurly. It does not matter what I said then ; what I say now is the thing. And I say that, earnest or not earnest, my promise was made to Sophy Tindall. Now, I put it to you, Hurly, whether the Sophy Tindall of our old days was not altogether a different being from your cousin, Sophy Bix ?"

" The difference is surely all in my cousin's favour. The Sophy of our old days was a poor cottager, with a better education, indeed, than generally falls to the lot of young women in her condition, but with no great degree of refinement, and with no pecuniary prospects for the future, except that of inheriting the scanty savings of the old gamekeeper. The Sophy of to-day is a well-educated young lady, lovely in person, amiable in disposition, and ample in fortune."

" Put it in another light, Hurly. Sophy Tindall had no vile scamp of a father (whatever she might have once had) to be sticking like a burr to her and her husband, and handing down to them his ill fame and the disgrace of his connexion. For, of course, every one believed he was dead, and out of mind. Sophy Bix, on the other hand, has—I need not tell you what she has in that way, because you know well enough without my help—but I tell you candidly, I have so much regard for my position, that no amount that he could lay down before me would induce me to become William Bix's son-in-law."

" And yet——"

" And yet we are such very dear friends, you would say. Pho! he would suck me dry to-morrow if he could; and I—well, I know how to use him to my advantage. Do you think I am not wide awake, Hurly?"

I shall not endeavour to recall what more passed between us; it is enough to say that the explanation I had sought was full and complete, while it brought to light so much that was utterly atrocious and abominable in the character of Marmaduke, that I wondered then, as I wonder now, how he could have ventured on thus exposing himself, while I felt glad for my cousin that she had escaped being united with so bad and base a man. Nor do I suppose that he would have been so candid and free in his revelation if he had not been excited by the wine he had previously drunk.

We parted coolly—he returning to the rooms above, to look for his friend Brown, and I remaining in the old office, to ponder in what way, and to what extent, I should communicate to Sophy's father the result of the interview.

I was saved the trouble of making any communication. I was still seated, in deep and painful thought, when the door softly opened, and William Bix entered the room, closing the door after him. I looked up and saw that his countenance was deadly pale, his dark eyes glaring with passion, and his lips nervously trembling.

"I have heard all," he hissed, rather than spoke. "I was there—there"—he pointed to a portion of the wall where had once been a door into a large closet, but which had since been blocked up, and an opening made into it from a passage leading into the hall. "I was there, and heard every word the wretch spoke."

"Don't be afraid, Hurly," he said presently, when he was calmed down. "I shall not take revenge. I shall not even quarrel with him. In fact, it is of no consequence. Sophy has no need to go begging for a husband, though she has such a father. Oh, no; we shall not quarrel with Marmaduke: he is too useful to me, and I am too useful to him for that."

CHAPTER L.

MEMORY'S TABLETS. THE BUBBLE INFLATED, AND THE BUBBLE BURST—RETROSPECTIVE.

MY story brings me now to the time when I was more than twenty-five years old. Many events had happened in the world around me since the day of which I wrote in my last chapter; but the intervening months and years had passed away quietly with me.

Let me pause and look back.

First, I see myself, in those years, gradually advancing in the confidence of my kind-hearted employer and friend, standing high in his favour, and receiving liberal remuneration for my services. Twice I have been abroad on important business connected with the house in Gracechurch Street, and have happily succeeded in my mission. I am Edwin Millman's chosen friend, too. In all the years we have known each other, since we were school-boys together, we have never had a serious disagreement, and there is no danger that we ever shall have. Edwin, I am happy to remember, has outgrown his tendency to pulmonary disease; or rather, it was a false alarm that he ever had this tendency: but we sometimes talk of our pleasant first holiday in Devonshire, and of its sudden termination. We have had many holidays together since then.

But, although we have never had a serious disagreement, there is one point on which I have not pleased him. He wishes to know why I will not, as in the days of my earlier connexion with his father's business, spend my evenings in his society at his own home. "You used to make one of us," he says, "and I am sure we were always so glad of your society; and now, if I ever do get you into the drawing-room, you seem in such a hurry to leave. You don't like aunt Rhoda, I am afraid; or is it Mary who frightens you away?" Of course I cannot tell him the true reason; and, as I do not choose to make false excuses, I altogether hold my peace; and, of late, he has ceased to remonstrate.

I still lodge with Mr. Filby and Betsy, in Fetter Lane. I have already said what a comfortable couple they were after their marriage. They are so still; but Filby is getting old, and he finds business worries him in a way it did not use to do. He has been examining into the state of his finances, and finds, on striking a balance, that he has three thousand pounds "to the good," and can retire on a hundred and fifty pounds a year—money being worth five per cent. at safe investment. This being the case, he talks of disposing of the lease of his house and good-will of his business, and taking a cottage at Islington or Somers Town. Betsy is agreeable to this, on condition that I will continue to live with them till I have a home of my own, and a wife to take care of me.

" Which will never be, Betsy," I say, with a sigh of resignation, to which she responds—

" And I should never have thought it of you, Hurly, that you would have lived so long without trying your hand at marrying."

" You lived twice as long before you made up your mind to it," I reply. And she says that hers was a different case altogether, as no doubt it was.

I turn over another page in my tablets of memory, and I see written down, Silver Square.

I have remembered my vow, and faithfully observed it, that I would never more go to any of William Bix's grand parties; and, indeed, after the evening of which my last chapter treated, I have carefully avoided William Bix. But I remember also my cousin Sophy's earnest entreaty that I would sometimes go and see her; and I do now and then look in at Silver Square.

I don't think that Sophy is much concerned at the desertion of her former boy-lover. She has long felt convinced that their folly (so she says) would have this termination, and has prepared herself for it. It might have been done in a kinder way, she admits; but it is best as it is, and she is contented it should be so. She is not deeply distressed, therefore, when she hears of Marmaduke's marriage with Eugenia, one of the fine, dashing sisters of Quercus and Philander Brown, which has taken place within six months of my last interview with him.

It is scarcely necessary for me to assure my readers that Marmaduke continues to *owe* me the five hundred pounds he promised to restore. Indeed, I have not seen him since the night (or morning) of William Bix's party, though I sometimes hear of him as being mixed up with William Bix in his many schemes for transmuting all kinds of base metals, and yet baser materials, into solid, substantial, pure gold. It is evident, therefore, that, however deep William Bix's resentment against Marmaduke may be, he does not allow his personal feelings to interfere with the ordinary course of business.   As a matter of delicacy, however, the recreant lover is never again seen in the Silver Square parties.   His visits, when paid, are always confined to the range of offices on the ground-floor of the renovated mansion.   Furthermore, I hear of Marmaduke that, since his marriage, he has begun to put into execution some of the schemes he broached to me.   He has bought the adjoining property which was to make his estate so much more valuable; and has begun to pull down his house that he may build a greater.

Apropos of Marmaduke and his apparent prosperity, I may remark that superabundant wealth seems to be pouring in, in a full tide, upon all who are fortunate enough to have become connected with William Bix in his numerous schemes.   Among these happy ones are the Browns, of Blackheath, the father and his two sons, whose mansion, doubled in size to suit their growing fortunes, glitters within—so I am told—with all kinds of frippery that wealth can purchase, and whose equipages are the envy and admiration of the little world by which they are surrounded.   As to William Bix himself, he has become the most popular man of the time.   His house and offices in Silver Square are crowded with grovelling worshippers.   High-born gentlemen, and proud, haughty dames, condescend to solicit his notice and favour.   A word from his lips fills their hearts with gladness for many a day, for that word may make them rich beyond their previous conceptions.   He has but to nod, and there is a wild rush of excitement in what is, *par excellence,* called "The Market."   If he deigns to smile on any new enterprise, its success is reckoned sure.   It matters not how wild may be the projects which he favours; everything he touches seems to turn to gold.   It may be that he is not in any high sense of the words a good man of business; but it is admitted by his detractors (for even William Bix has detractors) that he has boundless audacity, and daring, desperate courage, and a brusqueness of demeanour, which serves, for a time, the turn of blunt honesty.

Enough of this. Once more I turn to my tablets, and the scene in my mind's eye changes.

I see a tumultuous crowd gathering round the old house in Silver Square. There are pale faces, and angry faces, and sorrowful faces, and faces full of revenge, and hatred, and spite, and every evil passion. There are loud shouts, and subdued murmurs, and desperate threats. There are fierce gestures, and wringing of hands, and clenching of fists in impotent wrath. The crowd increases, threatens violence, and is dispersed. Then again it rallies; and curses both loud and deep may be heard, interspersed with invectives: Bix, the scoundrel; Bix, the swindler; Bix, the thief, robber, murderer; Bix, the everything that tongue can utter or thought frame, so that it is evil. What does it all mean?

It means that the big bubble has burst; that the enchantment is over; that the spell is destroyed; that the golden hopes, and the gold-producing magical papers which yesterday were thought to be worth thousands and tens of thousands of current coin, are of no more value to-day than dry and withered leaves. It means that William Bix has disappeared, no one knows whither; that the offices are closed; that his willing dupes are ruined.

Day by day I hear more of this—hear of widows and orphans whose scanty means, their living, their all, was intrusted to the marvellous magician, who was to multiply it tenfold; of quiet, plodding men, whose life-savings were invested in the wonderful projects which were to raise them at once beyond the need of further industry; of large and prosperous firms, whose fate is sealed the instant it is whispered that their principal had dealings with William Bix ; of reputed millionaires, who were said to turn pale on 'Change when the first whisper was breathed of things going wrong in the great house in Silver Square.

Every hour brings now its fresh rumours. One scheme after another has collapsed. As well try to make an empty bag stand upright, as to suppose that one of the multitude of projects with which the name of Bix is associated can maintain an equilibrium. Those who were mixed up with these schemes and projects are fleeing to every country in Europe, or beyond it ; officials, in dumb show, are replacing the huge ledgers on their shelves, and departing to their homes, wondering what they shall do on the morrow ; and poor deceived victims are rushing about from one high authority to another, to find that they have nothing better to do, and nothing worse, than to fold their arms in silent resignation.

There is nothing but ruin—dark, portentous, stark ruin—to be seen hastening on.

Every week increases the more perfect knowledge of the magnitude and completeness of the long series of frauds which have been practised upon the multitude that made haste to be rich. Whether Marmaduke Tozer has been a defaulter in intention, or merely a dupe, is not yet ascertained ; but that his ruin is complete and signal there is no doubt at all. He is reduced to abject poverty ; his estate is to be sold for the benefit of creditors; so are a dozen more estates to begin with, and among them that of Mr. Brown, at Blackheath. *Sic transit gloria mundi.*

It is reported that William Bix, the great negotiator, the enormous speculator, the wonderful charlatan, the gigantic swindler—for by each of these supplementary names is he spoken of—has been seen in America, in France, in Australia; that his corpse has been recognised in the Morgue at Paris ; in a parish dead-house near London ; in a hospital in Dublin ; but these are vague rumours. One thing is certain: he is never seen more near Silver Square. The sheriff of London holds possession of the grand mansion for a brief space, and then messengers from the Bankruptcy Court step in; and there are goodly pickings for the vultures of the law (so people say), but not a penny for the hundreds of ruined creditors.

And where is poor Sophy in all this din, and hubbub, and dire confusion? Go to the gamekeeper's cottage, and you will find her there, returned to the warm nest from which she was taken. Poor cousin Sophy!

CHAPTER LI.

AUNT RHODA'S CATECHISM.

T had become an old story of some year or more, this bursting of the grand bubble; and the busy world, taught wisdom for a little while by the things it had suffered in some of its members, had settled down for that time to the old humdrum method inculcated in the wise saws of "Honesty is the best policy," "Safe bind, safe find," "Small profits and quick returns," with many others of a like import, when Mr. Filby announced to me first of all, the intention of which I have already spoken, with the proviso which Betsy had introduced into the compact. Of course I agreed heartily with the proposal: and by-and-by, when the project was matured, and a customer was found for the lease and goodwill of the house and business in Fetter Lane, I was employed by my old friends in looking out for the quiet retreat on which they had determined.

" Let it be as near the old place where we used to go daisying and buttercupping as you can get it, Hurly; and be sure there are some green fields round about," said Betsy. These were the only instructions she gave me; all else was left to my judgment and liking.

Only those who have been engaged in a like errand can fully understand how many difficulties I had to surmount before I could find the cottage which I fancied would meet all the requirements of the case. At length, however, after the spare evenings of two or three weeks had been consumed in the quest, I believed I had discovered the very *ne plus ultra* which would delight my old nurse's heart, and, in natural sequence, that of her husband also. It was a pretty cottage, at a moderate rent, with a patch of garden ground attached. It was not far from a main road, but yet it was retired and in the country, or as much so as could be expected of a cottage within three or four miles of St. Paul's. There were green fields near, not the identical fields which had witnessed our former communings—Betsy's and mine —but sufficiently like them to answer every purpose; and there was a dairy close at hand, kept by the very woman (grown twenty years older) who had supplied my childish cravings for new milk and curds-and-whey. I verily believe—silly as it may seem—that this discovery hastened the conditional bargain I immediately made with the owner of the vacant cottage.

Returning to Fetter Lane with the good news of my success, I was mysteriously told by Betsy that I had got home just in time; that I was particularly wanted by a stranger lady who had alighted half-an-hour ago from a hackney-coach, and had taken possession of my sitting-room up-stairs, while awaiting my return.

" A lady, Betsy! What can any lady want with me?"

" She didn't say, Hurly; and I didn't ask."

" What sort of a lady?"

"I should say one of the right sort, by her looks," said Betsy; "but it's only to step up-stairs and see for yourself."

"True; but I may as well have some cue. Are you sure you don't know the lady?"

"Never saw her before, Hurly."

"And you did not ask her name?" said I.

"She had such a quiet sisterly way about her, that I never thought of asking her name till I was out of the room."

"Sisterly—um! A young lady, then?"

Betsy laughed. "I didn't say young. You may call me young if you like; but it doesn't make me so, does it?"

"Oh!—sisterly, then, as in connexion or comparison with yourself; there's one danger the less," so I said; but I was half disappointed, though half relieved. For I had begun to fancy that my poor cousin Sophy (whom Betsy had never seen) might have taken a journey to London, and sought me out for some service that I could render her. I was glad it was not so, for what would she meet with in London but mortification and sorrow? And yet I should have been glad to see her.

I went up-stairs, opened the door of my sitting-room, and met the kindly countenance and bright benevolent eyes, and was grasped by the hand of—Aunt Rhoda Millman.

"My dear madam," I began, but was instantly stopped by my visitor—

"Now, do not be alarmed. I see, by your looks, Hurly" (aunt Rhoda, like almost all the rest of my friends and acquaintance, had fallen into the habit of calling me Hurly)—"I see by your looks that you are afraid something painful has happened at Gracechurch Street since you left three hours ago; but there is nothing the matter. My brother is well, so are Edwin and his sister; and no unexpected intelligence has arrived from any quarter to trouble us."

I was very glad to hear it, and felt greatly relieved by her assurance.

"But you wonder all the more what has brought me away from home so late at night, and to your lodgings, of all other places."

I said that I felt both myself and my poor room very highly honoured by the visit. And as to its cause, I was sure it was "a sufficient and a good one, whatever it might turn out to be."

"I believe it is a good and sufficient one, Hurly. I know it is a benevolent one in intention," said aunt Rhoda.

I was not surprised to hear this. Aunt Rhoda was so kind-hearted that I think she would have looked upon a day as being lost in which she had not lightened some fellow-creature's burden, or softened some sorrow. She was not in the habit of being generous at the expense of others; and in general she shrank from asking any one, excepting perhaps her brother, for money to enable her to carry out any plan for which her own finances were barely sufficient. She preferred, I believe, making self-sacrifices in the accomplishment of her aims. I was sure, therefore, that the cause was urgent which brought her so far out of the way, to ask me (for, of course, that was what she came for) to co-operate with her in her benevolent design. I suppose my countenance expressed some gratification at the honour thus done me, for she said—

"I see you are willing to help me; but I hope you intend to sit down, Hurly."

I took the hint, and seated myself near to my visitor. "I will call for candles," I said; for, though it was a summer evening, and not nine o'clock, it was getting dark in Fetter Lane.

"No," she said, "there is light enough. I am not sure that I shall not get on better without the help of a candle."

She sat silent for half a minute, thinking how to open the matter on which her mind was set, I suppose. At last she said abruptly—

"You know that I kept school once, Hurly."

"I have heard that—that you were so good as to educate——"

"Kept school, Hurly," she repeated, with good-humoured peremptoriness. "I am not ashamed of it, nor ashamed to call things by their ordinary names; why should I be? It is a very useful employment, and I look back upon it now with gratification —with real pleasure."

"I have not the least doubt, dear madam, that your former pupils share in that feeling with yourself," I said, wondering what was coming next; but rather imagining that one of those former pupils had fallen into adversity, and was needing more help than her old teacher could give without assistance from others.

"I kept school," she repeated; "and sometimes I had occasion to put rather embarrassing questions to my pupils as to their motives for pursuing certain courses of which I might or might not approve, and as to their feelings and intentions too. I was a very strict disciplinarian, I assure you, Hurly; and a very severe catechist."

"A very kind one, I am sure, Miss Millman."

"I am glad you think so, Hurly," the lady went on; "for it gives me hopes that you will still think me kind. For you must look upon yourself, for the next half hour at least, as my pupil."

"Very willingly indeed. But should I not take a lower position?" I drew towards me a footstool, and would have seated myself near her feet, but she prevented me.

"No, no," she said hastily, "we will have no show of humilia-tion. It is I who should be humble; but there is no need to parade it. Let us be true to one another."

What could it all mean? What benevolent design was she set upon which needed so singular a preface? All I could say was that I accepted the terms she proposed, and would honestly and truly answer any questions aunt Rhoda might see right to propound.

"Thank you, Hurly," she said; "and now, to begin my inquisition, you must tell me honestly and truly whether you intend to remain single all your days?"

I almost started from my chair in sheer amazement. The question was so entirely unexpected; so beyond the range of any previous conjectures; so indelicate almost, or at least would have seemed so indelicate from other lips than those of a motherly, matronly friend; and yet it was asked so calmly and quietly that I was utterly astonished. I was very glad that lights had not been brought; that the room was so gloomy that the expression on my countenance was shaded.

"You did not expect to be asked such a question, of course I know that," said my *extempore* schoolmistress, "so I will give you time to think; only be honest."

By this time I had recovered composure enough to reply that I had formed no express intention on the subject, but that, as far as I could see, I had no prospect of being otherwise than in the state to which she had referred.

"Cautiously worded," said aunt Rhoda; "but I must be satisfied with the answer, I suppose. I come to the next question, therefore: Your prospect (I will not say intention) does not arise from any repugnance, any dread, I should rather say, of a married life?"

"Very far from it."

"Why don't you marry, then?" demanded the lady, with startling abruptness, almost sharply, it seemed to me.

Rather amused, and yet a little annoyed, I replied that among other reasons I might mention the very sufficient one, that my finances were not in so flourishing a state as to warrant such a bold step.

" In other words, you think you are too poor to keep a wife," said the out-spoken questioner. " But this is only one objection, and one which possibly might admit of a satisfactory solution. Now, answer me, sir; is it another objection that you have never yet met with the person whom you——"

" Pardon me, madam," I said, hastily interrupting her; " I must entreat you to spare me that question."

" I won't spare you. I told you I was a strict disciplinarian, and a severe catechist; and I intend that you shall find me so. You *must* answer me." She said this with an assumption of authority which—however unlike the gentle aunt Rhoda I had hitherto known her to be—I thought very well became her. And, at any rate, I determined to humour her present bent, so I said, with mock humility and abasement, that, since I must confess, I would acknowledge, with due contrition, that I had permitted the citadel of my heart to be taken by storm, or, to be more correct in my simile, by sapping and mining unawares.

" In other words, you confess to having been or being what is vulgarly called in love?" said my interrogatress.

" If to be in love means heartily to admire and——"

" You need not go on with your definition, sir," said the lady. " It is enough that you acknowledge the fact. Now, I ask you another question; please to answer me. Have you ever sought to make the—the young person, whoever she may be, aware of your—what shall I say? your predilection?"

" Never, my dear madam."

" Why have you not?"

" Because,—but, madam, I ask you once more not to press that question."

It was getting darker and darker in the room, and I could not catch the expression on aunt Rhoda's countenance. I observed, however, that she rested her head for one moment or two on her hand, as though in the act of considering. Then she spoke again,—

"As you wish it, and have answered so openly my other questions, I will remit this, for the present, at least. But you must reply to the next. Have you reason to suppose that the young person—I take for granted she is a young person, you see—has indulged in a reciprocal predilection, attachment, what you please, towards yourself?"

"I have no reason to suppose it, madam."

"On the other hand, you fear, perhaps, that you do not please —that she has a prejudice against you, and therefore you have determined to abandon the pursuit of your wishes?"

"I have determined to abandon the pursuit," I said, "but not for the reason you suggest. I have no reason to suppose that the person in question has any personal dislike towards myself; I cannot think that, but I really do not know."

"You are a strange, cold-hearted lover, surely," said aunt Rhoda; "and, perhaps, I am wasting time on you. But I must go on with my catechism to the end; and I may understand, I suppose, that the reason why you have determined to subdue your affection is what you think to be an honourable reason?"

"I do, indeed, think it to be so," I said.

"For instance, your affections are misplaced."

"I have reason to believe——"

"Do not answer me yet. You have loved unwisely; you have been attracted by a pretty face and fair brow, lacking brains behind it? or you have discovered that the young person has faults of temper which would mar your domestic happiness? or she may be in too lowly a position in life, and your pride revolts from the humble connexion? or she is uneducated and vulgar? or, with many amiable, moral qualities, she may lack the one thing needful? All of these are grave considerations, I am quite ready to admit. Tell me which conjecture is the right one."

A wild, strange thought—not a hope exactly, but something near it—crossed my puzzled brain, but I instantly dismissed it, and replied with as much composure as I could command, that all my querist's conjectures were wide of the mark. "I have before said, madam, that my finances——"

"That you are too poor to marry. Isn't this a subterfuge, Hurly? Or, am I to understand that your affections are fixed so much above you, as to bring out your comparative poverty into strong relief, and that, therefore, you are determined to subdue and root out those affections?"

"You are right," I said, "my affections are placed very high above my merits or my hopes."

"Have you subdued them? Are they uprooted?"

"Alas! no."

"Poor Hurly! poor Hurly!" She spoke very softly; "I can understand you, I think. But it may be that you are imprudent. You venture too frequently within the influence——"

"Spare me, I entreat you, my dear madam. And yet I will answer this one question, for I am not ashamed to reply that, as far as I can, I do avoid her presence, and, and—Be kind, my good and honoured friend; do not urge me further."

"One—only one question more." Aunt Rhoda's voice trembled a little as she spoke. I know she was agitated. "You avoid her presence, you say. Are you speaking of my dear niece—of Mary Millman?"

*   *   *   *   *   *   *

"Hurly," said aunt Rhoda, presently, "I have taken a very unusual course; a very indelicate course, some may say; and have acted and am acting quite unconventionally. But I am an old woman, or soon shall be; and I have learned this, that many a trouble would be smoothed down if people were not so fearful of being unconventional. You don't imagine that your supposed and cherished secret of so many years has been a real secret. Bless you, Hurly, why I knew it five years ago. But you should never have known that I even suspected it, if it had not been for a little circumstance which let me, not long ago, into another secret. My dear, you are not the first penitent I have brought to my confessional to-day; and I said to myself, why should two such dear friends of mine be unhappy, when a few words of mine —a little unconventionality—would make them both happy— rationally and naturally happy?"

"May I hope, then," I said, eagerly, "that your niece——"

Aunt Rhoda laid her hand on mine. "Go and ask her, Hurly."

Yes, I was very happy, I confess it; but the joy was transitory.

"You have meant very kindly, very benevolently, very generously," I said; "but it cannot be. Your brother, Mr. Millman, Mary's father, and my friend and employer—it would be a poor requital for all his goodness to me, were I to put it in his power to say, ' You have taken advantage of my confidence.' "

Aunt Rhoda fairly laughed. "You don't think I am here without my brother's knowledge?" she said. "Why, my dear, he sent me. He has known your secret longer than I have. He will tell you so to-morrow. And, Hurly, please to look out and see if the hackney-coach is at the door below. I told the man to return for me in an hour."

CHAPTER LII.

I AM MARRIED; SET OUT ON A WEDDING TOUR, AND RENEW AN
OLD FRIENDSHIP.

SHALL not trouble my readers with a particular account
of my private interview with Mr. Millman, on the day
following his sister's visit to my lodgings. It is enough
to say that it was eminently satisfactory, I believe, to us both.

I have still less inclination to dwell upon my subsequent interview with Mary Millman. So long as the world lasts, such
passages in personal histories will, no doubt, take place; but that
is no reason why they should be made public property. I shall
only say, therefore, that I was very happy, and heaped blessings
mentally on the head of aunt Rhoda, for being " unconventional."

Edwin Millman was in ecstasies—so he said—and wondered
where his wits had been that he had not seen why I had so long
avoided meeting his sister.

The long and short of the matter is, that I and Mary were
quietly betrothed; and our wedding-day was arranged for the
ensuing autumn.

There is no earthly happiness without its alloy; and the alloy
to mine was that I should have to break up my home with the
Filbys, just at a time, too, when our joint occupancy of Rose
Cottage (for so was their new house named) was almost decided
on. But my old friends, and especially Betsy, took the disappointment very philosophically. Or rather their hearty rejoicings at my pleasant prospects neutralized their vexation at the
disturbance of our former plans. They were, perhaps, the more
easily reconciled to my leaving them, by reason of my taking a

house in the neighbourhood of Rose Cottage; so that, as Betsy said, we should be all one family like, after all.

And so, time swiftly gliding on, our wedding-day came in due course.

It was a whim of mine, and Mary indulged me in it, that our honeymoon, or part of it, should be spent in Kent, amidst the scenes of my boyhood of which I have spoken. Accordingly, after the ceremony was performed, and a hasty wedding breakfast despatched, and travelling gear put on, a modest postchaise drove up to the door of the house in Gracechurch Street, and, amidst the hearty congratulations of the wedding guests, we started on our journey: we—that is to say, my darling Mary, her brides-maid—a certain Lucy Lascelles, of whom I have no more to say here than that, before another year passed over her head, she was Mrs. Edwin Millman—and myself.

Dr. Johnson is said to have declared that there is no earthly pleasure superior to that of travelling in a postchaise over a smooth road, at the rate of I forget how many miles an hour. He did not think of adding, with a newly-married wife by one's side. But, transcendent as is the pleasure, it palls by long continuance; and when, late in the evening, we arrived at my old quarters— the "Lion" at Wingham (the landlady of which had been duly notified of our intended visit)—we were not sorry that our journey was over.

How royally (as became the reputation of the old inn) we were entertained; how the genial hostess feigned to believe that I could not be the whey-faced—yes, she called me whey-faced—boy she remembered to have entertained more than fifteen years before; how she inquired with much interest after the gentleman with the white beard, and sighed when told of his death: all this, and more, needs no comment.

I have said that it was a whim of mine to spend the very earliest few days of my wedded life in Kent. Yet not altogether a whim. There was, at least, a serious reason at the bottom of it. During the last two years I had heard neither from nor of my poor cousin Sophy; and I wished very much to see her. Mary also—after she had heard the story from my lips—felt a kindly interest in her new cousin.

"Why shouldn't she come and stay with us? at least, why not pay us a long visit?" she had asked. And, though I had some doubts as to the desirableness of this plan, there could be no doubt that the proposal was kind; and it strengthened my desire to renew my old friendly intercourse with Sophy and her grandparents.

Accordingly, after one day's rest at the famous old "Lion," we took our way towards the distant village, by the well-remembered foot-path through the parks, and entering the village street near to the "Four Horseshoes," we walked on. Presently the house in which Mrs. Tozer formerly lived loomed in sight; and as we passed it, and looked up at the windows, I was struck by seeing, framed and glazed, the information that *Miss* Bolster sought patronage as a milliner and dressmaker; also that she occupied some portion of her time in cleaning and turning and trimming straw and Leghorn hats and bonnets. Furthermore, by a plain card in the same window, passengers were told that Miss Bolster had genteel (a particularly large "genteel") lodgings to let.

"What a funny name," said Lucy Lascelles; "Bolster; Miss Bolster!"

"I made the same remark a good many years ago, Lucy. We will see, if you please, whether the name and its owner are well matched," and I opened the gate.

"My dear Hurly," Mary remonstrated; but I told her that I had a special desire to see the lady with the funny name, and we walked up to the door, which was speedily opened to us by a neat-handed damsel, who, on my inquiring for Miss Bolster, ushered us into the same parlour in which, when a boy, I underwent on one occasion the searching examination of Mrs. Tozer.

Miss Bolster soon made her appearance; the same Marianne Bolster whom I had known in those boyish days; there was no doubt of that remaining: but wonderfully smartened up and improved, nevertheless. A little sprightly woman of some thirty years old, with bright eyes and modest curls, and in a fashionable morning dress. And yet I instinctively looked at her left cheek, as though almost expecting still to see there the red streaks left by the sounding slap I had heard bestowed upon it by its owner's angry mistress more than sixteen years ago. There were no red marks, however; but pretty blushes on both cheeks, as the little woman curtsied to her lady visitors, and seemed to be waiting their pleasure.

"You don't remember me, ma'am," I said.

Miss Bolster looked up in my face, and very demurely answered in the negative. And then a half light broke in upon her suddenly—"Why, it isn't—it isn't *you?*"

"Yes, it is I—I, Hurly; and this lady is"—I laid my hand on Mary's arm—"my wife."

"Oh, the darling! I must kiss her, then, for old sake's sake." And, suiting the action to the word, Miss Bolster sprang forward, and, throwing her arms round Mary's neck, embraced her with hearty good-will. Having subjected Lucy to the same ordeal, Miss Bolster apologized for the freedom she had taken. "But Master Hurly—I beg his pardon, Burley, I mean —and I were always such good friends that I really couldn't help it."

As the "always" was comprised within the space of one week, I was rather surprised, at first, at the little woman's ardour, and even at her remembrance of me, until I painfully reflected how desolate her life must at that time have been that so deep an impression of my boyish sympathy remained. Passing by this, however, I congratulated Miss Bolster on her present apparently comfortable circumstances. And then I found, what I have since observed, again and again—that there is a crook in every lot, and that even unexpected prosperity has its vexations and drawbacks.

She was very well off, considering; she could not deny that, said Marianne Bolster; she had worked hard, and had gone through no end of worries; but she had made up her mind to hard work and worry, so that didn't signify. Then she had—but there is no need to tell at full length the story how she had saved enough money to apprentice herself to a dressmaker; how her genius in cutting out and her genteel taste in costume were developed; how, in time, she rose to be forewoman in a certain fashionable establishment, and again saved money; how, just at a fortunate juncture, two or three years ago, on paying a visit to her native village, she found that her old house of bondage was vacant by the death of its once owner, and that it was to be sold in consequence of the failure of Marmaduke—"and a pretty mess he seems to have made of it," said Miss Bolster, interjectively—and how the fancy took her to invest her savings, together with two or three hundred pounds she was able to borrow, in the purchase of the house, and the establishment of her present business.

She was doing well, too; oh, she had nothing to complain of on that score. She had always her hands full of work, and employed apprentices and workwomen, I forget how many; and had no difficulty in making her way, and expected soon to pay home the mortgage-money. It was not *that* that worried her. Low people *would* call her Marianne, and *would* remember the time when she

was only a servant, and was knocked about by such a mistress as
Mrs. Tozer.   This was her trouble.

It was very vexatious, no doubt ; but I could suggest no remedy
for the grievance but patience ; and then I turned the conversation
by asking if Miss Bolster had heard any particulars concerning
the closing days of her former mistress's life.

Heard !   Oh yes, she had heard more than was true, perhaps ;
but at any rate it was currently reported that Mrs. Tozer
became at last so fretful and unreasonable that she could get
no one to "put up with her tantrums ;" and that even when
she lay on her death-bed, her temper "wasn't a bit mended,"
for with her little remaining strength she threw into her
nurse's face (a parish nurse, for she could get no one else to
stay with her) a glass of toast and water because she detected
that it was stale.

" And Marmaduke ?" I asked.

" Oh, Marmaduke never came near her, though she was moan-
ing and crying out for him all day long, and all night too, for
days before she died.   He was too busy with the new estate he
had bought.   And after all," said Miss Bolster, with a good deal
of truth, " it isn't much to be wondered at that Marmaduke Tozer
turned out as he did.   He wasn't led on to love his mother when
he was a child ; his love was crushed down then and turned to
fear ; and it wasn't to be expected that fear would turn to love
again when he grew older.   You may burn an old stocking, and
make tinder of it easily," the little woman added, " but you can't
unburn it, you know."

Acknowledging this, I told Miss Bolster that we were on the
way to the gamekeeper's cottage, and asked could she give me
any information respecting Sophy.

The reply was sorrowful and unexpected.   My poor cousin was
sinking in a rapid decline.   Doctors had given her up.   It was a

hopeless case, they said, so everybody could see; and that was Marmaduke's doings again.

I had no heart for further communications; and declining Miss Bolster's polite and pressing entreaties that we would take "a little something" to refresh us after our long walk, we soon afterwards took our leave, and went on our way.

CHAPTER LIII.

HOW MY HONEYMOON WAS SPENT, AND THE MONTH AFTER—THE LAST OF MARMADUKE TOZER.

S we drew near to the gamekeeper's cottage, I asked Mary and her friend to walk on slowly under the shelter of the park fence; then I turned in at the little wicket-gate alone, and gently knocked at the door.

It was opened to me by Dame Storks—so aged, and feeble, and careworn, that I had some difficulty in recognising her. She did not know me; but her anxious solicitude for her granddaughter led her at once to the conclusion that I was a new doctor who had promised some day to call and see what could be done: and she tremblingly invited me to enter, whispering cautiously in my ear, as she did this, "I don't think my poor girl is so *very* bad as they say, sir. You will try to cure her, won't you? Poor dear! poor dear!"

I did not care to let my old acquaintance see how deeply I was moved by the simple pathos of her entreaty; and I followed her silently into the well-remembered kitchen, which had scarcely changed its appearance during the ten years which had elapsed since I last stepped across its stone floor.

Sophy was not there; she was out in the park, Dame Storks said. "She manages to walk out in the sunshine, sir, and it does her good; so, you see, she can't be so very bad," she added.

"I'll go to her; don't trouble yourself, I know the way," I said, hastily; and in another minute I was in the park. It seemed not long since I was last there, watching Sophy and Marmaduke as they strolled among the trees, and made themselves happy with their deceitful dreams—day-dreams of future pleasures; no, not long since. But how changed the reality now! It was too painful to dwell upon, and I hastened towards the slight, drooping figure I saw far distant, seated on a rustic chair, which had probably been placed there for her comfort. She did not see me till I was very near to her, and then she uttered a faint cry, first of terror, and then of delight, as she rose, and almost fell into my arms.

It was too true. It was a hopeless case. Oh, that light burden—almost lighter than when she was a hearty, healthy, romping child! That death-pale countenance, flushed only on each cheek into one deep crimson, burning spot! Those large eyes, so preternaturally bright, with those dark rings around them! Yes, too true; consumption had marked her as its prey, and would never loosen its grasp till its fatal work was done: never.

"Oh, Hurly! how good of you—how good—to think of your poor cousin in her great sorrow!" she said, smiling through her tears.

"Think of you? I have thought of you every day, Sophy, these many years. But I did not know you were ill."

"I have been poorly, very," she said; "but I am getting stronger and better. I shall soon be well now. If it were not for this nasty cough which I cannot get rid of, I should soon gain strength; but it hinders me from resting."

The common delusion—I should be quite well if—if it were not for this or the other symptom, which proves how ill I am. Poor Sophy !

"And I have such thoughts," she continued, "which keep me awake at night. Oh, Hurly ! if I could but be sure—quite sure, I should not care then how ill I might be. There is not much left for me to live for now, is there ?"

She said this very mournfully.

"Much to live for, my dear cousin, but more to die for ; oh, how much more ! But you say, if you could be sure—sure of what, Sophy ?"

"Hurly, you told me once, it was almost the last time I saw you at that dreadful Silver Square"—she shuddered as she said this— "that all the riches and pleasures in the whole world were not worth a thought in comparison with the love of Christ."

"Yes, dear cousin, yes ; I said this."

"And I partly believed it then. At least, I thought that the love of Christ must be very poor indeed, if it were not worth more than I had ever found in riches and pleasure."

"And you think so now, Sophy ?"

"More now than ever. If I could I would not live again those miserable years I spent in London. But you told me something else, Hurly. You said that that love was waiting for me, wooing me, seeking admission into my soul. That I had but to——" Her voice failed her here. We had been returning to the cottage— she leaning her light weight on my arm, and I, forgetting how weak she was, had hurried her beyond her strength.

"One moment, Hurly," she whispered feebly. "I shall be better soon. These fainting fits come upon me sometimes suddenly."

She did not recover immediately, however ; and I had almost to bear her in my arms into the cottage.

"You are not the new doctor, then ?" said Dame Storks, trem- blingly, when I endeavoured to explain who I was, "I don't understand it," she added; "I dare say 'tis all right, but my memory fails, and trouble comes so thick and thick that I can't think of much else. And people come and go, come and go, just as they like. It didn't use to be so."

"Grandmother, you know George Burley; you remember him, do you not?" said Sophy, rousing herself to speak. It was of little avail, however. Sorrow and age had not only impaired the memory, but dimmed the intellects also, of Dame Storks, who knew no one distinctly but her husband and her granddaughter. So Sophy told me; and added that her grandfather was now laid up with rheumatism, and almost bedridden.

"Sophy," I said, presently; "I have news to tell you. I am married."

"Married! Oh, Hurly, I am so glad; so very glad."

"Married; but only two days ago. My wife is with me now— she is waiting outside—she would like to know you; she loves you already. May I bring her in?"

There was no need to ask permission; no need, at least, for an answer in words. Sophy's eager countenance was the answer. As I was about to leave her, however, she laid her hand on my arm, and whispered, "I want to ask you one question, Hurly, now we are alone. Have you heard anything, do you know anything of *him?*"

"Of him? of Marmaduke?"

"No, no;" she smiled faintly. "Oh, Hurly, how foolish we both were! Poor Marmaduke! I hope he will be happy. I am afraid my father took his revenge on him as he said he would, though I begged him not to do so. But it was not of Marmaduke I was thinking then. I meant my father. Do you think that what they said is true?—that he is dead?"

"I cannot tell, my dear cousin. I know only that he has not been heard of since that sad time."

"My poor father!" she rejoined. "He was kind to me, or meant to be. He loved me, I am sure. I am sorry I could not be more fond of him, or more grateful to him than I was. But was it very wrong that I was not? I could not respect him, you know."

I thought of this long afterwards. I think of it now sometimes. There can be no true, pure love and gratitude where there is no respect. I said something like this, and then I called in my wife and her friend.

I shall not lengthen my story by an account of this their first meeting, except by saying that Mary and my cousin soon understood and loved each other. There were no barriers of ceremony to break down, or what few there were, were easily broken; so that, when we presently retired, it was with the understanding that we were to see Sophy again on the following day.

But I must not omit to record that the old grandmother's homely hospitality had survived her memory, so that we could not be permitted to leave the cottage without partaking of its owner's cake and currant wine.

We returned to the cottage on the following day, but not till we had seen the doctor, who, as a matter of form, still visited the patient. Our strongest and saddest impressions were confirmed by him. There was no hope—none. He comforted us, however, by an assurance, which I saw no reason to doubt, that all had been done for my cousin's restoration that skill could suggest, that she needed no comforts, and that her disease, though probably hastened on by trouble, was hereditary in its source, and, sooner or later, would most likely have claimed her as its victim.

At Mary's request, I left her with my cousin and her friend Lucy. At the termination of an hour I returned.

"You will come and see me again," said the invalid, as my young wife kissed her, and wished her good-bye.

B B

"Yes; again and again."

And she kept her promise; for that day we paid another visit to Miss Bolster, and engaged her lodgings, that we might be nearer to poor Sophy.

We have never regretted that the month which we had designed for entire recreation, and desultory pleasure-taking, was turned aside from this object, and devoted to the sacred duty thus unexpectedly set before us. We have no happier memories now, of our early married life, than those connected with my dear dying cousin. We took a few excursions from our temporary lodgings, visited my old schoolmaster and St. Judith's Bay, and one or two of the neighbouring towns; spent a day in a jaunt to the Reculvers, and part of another in exploring the ruins of Richborough Castle; but besides these we never left the little village, and not a day passed which did not take us, sometimes singly, sometimes together, to the gamekeeper's cottage, and bring us into quiet and solemn communion with dear Sophy. At length my month of absence had expired, and it was needful that I should return to the business house in Gracechurch Street. Our cottage, also, was waiting for its new occupants; and, under the joint superintending care and zeal of aunt Rhoda and my old friend Betsy, was gaily decorated against our arrival. So we were told in a brief note from Edwin Millman.

"I have a favour, a great favour, to ask of you, Hurly," said my wife, an evening or two before the day appointed for our return.

"A favour of *me*—a favour? Why not say that you have a claim to make upon me? or, at most, a wish unfulfilled that I can gratify?"

"Because, dear Hurly, it is best to call things by their right names. It is a *favour* that I have to ask."

"It is yours, Mary, before you name it."

Mary shook her head. "It involves a sacrifice, Hurly, on your part, and on mine too; I am sure it involves a sacrifice for us both," said she. "I want you to leave me here—to consent to my remaining here while I can be of any use or comfort to your poor cousin. Will you grant me this?"

"What? and go back to London without my dear darling wife? Oh, Mary!"

"It will not be for long," she pleaded. "Have you not seen how Sophy fails from day to day?"

"I have seen it, indeed."

"A few weeks more, and, if God will, we shall meet again; and will it not make us happier then to think that we were not so selfish, dear—so very selfish—as to set our own present joy against a solemn Christian duty?"

"What will be thought of us, Mary," I asked, in sore dismay, "if I go back without you? It will be said that we quarrelled in our honeymoon, and even, perhaps, that I have deserted you. Besides, it will be so strange for you to be left here alone."

"Not alone, dear husband, because Lucy is willing to remain with me; and I shall have your old friend, Miss Bolster, to take care of me."

"But the appearance of it, my dear Mary!"

"I know it will not be quite conventional," she replied; "but if it is right——"

"Do not say any more, dear. It shall be as you please," I said, with a sigh of resignation.

So I went back to London without my wife, solitary and troubled—troubled, because I had taken what I knew must be a last farewell of my cousin.

I did not go to my own house, but quietly occupied a room in my friend Filby's Rose Cottage; and it seemed almost as though the events of the past month had been but a dream.

Nevertheless, I had the consolation of hearing every day from Mary, whose letters gave me the happy assurance that my dear cousin was ripening fast for heaven, that her fears of death were taken away, and her hopes firmly fixed "within the veil." What can I say more?

Then came a letter, after our separation had endured about a month, to say that the last scene of all was evidently drawing on; and at the close of that day I was once more travelling over the Kentish roads. It was early on the following morning that I arrived at Miss Bolster's house. My wife was not there; she had been all night at the gamekeeper's cottage; so had Miss Lascelles; and I bent my steps thither. My dear wife heard them, and hastened to meet me in the little garden.

It was all over. Disease and death had done all that they could do.

Five days later, and the mortal remains of my poor cousin were committed to the grave, in sure and certain hope of the resurrection to eternal life through our Lord Jesus Christ.

We lingered a few days longer in the village, partly that we might comfort the mourning grandparents—who by this time had recalled George Burley to mind—and also that we might make some arrangements for their future requirements. It was on the evening of the third day after Sophy's funeral that I strolled alone and pensively into the churchyard to see that some directions I had given respecting her grave had been attended to. It was late, and the evening would have been dark if the moon, almost at full, had not shone down brightly on the scene.

I had looked at the little hillock beneath which my poor cousin lay quietly at rest, and had almost reached the churchyard gate on my return, when it was opened by another person who approached hastily until we were almost face to face. Scarcely face to face, however, for the stranger's hat was so pulled down over his brow, and the collar of a loose cloak which he wore was so closely fastened round his mouth and chin, that his features were almost concealed.

Supposing him to be a romantic or a thoughtful resident in the village who cultivated a taste for moonlight rambles, I should have passed him silently if he had not laid his hand rather rudely on my arm, and accompanied the action by asking sternly and abruptly—

" Where have you laid her ? "

I knew the speaker now. There was no need for him to lift his hat and unclasp his coat collar (which, however, he did), to enable me to exclaim, in the first moment of surprise—" Marmaduke ! You here ! "

" Yes, here ; " he said, impatiently. " You have no malice against me, Hurly, have you ? " he asked.

" None, my poor friend," I replied.

" Thank you ; but I don't want your pity, either," he went on, haughtily. " I saw you enter the churchyard, and knew you," he added ; " but I don't want to disturb your solitude. Only show me where the poor girl lies buried, and then you may leave me, if you please."

I took him by the arm, and walked silently back to the grave. There he shook me off, but not roughly ; and I was able now to look into his countenance, for the moon shone brightly upon it. My readers will recollect that, in my first description of Marmaduke, I wrote of him as being exceedingly handsome. He was handsome still ; but his beauty was like that which is sometimes pictured of a fallen angel. Sensuality was stamped upon it, and discontent, and remorse. He was, or seemed to be, ghastly pale ; but this might have been partly attributed to the peculiar light by which he was seen. It was no deception, however, which made me only fancy that I perceived the strong muscular workings of his face as he stood gazing down on the cold mound at his feet. Presently he broke the painful silence. "Call me fool, call me villain," he said, passionately.

"I call you neither," I said; "nor did Sophy even reproach you. It will surely be some comfort for you to know that you had no share in her early death. She was not heart-broken by you. She remembered you kindly, and almost her last expressed wishes were for your happiness."

"Poor Sophy! dear Sophy!" he groaned, and tears rolled down his pallid cheeks.

"It will add to your comfort," I went on, "that my cousin died rejoicing in hope of a better life. Her tried spirit is happy now."

Marmaduke made no reply, but walked slowly away, and I by his side.

"Thank you, Hurly," he presently said, when we reached the gate; "here then we part," he added.

And there we parted; for I could not ask him to accompany me to his old home; and he proffered no explanation as to whence he came, or how he had heard of Sophy's death and burial. I never saw him more.

CHAPTER LIV.

ANOTHER RETROSPECT—THIS HISTORY PARTS WITH SOME OLD
FRIENDS—BETSY HAS "A TURN" GIVEN HER.

YEARS and years and years passed away. I was a happy
husband and father—happy, too, in my relationships in
life. With Mr. Millman and aunt Rhoda I had maintained a reciprocal and, on my part, a grateful friendship. With
Edwin Millman I was on terms of the closest intimacy. He, too,
as I have elsewhere hinted, was married; and, as he had taken a
house very near to mine, it was natural that his Lucy and my
Mary should be very sisterly towards each other, as indeed they
were. Then there was my old friend Betsy with her husband,
who still inhabited Rose Cottage, and who thought it hard, they
said, if I did not look in upon them at least three times a week.
They were both of them waxing old; but theirs was a kindly
winter of age, not at all cold or frosty; nothing pleased Betsy
better than to entice our children into her companionship away
in the green fields, where she told them the same exciting
histories of her younger days which had formerly pleased their
father. Oh, she was a nice old lady, so all my youngsters declared,
and I perfectly agreed with them.

As to my circumstances,—well, they were almost as prosperous
as in the thoughts of my boyish days I had occasionally pictured
to myself that they would be; and this, I am aware, is saying a
good deal. Edwin and I were partners in the Gracechurch Street
house; and our transactions were considerably extended and
expanded. Consequently our names stood respectably high in
mercantile circles; for "men will praise thee when thou doest

well to thyself." I am happy to think, as I look back upon this past, that neither Edwin nor myself were unduly elated with our success, and that we did not put our trust in uncertain riches. If we had done this, we should have laid the groundwork for future unnecessary sorrow; for we have known reverses and losses since then. But the history of these does not come within the scope of this narrative.

With regard to other persons who, with more or less frequency, have figured in the past pages of my written history, a few lines may suffice. The old gamekeeper, Storks, and his wife, for instance, had long since been laid beside their daughter and granddaughter in the village churchyard. I am glad to remember now that while they lived they never wanted any of the comforts their age and circumstances required, or that money could purchase. Indeed, a small pension awarded to them by the family at "the great house" in the park, together with their rent-free cottage, would have kept them from destitution; and the additional provision which I was able, and felt it my duty, for Sophy's sake, to make for them, added to their moderate income. So far, therefore, all was well; but they went to the grave sorrowing for their later loss, and reflecting very bitterly, I fear, on the author of the wrongs they had suffered.

I and my dear wife occasionally, during the lifetime of the old couple, went down into Kent, and thus kept up our acquaintance with Miss Bolster. The bustling, industrious little woman evidently prospered in her millinery and dressmaking business; but at our last visit she confided to us that she contemplated making a change in her condition and removing from the village. A bachelor mercer, named Grace, some years younger than herself, of whom she sometimes bought her "fancy articles" (her own expression), and whose shop was in the neighbouring town, had made her an offer of marriage, which she had accepted. She was therefore shortly about to transfer her own business to the town, and to carry it on under a new name and proprietorship. It was very natural and proper; and Mary and I had found so much real happiness in a married life that we cordially rejoiced with Miss Bolster, and congratulated her on her prospects. She did not seem very sanguine, I thought; but she said she was satisfied that she was "doing the proper thing," for "women were poor creatures standing alone;" and my Mary agreed with her in this sentiment. I rather think, however, that one of the great inducements on the part of Miss Bolster to taking this step was that she should get rid for ever of her odious name and its early associations. Be this as it might, we parted with her, reiterating our good wishes, and shortly afterwards we received from her, by favour of a London friend of the husband, a small packet, done up very neatly in white paper, tied round with white ribbon, and containing, with Mr. and Mrs. Grace's compliments, a conglomerate mass of soft, dark-coloured, and (probably) indigestible plum-cake, with a due proportion of iced sugar half dissolved. Poor Marianne! I am afraid her confectioner did not do her justice. It was a failure that wedding-cake of hers, I fancy; but no matter.

In my occasional trips to Kent I had never neglected to visit St. Judith's Bay, and St. Judith's School, which, I am pleased to remember, continued to flourish. When in conversation with my old schoolmaster, I sometimes heard tidings of former schoolfellows which surprised me. Some of the cleverest boys of my time had from different causes, but mostly from want of perseverance or principle, sunk into obscurity, and were struggling in life without much hope of recovering their former position in society, while others who were reckoned stupid and unambitious, had plodded onwards and upwards to great success. I expressed surprise at this, but my old schoolmaster sagely shook his head. " It does not surprise me at all, Hurly " (he too called me Hurly when I was at school, and he retained the habit to the last)—" It does not surprise me at all. It is the old story of the hare and the tortoise exemplified,—

> " ' 'Tis the plain, plodding people, we often shall find,
> Who leave the inconstant and clever behind.' "

And speaking of this reminds me of William Bix, the sharp and clever, or who had been reckoned so sharp and clever, in his boyhood. He had been so long unheard of, and was so confidently reported as being dead, that we all believed it. I have spoken of the various stories which were current respecting his fate, soon after his disappearance: but there was another and a later one which bore such apparent marks of authenticity and personal identity that I was fully assured the unhappy man, under one of his many aliases, had ended his life miserably in a foreign land, leaving behind him a reputation which exactly coincided with the history of his past wasted and evil life. It seemed to be a fitting, though a sad conclusion of that history; for " he that being often reproved, hardeneth his neck, shall suddenly be destroyed, and that without remedy."

Of Marmaduke Tozer, as I have already said, I never heard after our meeting by the grave of my cousin; and of the Browns I knew, only incidentally, that, after collecting together the wreck of their once flourishing fortunes, and receiving some assistance from former City friends, they emigrated to America. Many years afterwards, however, I happened to see the names of Quercus and Philander Brown as the principals in a mercantile firm of some repute there; and it is fair, therefore, to believe that they had profited by the things they had suffered, and had bent their energies in a new sphere towards the restoration of their shattered fortunes and hopes.

I turn from these reminiscences to my own more directly personal narrative.

One evening, about ten years after poor Sophy's death, on returning home from business, I found my old friend Betsy waiting my arrival; and, as I saw, or fancied I saw, an extra degree of importance combined with an unaccountable agitation on her expressive countenance, and as also she asked to speak to me in private, I invited her into my library.

"What is the matter, nurse?" I asked her, when we were seated.

"Oh dear, oh dear! I have had such a turn given me. Who do you think I have seen, sir?"

"I am a poor hand at guessing, Betsy. Not Marmaduke?"

"No, no: a worse than him. But you'll never guess. I have seen—William Bix."

"Impossible!" I exclaimed.

"Yes, that's what Filby said; and he tried to persuade me that I had lost my eyesight. It isn't so good as it used to be, I know: but it is good enough to see a man with in broad daylight, as I have seen that man twice this very day passing outside my window. It is true, Hurly, I have, indeed."

"But, my dear Betsy, you know that William Bix has been dead these many years, and you are too wise to believe in ghost-seeing."

"It was no ghost I saw, sir; but William Bix, in flesh and blood and bones. I should know him in a thousand, or ten thousand either. I ought to, I think, considering all the trouble he used to give me as well as others."

"But you forget. We heard of his death in Paris."

"We thought we did; but it couldn't have been him that we read about in the papers. At any rate, he is alive now."

"You saw him pass your cottage, you say?"

"Twice this very day, Hurly," said Betsy, giving me for the second time, in her earnestness, my old familiar name. "Twice. I thought I must be mistaken the first time; but when he passed again—shuffling along on the pavement—and I caught sight of his face, and heard that little disagreeable cough he used to have, I was sure of him then. I am as sure it was him as I am sure that I am talking to you, sir."

"How was it—I mean what time was it you saw him, and what sort of appearance did he make?"

"I'll tell you as near as I can all about it, Hurly," said Betsy. "It was about ten o'clock this morning, and I was just sitting down to work at my window, when I looked up, and saw an oldish-looking, shabby-genteel man walking by, as if like he was going into the City—at least, he was going that way. He was shuffling along, as I said, but pretty quick too, and there was something in his walk that made me notice him. I think it put me in mind of your poor old grandfather in his last days."

"Ah! and being struck with that familiarity, you were naturally prepared to trace other resemblances."

"No, but listen, Hurly. I was turning my eyes down again to my work, when the man gave that sharp dry sort of cough you remember, as if he was clearing his throat, and it gave me such a startle, for I never heard anybody besides your uncle William cough just like it. So I looked up again, just as the man had reached the corner, and I could only see his back."

"Only his back, Betsy! But one back is so like another, you know——"

"I have not done yet, sir; I saw only his back till he got quite to the corner. Then he stopped all at once, and looked back the way he had come in a half-frightened sort of manner, as if he was afraid of being followed or watched; and that was how I came to see his face."

"And it was William Bix's face; you are sure of that, Betsy?"

"I am sure of it now, Hurly; now that I have seen it a second time. I was not quite so sure then, because it was too far off. But I said to myself, 'If I had not heard of his being dead, I should say at once, there's my poor old master's good-for-nothing son.'"

"And that second time, Betsy?" I asked, with complete conviction that my good old nurse was perfectly sure in her own mind that she had had this vision, and half convinced that it was not altogether impossible; "when did you see the man again?"

"This afternoon, Hurly; only two or three hours ago. I was still sitting at my window, working, when I heard the same shuffling footsteps on the pavement outside and the same cough; and I looked up; and as plain as I see you now, sir, I saw William Bix then. I am sure I am not mistaken."

"Strange! How was he dressed?"

"Very shabby, sir. He had got on an old camlet cloak, with a high velvet collar, a white hat, greenish trousers, and a pair of cobbled shoes. I had time to notice all this; but it was his face I looked at most of all. It was the same face as ever, only grown older; the same wicked look of the eyes, and that nasty deceitful smile, that he used to have, particularly when he was half—not quite sober. And as to that, he was not quite sober this afternoon. I could tell that by his unsteady way of walking, and his watery eyes."

"But, Betsy, you know that William Bix gave up that bad practice years ago, and drank nothing stronger than tea——"

"Yes, I know," she replied; "but there's a text in the Bible that tells us of a hog being washed, and then going back to roll in the mud. And if William Bix is alive—as he is—and has taken to drinking again, he won't have been the first, and won't be the last reformed drunkard who has done, or will do, the same thing."

"Quite true, Betsy," I said; "for no reformation is really genuine and to be trusted which does not spring from the heart, and which is not produced there by Divine power. It is the grace of God which brings salvation, that teaches men to live soberly, righteously, and godly, and to deny themselves; and nothing else will do this effectually. But the news you have told me is very surprising. I cannot understand it. So long as we have believed that unhappy man dead too!"

"I cannot understand it either," said my old friend. "But one thing is quite certain, or next to it, that William Bix is come to life again for no good. There's some mischief going on wherever he is. You may be sure of that, my dear."

"I am afraid you are right, Betsy," said I; "happily, however, he has done you and me all the harm he is likely to be able to do; and we have survived it, and are none the worse for it now. I do not think it is in his power to injure us any further."

Betsy shook her head dubiously. She had naturally a strong terror of and belief in my uncle's power for evil, and she reminded me that if he could not injure us he might be injuring others.

"Very true; and, if it be as you say, we must try to prevent it. Do you think, by-the-bye, that my uncle, if it were he that you saw, saw you?"

"No, I took care of that: though he might not have known me if he had, Hurly."

"Don't trust to that. You had better not let him see you; for, having passed your house twice, it is not unlikely he will pass again. If he should do so——" I paused here, for I did not like to suggest that Betsy should follow him as a spy. She, however, had no such extreme delicacy.

"If I see him again, I'll know something more of him, depend on it, sir; and I'll come and let you know directly." Saying this my old nurse soon afterwards departed, greatly relieved in her mind by having bestowed her confidence on me.

CHAPTER LV.

TRACKING THE CAMLET CLOAK—ANOTHER SURPRISE.

BETSY set about her task in right earnest. She made herself a screen of potted geraniums in her window, through which she could look out upon the road and take a deliberate view of every passenger without danger of being observed in return. At this window she stationed herself early on the following morning, and was rewarded for her pains by seeing the old camlet-cloaked stranger pass, about the same hour as on the previous day. There was little doubt, therefore, that William Bix—if he were indeed the man—had some object in going towards London in the morning, some petty employment there, perhaps; and that his lodging or home was not far distant from Rose Cottage.

Betsy laid her plans accordingly. Quietly pursuing her household occupations through the middle of the day, she returned to her post of observation in the afternoon, in bonnet and shawl, ready to slip out and follow the object of her suspicion before he could have time to evade her pursuit. She was successful: about five o'clock he made his appearance, walking more unsteadily than on the previous afternoon, and in another minute Betsy was in the road also. She followed him, at a safe distance, for about a mile, until he arrived at a cluster of small dirty cottages, called Paradise

Row, in a very mean neighbourhood. Here he took a key from his pocket, unlocked one of the cottage doors, and entered. Betsy observed all this, and not caring to carry on her investigations further that evening, she returned home. On the following day, however, having once more watched the camlet cloak and its wearer on their way towards London, she again sallied forth, and, making acquaintance with a woman who kept a huckster's shop almost opposite Paradise Row, she learned that "the old gentleman in the camlet cloak" had resided in that neighbourhood about a month: that his name was Howard; that he lived alone, and "did for himself;" that he was supposed to be poor, first, from having chosen such a place for his home, and next, because all the household goods he was known to possess were barely sufficient to furnish one room scantily. Possibly, however, the woman suggested, the man might be a miser; and, in that case, there was no telling but he might have heaps of money hoarded up; but, any way, it was no business of hers.

Having obtained this information, Betsy's task for that day was ended; and she set her husband to work the next morning, to follow in the wake of Mr. Howard towards the City. Our friend Filby was not so successful, however, as Betsy had been. He tracked the camlet cloak, indeed, into the crowded thoroughfare of Tottenham Court Road, and through that into St. Giles's; but there he suddenly lost sight of him; a circumstance not to be greatly wondered at, perhaps, when it is considered that Mr. Filby was over seventy years old, and, though active enough for that age, yet stout, rather short-winded, and puffy. At all events, he returned to Rose Cottage, after an absence of three or four hours, bathed in perspiration, to report his want of success, and to express his opinion that William Bix was not worth so much trouble, with which I coincided when I received the report.

But Betsy was not satisfied. Where William Bix was, there

was mischief afoot, she was sure of that; and she would search it out. Accordingly, after allowing a day or two to elapse, she herself sallied forth and gave chase to the camlet cloak, and did not lose sight of it till she had seen its wearer safely housed in a low public-house, not far from the Seven Dials, after having made a short call at a small pork shop in one of the intervening streets, probably to purchase his provisions for the day. All this Betsy faithfully reported to me in the evening; and then, by my persuasion, the matter was permitted to rest. We had gained some knowledge of the haunts of the wretched man, though to what purpose the information might turn I had not the slightest idea. I certainly had no intention of renewing my acquaintance with him; and had so little curiosity on the subject, that I declined to convince myself of the personal identity of Mr. Howard by ocular demonstration. Nevertheless, taking for granted that Betsy was not mistaken, I was not sorry that it might eventually be in my power to send relief to my poor unhappy relative, if I should be convinced of his being in actual want.

Some weeks wore away, and, excepting that we were constantly reminded of William Bix by the regularity with which he, or his double, twice a day shuffled by Rose Cottage, nothing arising out of his reappearance occurred to disturb the equanimity of our little circle. Indeed, even Betsy became so accustomed to the sight of the white hat and old camlet cloak that she saw them pass and re-pass with comparative indifference; taking care, however, not to make herself visible to their mysterious wearer.

One day, when seated in my private room at Gracechurch Street, I was informed, by a clerk in the outer office, that a lady who particularly wished to see me had sent in her name. It was not a very usual occurrence for ladies to invade our house of business; but such things had occasionally happened; and, merely inquiring the lady's name, which the clerk pronounced to be Greece, or Grease (information that did not at all enlighten me), I told the young gentleman to usher in the visitor, who proved to be none other than my Kentish acquaintance and friend, Marianne Bolster, transformed into Mrs. Grace, wife of the country draper, and further translated by the rather affected cockney clerk into Mrs. Grease.

"My dear Mrs. Grace, this is an unexpected pleasure," I said, as I shook hands with her, and begged her to be seated. The little woman looked so comfortable and respectable that it was a pleasure to me even to look at her, especially when I remembered the circumstances under which we first knew each other. Nevertheless, when I looked closer, I fancied I could detect some marks of anxiety on the lady's countenance; and I was not deceived.

"It is a great liberty I have taken," said she.

"No liberty at all; or rather a very proper one. I should have considered myself slighted if I had known you had been in London without calling on me," I said.

To which Mrs. Grace replied that I was very kind, and that she felt encouraged to tell me her trouble—for she *was* in trouble —and she had been so impressed with the hope that I could help her out of it, that she had come to London almost on purpose to see me.

Naturally I was sorry to hear that my old friend was in trouble, and equally willing to give her all the assistance in my power.

"It is ⬛⬛money, Mr. Burley," said the lady; desperately ⬛⬛, I have got it out easier than I expected."

⬛⬛was about money, I expected this when she began ⬛⬛ouble; but this said but little, and I entreated Mrs.

Grace to take time (for she seemed agitated) and then further to explain.

"Thank you, sir; you are very good, and I knew you would be; but it is a large sum I am in trouble about—as much as four hundred pounds." It required an effort to get this out; and when she had said it she looked down and, in a bewildered sort of way, began to twist the tassel of a neat little pelerine she had on.

"Let us understand one another, Marianne," said I. "Do you wish to borrow four hundred pounds?"

Oh no, it was not that; but Grace (her husband) had been so foolish. If he had but consulted her it would not have happened.

"What would not have happened, my good friend?"

Why this,—Grace would not have become security as he had, for a friend, and so got into this trouble.

"Oh, I think I understand." But I did not, until the little woman further explained that her husband had been goose enough (the words are hers) to sign his name to certain acceptances for four hundred pounds, for the benefit of an acquaintance who was desirous of doing business without any capital of his own.

This looked rather bad, and I shook my head. "It was unwise, certainly; for, as a matter almost of course, the four hundred pounds has gradually vanished, and your husband will have to meet the bills as they become due?" I said this interrogatively, but was not prepared for the reply—

"Vanished! Oh dear no, sir. The money has never been sent."

"Never been sent?"

"Never been sent from London, though the people have had the bills more than a month."

"My dear Mrs. Grace, I thought I understood you a minute

ago ; but now I do not understand you at all. Suppose you begin at the beginning and tell me all your trouble."

Upon this hint the little woman spoke ; the gist of her story being that her husband's friend, captivated by an advertisement he had seen in a London paper, proffering money accommodation to any amount, on extremely reasonable terms, and being anxious either to commence a business, or to increase one already commenced, persuaded the country draper to assist him in procuring a loan. "Here is the advertisement of the money-lender," said my visitor, opening her pocket-book and handing me a slip cut out from the advertising columns of a Sunday newspaper. It ran thus :—

"MONEY ! MONEY !! MONEY !!! Money to any amount from Ten pounds to a Thousand, may be obtained for any number of years, at Five per cent. interest, by any person of respectable character, on the security of the borrower and a responsible friend. The object of the advertiser being to assist struggling merit rather than to accumulate large profits, the utmost consideration and inviolable secrecy will be observed in every transaction. Application to be made (by letter only) to A. Z., —— Street, Bloomsbury."

"Very inviting, I must confess," said I, giving back the paper to Mrs. Grace. "Well, and so——"

And so her husband's friend, who wanted money, wrote to A. Z., proposing to borrow four hundred pounds ; and, in due time, after some further correspondence, the proposed borrower was informed by A. Z. that his references were eminently satisfactory, that all he had to do was to post the acceptances, with a certain amount of commission, in cash, to the address in Bloomsbury ; and that the loan should be immediately transmitted through the same medium.

"And your husband's friend followed these instructions, I suppose ?"

"Yes, he did," said the little woman, energetically.

"And, of course, has heard no more of A. Z."

"Not a word more, and this was a month ago," continued my visitor. And then, in reply to my further inquiries, she told me that eight acceptances of fifty pounds each, with interest added, running over a space of four years, at six months' intervals, were given. Also that the commission demanded beforehand, amounting to ten pounds, had duly accompanied the bills on their transmission by post.

"A ten-pound note, good Bank of England," Mrs. Grace added, with a sigh which led me to conjecture that this had been borrowed for the nonce from her husband; a conjecture which I afterwards found to be correct.

"I am afraid," said I, "that the ten pounds are hopelessly lost. How could any person be so blind as not to see, on the very face of the transaction, that the primary object of the benevolent advertiser was to obtain possession of the money?"

"That's just what I said when I came to know about it," said Marianne. "'How could you be so blind?' I said. But there's nobody so blind as those who won't see," she added.

"Very true; but now that your husband's and his friend's eyes are opened, they wish, I suppose, to avoid further loss and exposure?"

"Yes, sir."

"But there are difficulties in the way. In the first place we have to find A. Z.; and then—but we won't talk about difficulties. Depend upon it, I will give you what aid I can; and I trust we may be able to recover the bills."

My old acquaintance thanked me very heartily and with tears in her eyes. As to the ten pounds, she said, she never expected to see them again, and it would be a good lesson to her husband against doing such things in future without her knowledge;

plainly intimating that it would not have been done at all if he had first consulted her, which I thought likely; but, without entering into further particulars, I proposed that we should at once repair to Hatton Garden, where my old friend Mr. Fawley, the lawyer, still had his offices; and afterwards to my own house, which I desired should be the lady's home while she remained in London.

CHAPTER LVI.

A. Z.

MR. FAWLEY, grown very grey and rather infirm with age, but as keen as ever in his professional avocations, received us very graciously, and listened with a good deal of good-natured patience to the explanations of the lady client I had introduced to him.

"A very commonplace piece of swindling," he remarked, coolly, when she had finished her story, and he had cursorily glanced at the letters of A. Z., which his client laid before him, and which, I may remark, I had previously seen. "A very ordinary piece of swindling, and so transparent that it is a wonder there are people to be found who can be taken in by such tricks. But it makes good the old adage, that 'the pleasure is as great, of being cheated as to cheat.'"

"No doubt there is some truth in that," I said; "at any rate, there are plenty of people who stand ready to be victimized. The question is, what is to be done in the present instance?"

"The thing to be done—or that your friend wishes to be done —is to get back those acceptances, I suppose."

" Undoubtedly."

" But you see this is easier said than done," remarked the lawyer. " First, you have to follow Mrs. Glasse's sensible advice, and catch your hare before you cook it. In other words, you have to find A. Z., which may not be an easy matter. Next, you have to bring home to him the charge that he ever had those bills in his possession ; you have also to prove that no consideration was given for them. Then, probably, A. Z. is only a tool in the hands of others who are behind the scenes, and the bills were passed into those hands as soon as they reached him. Most likely, by this time, they have been negotiated, and nothing more will be known of them till they arrive at maturity; and then the holder will be ready to swear that he believed the bills to be perfectly honest bills, and that he discounted them in the way of ordinary business. Consequently, barring any proof of fraud or collusion, which will be very hard to get at, the acceptor will be held legally responsible."

" I am aware of all that, and foresee the difficulty of gaining repossession of the acceptances ; but it must be done if possible."

" It seems to be a case more suited to a police court than a lawyer's office," said my old friend. " Why not get the help of a detective, and see what you can make of this A. Z., when you have laid hands on him ?"

" It may come to that if other means fail," I replied; " but I have a reason for wishing, if possible, to avoid the exposure of a police court ; and if you will favour me with a word or two in private"—I whispered this in an aside—" I will tell you why."

Mr. Fawley rose and conducted me into another room.

" You did not particularly observe the handwriting of those letters ?" I said.

" Letters ?"

" Those you still hold in your hand—the letters of A. Z."

Mr. Fawley looked at them again, and shook his hand. "A common sort of commercial hand," he said, adding, "I see nothing particular in it. No, I don't identify it, Mr. Burley."

"I do. Those letters were written by William Bix."

The lawyer started. "You don't mean your good-for-nothing uncle?"

"Well, I suppose I cannot deny the relationship—yes, by my uncle, William Bix."

"But, my dear sir, William Bix is dead," continued the lawyer.

"We thought him to be dead; but I have reason to know that we were mistaken. He is undoubtedly living, and has been seen and recognised by both Filby and his wife, who ought to know him," said I.

"What! my old friend Betsy. Oh, if she has seen him, there's an end of all doubt. But how was it, and when, and where?" Mr. Fawley asked, with unprofessional eagerness.

I told him what the reader already knows.

"And so he is alive, is he? And the creature's at his dirty work again. But how do you trace a connexion between Bix and A. Z.?"

"By these letters. Remember, he was my writing-master at St. Judith's; and, though he has or had as many hands as Briareus——"

"And he had a hundred, they say," interposed the lawyer.

"—— and as many various styles of handwriting as a hundred hands could produce, there is one peculiarity about them all which I detect in these letters. I detected it the moment I saw them."

"Admitted; and admitted that your conjectures are certainties, which appears possible—what then?" asked the lawyer.

"Why, it narrows our field of operation. We know where

William Bix is to be found ; and the only thing is to obtain positive proof of his identity with this writer——"

"The first thing, you mean, friend. And, that done, what then ?" demanded Mr. Fawley.

"Nay, sir. I came to you for advice," said I.

The lawyer mused. " Your object is to get back these acceptances for your friend ; and you wish to let the swindler off scot-free : is that what I am to understand ?"

I also paused. "You have stated my object correctly. As to my wish—well, I have so much tenderness for the memory of my poor grandfather that I confess to a reluctance to being the means of inflicting upon his son the punishment which we know he justly merits."

"A foolish weakness," said my legal adviser ; "but it must be humoured, I suppose—the more so that I don't know what good could be done by bringing the scoundrel into open court, even if we could get him there. I am to understand, then, that, with this proviso, you put the matter into my hands ?"

"Undoubtedly, if you will be kind enough to undertake it," I replied.

"It may cost your friend another ten-pound note," he continued.

"For which I hold myself responsible."

"Good," said Mr. Fawley, and he rang a handbell.

"Tell Jackson I want him," he said to the boy who attended the summons. The boy disappeared, and in another minute entered a strange-looking, middle-aged, weak-eyed and sallow-complexioned man, shabbily dressed in on old office coat, which had seen long and hard service, apparently. I don't know that any further description is needed.

" Read those letters and that advertisement, Jackson," said Mr. Fawley.

He silently obeyed.

"You want to find A. Z., I suppose?" he remarked, when his task was finished.

"Of course. Will you be kind enough to tell Mr. Jackson what you have told me?" continued the lawyer, turning to me.

I repeated my story, and the man listened with a sort of stolid indifference.

"It will cost something," he said.

"Ten pounds. Mr. Burley will put ten pounds in your hand, for expenses, when you place the acceptances in his."

"Very good, sir. I'll set about it at once."

"And you had better communicate with Mr. Burley—take the address, Jackson. I am not to appear in it, mind."

"Very good, sir," he repeated. "I had better take these documents with me."

I wrote my business address on a card, and gave it to Mr. Jackson, who then silently withdrew.

"An invaluable man that," said the lawyer; "a first-rate copying-clerk, and a wonderful fellow for mysteries. Knows every dodge in London, and, I had almost said, every dodger. He will do your business for you if anybody can. He has only one fault."

"I can guess it," said I.

"He might have been rich, respectable, and respected, but for his besetting sin. Poor Jackson!" sighed the lawyer.

"Nevertheless, you think he is to be trusted?"

"Every whit."

"He looks a miserable object," I remarked.

"He *is* a miserable object; he is wretched in the extreme. He is killing himself as fast as a horse can gallop, and he knows it."

CHAPTER LVII.

A BARBER'S SHOP—MR. JACKSON.

N rejoining my Kentish friend in the outer office, I briefly informed her that Mr. Fawley had put matters in train for the recovery of the acceptances, and then, handing her into the carriage, which I had kept in waiting, I ordered the driver to proceed to my house in the suburbs.

"You know my Mary, and she knows you," I said to Mrs. Grace; "so you won't need my introduction. I shall be home to tea." Having thus disposed of my friend, I turned my steps eastward, and for the rest of the day was immersed in foreign correspondence. In the evening, according to our general custom, Edwin and I left the counting-house together, and commenced our walk homewards.

Our route did not lie exactly through Holborn and Bloomsbury, but, yielding to a feeling of curiosity, which was encouraged by my companion when I told him of my morning visitor and her errand, we made a *détour*, and presently found ourselves in the street, and opposite the house, to which the letters for A. Z. were to be addressed.

It was a dingy, disreputable-looking house, in an equally miserable back street. Children—very dirty ones—were playing in the gutter-mud, and women, as dirty and unkempt, and in many varieties of disarray, were lounging about their door-sills, seeking, perhaps, for fresher air than they could obtain in the interiors of their habitations. A few men were lounging about also, smoking strong tobacco from filthy pipes.

The house itself, to which our curiosity was directed, was occupied on the ground-floor by a barber, whose striped pole projected from the door-lintel, and whose shop-window, half-obscured by dirt, displayed (in addition to a few articles belonging to his trade proper) a number of coarse prints of theatrical personages in professional costume, and a few fly-spotted weekly numbers of cheap periodicals; also some broadsides of popular songs, such as at that time were produced and circulated by the well-known Mr. Catnach of the Seven Dials. We had time to note all these particulars while we lounged on the pavement, puzzling ourselves for a decent pretext for entering the shop, and conscious that the keen eyes of the shop's proprietor—a pale-faced old man, in dirty shirt-sleeves and apron—were fastened on us as he stood at his shop door. To avoid or avert his suspicion, I boldly entered the shop, followed by Millman, and, on the spur of the moment, asked to be served with a pot of pomatum.

It was a clumsy expedient, and I felt it to be so. In fact, it was ill-considered of me to venture into the place at all; for, supposing I had happened to light upon William Bix in these haunts of his, no possible good could have arisen from it, and the very object I was set upon might probably have been defeated. I had not acted altogether without premeditation, however; for I knew that the old camlet cloak and its wearer would have left the neighbourhood two or three hours earlier in the day.

The man served me with the pomatum without verbal remark, but not without a glance of derisive intelligence, so manifest that I was not sure whether he had not made himself master of my thoughts.

"Is there anything else I can have the pleasure of doing for you, sir?" the barber asked, in a tone somewhat betwixt civility and impudence, as he wrapped up my purchase and pocketed the sixpence.

"I believe nothing else," said I, looking round his little shop, not, as the reader may suppose, to see if any other want could be supplied from that emporium, but to detect, if possible, any traces of A. Z. in the shape of unopened letters on counter or shelves.

"You are quite sure, are you, sir?" continued the man of lather: "nothing in this way, now?" whipping from his window one of its coloured attractions, familiar to every one as "Paul Pry." "Nothing in this way, now?" said the fellow, looking knowingly in my face.

"Nothing," said I.

"And there's nothing you would like to ask me? You haven't any questions to ask, have you?" continued the man, abating a good deal of his former civility and increasing in his impudence.

"My good sir, what should I have to ask you?" said I, rather nettled at the barber's manner, and not the less so because of my consciousness of being seriously acting the part of Paul Pry in real life.

"Oh, sir," said he, with a palpable sneer, "it isn't for me to say what; only, if all you wanted was a pot of pomatum, you could have got that nearer home, I should think. Gentlemen such as you don't often come into such parts as these for their pots of pomatum; and sometimes they do come to make inquiries —inquiries, you know."

"Pho!" said I, laughing; "you mistake: I am not a detective."

"No, sir, I should think not," said the barber; "I shouldn't take you for one, nor your friend for one either, though he has been searching with his eyes all over my shop all the while he has been in it. Not but what he is very welcome, and you too, mister."

"I beg your pardon, friend, if I have offended you," said

Edwin ; and I was about to make a similar apology, when a porter entered the shop and laid a letter on the counter, saying, as he did so, "That's all right, I suppose."

The barber nodded, and whisked the letter away into a drawer, but not before I had seen on the direction the cabalistic letters A. Z.

Meanwhile I had pocketed my pomatum, and, buttoning up my coat, followed Edwin out of the shop, the barber, with mock politeness, making me a low bow, and ironically begging that, if my purchase gave satisfaction, I would be kind enough to recommend my friends to him.

"We have done your friend Mrs. Grace no good by this move, I am afraid," said Edwin, when we were at a safe distance from the barber's shop.

"We have found out something, at all events," said I.

"Yes, that letters for A. Z. are left there, and that the cunning-looking old shaver is in league with that mysterious capitalist. But I am sorry I advised you to come out of your way to make the discovery."

"It will do no harm, I hope, if it does no good," I replied ; and then we dropped the subject.

It *had* done harm, however ; that is to say, an alarm had evidently been taken by the wearer of the camlet cloak, who, on the following morning, having been observed by our indefatigable friend Betsy, as he passed Rose Cottage on his way into London, did not return that afternoon, and was no more seen after several days' anxious watching. Meanwhile our country visitor, in spite of my assurance that her affairs were in good hands, became nervously anxious about the result.

A week passed away, and I also became anxious, for it was almost certain that A. Z. had shifted his quarters, at least for a time, and I was the more worried and annoyed when one morning poor Jackson called on me, with a very lugubrious countenance, to report his non-success.

"The fellow must have slipped out of the world altogether, I think," said he.

"You can find out nothing about him, then?"

"Oh yes, sir, lots *about* him, but that is not the question. I cannot find the man himself. He has forsaken his old haunts, his cottage in Paradise Row is shut up, and he has left no traces behind."

"Strange, isn't it, Mr. Jackson?"

"Not so very strange, sir, considering where I saw *you* last, Mr. Burley," said he.

"Me! saw me!"

"You remember the barber's shop in —— Street, Bloomsbury, sir? and the porter bringing in a letter?"

"Of course I do; but do you mean to say that you were that porter?"

"I was that porter, sir. I had laid a capital train for liming the old bird; but you and Mr. Millman just spoiled the sport."

"It was a very foolish thing of us, I confess," said I, after I had expressed my astonishment at the disguise which had so deceived me, and had had explained to me the well-laid plan which, according to Mr. Jackson, would have placed A. Z. in our power; "it was foolish in me to interfere; but what leads you to suppose that our visit to the barber's shop interfered with that result?"

"Oh, sir, that barber is an old hand; one of the craftiest dodgers in London. *I* know him. There's no doubt of his being confederate with A. Z., and your visit raised his suspicion. He knew what you were after as well as I did, and he saw how you started when I laid that letter on the counter. I knew at once that it was a done job for us for that time."

"I am very sorry," said I, apologetically, and humbly acknowledging the superior genius before which I stood rebuked.   "But
you do not give up the cause altogether, I hope?"

"Not a bit of it, Mr. Burley; it will take more time, no
doubt."

"And more money, perhaps?"

"No, no, sir; I don't say that.   A bargain is a bargain," said
Jackson.

"At any rate, don't spare money; and look to me for payment,"
I said; and there the conference ended.

Another week, and then another visit from Mr. Jackson.   He
was in better spirits this time.   He had a clue, he said, to the
present retreat of A. Z., and hoped, in a few days, to report successfully.   Meanwhile I was desired to rest satisfied that the grass
was not growing under his feet.   By this time, I may as well say,
our Kentish visitor and friend had returned home, disconsolate
enough that her errand had, so far, proved a failure, but declaring
that her business would go to wreck and ruin if she prolonged her
absence from it.

A month passed away before I saw Jackson again, and I began
to fear either that he was "at fault," as huntsmen say when their
hounds have lost scent, or, perhaps, that he had given up his
quest as hopeless.   It was not so, however; for at the end of that
time he once more made his appearance in my office, and quietly
laid on my desk the acceptances.

"Examine them and count them, sir, if you please," he said.

I did so; they were all there, eight in number.   As they were
not endorsed, except by the drawer, they had evidently never
been out of the hands of A. Z. since he received them.   I remarked
this to Mr. Jackson, and expressed my satisfaction and, at the
same time, my surprise that they had not been negotiated.

"There might have been some difficulty, if not danger, in

attempting so large a haul at one time," said Mr. Jackson; "and I dare say the old rogue knows how to calculate chances pretty well, and preferred keeping the thing snug in his own hands, unless he had wanted money at a pinch, which he does not seem to have done. But what reason do you think *he* gave for his keeping back the bills?"

"It is impossible for me to say."

"And you would never guess, sir. Mr. A. Z., in fact, pretends to have had conscientious scruples. He had found out something about the acceptor, or the acceptor's wife, I think he said, since the bills came into his hands; and, claiming old acquaintance with her, didn't wish to push the matter too far."

"Um! He might have returned the bills then."

"No, that would not have answered his purpose either. I fancy he retained them with the intention of making the best bargain he could for himself as they consecutively arrived at maturity."

"May I ask, Mr. Jackson, how you prevailed upon him to part with the bills to you?"

"Well, sir, there are secrets in all trades," said Mr. Jackson, musingly; "and I am not at liberty to enter into particulars exactly. I may say this much, however, that this billing trade is not the only dodge A. Z. is practising, though he makes use of other names; and in one of these he has lately brought himself too near the windy side of the law to be safe. In fact, I fortunately got a hold upon him for another trick he has been up to lately; and it was, 'Either deliver up those bills or take your chance of Bow Street.' My word! the old fellow did not hesitate long then."

"And so you sacrificed public justice," I began, but Mr. Jackson stopped me.

"It was your wish that he should be spared, sir; so I understood from Mr. Fawley."

What could I say then?

"But there's no fear, sir," continued Jackson; "he will come in for it some of these days without our dirtying our hands with him."

"Can you tell me where the man is to be found now?" I asked.

"No, sir. I don't think he will go back to his old quarters. In short, I fancy I have frightened him away from London altogether for a time, and——, but I am taking up your time, Mr. Burley."

Interpreting this to mean that Mr. Jackson had no more to tell me, or that he did not wish to be questioned any further, I placed in his hands the stipulated ten pounds, with a further gratuity for his diligence and skill; and he bade me good morning. It is almost needless to add that I transmitted the bills that day to my friend Mrs. Grace, from whom I shortly afterwards received a letter overflowing with thanks for helping her and her husband out of their great trouble.

It will have been observed that, throughout the whole of this confabulation with Mr. Jackson, he did not once mention the true name of A. Z., nor did he intimate any knowledge of my relationship to him; and yet I felt sure that the clerk well knew A. Z. to be the William Bix of Silver Square former notoriety, and my own uncle. I felt grateful to Jackson for his delicacy, and should have been pleased to have shown my sense of it if I could have done it without injury to himself. I never saw him again, however. A few months later, having occasion to call on my lawyer, I inquired after my useful ally, and was shocked to hear of his death.

"I told you how it would be, Hurly," said Mr. Fawley; "poor Jackson drank himself into the grave—died a month ago of *delirium tremens.*"

CHAPTER LVIII.

DEATH OF WILLIAM BIX, AND END OF GEORGE BURLEY'S STORY.

BOUT a year after the occurrences which have filled up the last three chapters of this history, I was some weeks absent from London on business. On my return, and when first happy greetings with wife and children were over, I learned that my old nurse had been anxiously inquiring for me several days past, and had left a particular request that I would go to her house as soon as I conveniently could after my return.

"I will look in in the morning," I said.

"Why not this evening?" asked my wife. "It will not take you long."

"Are you in such a hurry to get rid of me again, Mary, after our having been parted for an age?" I asked.

"Do you not think I am?" Mary retorted, adding, "But, seriously, the good old body seemed so anxious to see you that it will be almost cruel not to indulge her. Besides, she said she had a particular reason for making her request."

"And did she not tell you her reason?"

"I did not ask her; although I did ask her if I could do anything for her in your absence. But she said no, she wished to see you very particularly."

Reluctantly enough, for I was tired with my journey, and had calculated on a quiet evening with my family, I put on my hat and proceeded to Rose Cottage.

"I am so glad you are come, Hurly; so glad!" was Betsy's first greeting, and I could see that she was in great agitation; "so glad; I was afraid he would be gone before you could see him, but he has held out, though the doctor says he can't last more than a few hours."

"He! Of whom are you speaking, Betsy? Not, surely, of my good old friend Filby?"

"No, no; but come with me, dear. Oh, to think of his coming to my house to die, after all. Poor William! Your uncle William! Your uncle, William Bix, Hurly." And the good creature burst into tears. "It is very weak of me," she said, "but I cannot help it."

I followed her up-stairs, and into her spare bed-chamber. The first person I saw there was old Filby, sitting at the bed-head, with sorrowful solicitude marked on his countenance, which was a little bent downwards, with his eyes fixed on the ghastly form of the dying man, whose eyes were closed, and whose breath was heaved in painfully convulsive spasms.

"You saw his father die, Hurly," whispered my old nurse, as we drew near the bedside.

He was past all power of recognition. He did not know who stood by when the feeble fluttering pulse ceased to beat, and the once busy, misguided heart and brain once for all gave up their mortal functions.

"We all loved his father, Hurly," said Betsy, sobbing, as she laid her aged head on my shoulder, and gave way to a paroxysm of sorrow. "We all loved his father; and we would have loved him, too, if he would have let us. Poor fellow! poor, poor William!"

*   *   *   *   *

It was not till we had laid him decently in his last earthly resting-place that Betsy explained to me how it came to pass that she had received William Bix into her house to die.

About a week previous to my return home, she said, she took a fancy to go as far as Paradise Row to satisfy her curiosity as to whether anything had recently been known or seen of the man in the camlet cloak and white hat, who was known in that neighbourhood as Mr. Howard. As a matter of course, she made her inquiries of the woman at the huckster's shop with whom she had once before held some conversation.

The first question was met by a hasty retort.

" Are you a friend of that man ?" she demanded.

" Not very much of a friend," returned Betsy, shortly ; " but I have known something of him in old times."

" Well, friend or not, it's time somebody was looking after him," continued the shopkeeper. "He came back to his old house more than a month ago, looking more dead than alive, though he managed to crawl about till this last day or two. But since then he hasn't been seen ; and it is my opinion he is starving to death. It isn't any business of mine, you know ; but it may be of yours."

It was too true ; William Bix *was* starving to death. Betsy found him in his wretched den, lying on a miserable mattress, too weak to move, and with no one to help him. There was not a scrap of food in the cottage, nor a farthing in his pocket. He had given up all in despair, and had laid himself down to die : so he said.

How Betsy then enacted the good Samaritan, and supplied immediate nutriment ; how she sent a messenger for her husband ; how they agreed together to forget all the former misdeeds of the poor starving wretch ; how they had him moved the next day to their own abode, that they might watch over him and, if possible, restore him to life ; how these benevolent efforts failed because, as the doctor said, the patient's stamina was gone ; and how, as far as lay in their power, they smoothed his rugged passage to the grave, and soothed his last hours with their tenderness, while they strove to raise his flickering thoughts to Him whose blood cleanseth from all sin, and whose almighty power and infinite love redeemed the dying malefactor on the cross from the pains of eternal death, and raised him to life and happiness everlasting: all this need only be told in the few sentences thus written.

And now the task I set myself to perform is completed, and my story is told. That I have given a faithful delineation of some phases in human life and character, I know: and if the pages I have written should afford amusement for a few of the leisure hours of my readers, it is what I have desired. But, better still, if a single lesson should have been taught (as I earnestly hope and believe it has), indicating the path of true wisdom in contrast with that of the deepest folly and degradation, my end will have been more fully answered.

LONDON : ROBERT K. BURT, WINE OFFICE COURT, FLEET STREET, E.C.

BY THE AUTHOR OF "*Jessica's First Prayer.*"

LITTLE MEG'S CHILDREN.

Royal square 16mo.   With numerous Engravings.
1s. 6d., gilt edges, cloth, bevelled boards.

PILGRIM STREET:

A STORY OF MANCHESTER LIFE.

Fcap. 8vo.   Engravings on Toned Paper.   2s. cloth boards;
2s. 6d. extra boards, gilt edges.

FERN'S HOLLOW.

Fcap. 8vo.   Engravings on Toned Paper.   2s. cloth boards;
2s. 6d. extra boards, gilt edges.

ENOCH RODEN'S TRAINING.

Fcap. 8vo.   Engravings on Toned Paper.   2s. cloth boards;
2s. 6d. extra boards, gilt edges.

THE FISHERS OF DERBY HAVEN.

Fcap. 8vo.   Engravings on Toned Paper.   2s. cloth boards;
2s. 6d. extra boards, gilt edges.

THE CHILDREN OF CLOVERLEY.

Fcap. 8vo.   Engravings on Toned Paper.   2s. cloth boards;
2s. 6d. extra boards, gilt edges.

JESSICA'S FIRST PRAYER.

Royal square 16mo.   Engravings.   1s. cloth boards;
1s. 6d. extra boards, gilt edges.

www.ingramcontent.com/pod-product-compliance
Ingram Content Group UK Ltd.
Pitfield, Milton Keynes, MK11 3LW, UK
UKHW030621291224
453057UK00007B/42